Upgrade Your Computer Printer and Save a Bundle

Upgrade Your Computer Printer and Save a Bundle

Horace W. LaBadie, Jr.

WINDCREST®/McGRAW-HILL

FIRST EDITION
FIRST PRINTING

© 1993 by **Windcrest Books,** an imprint of TAB Books.
TAB Books is a division of McGraw Hill, Inc.
The name "Windcrest" is a registered trademark of TAB Books.

Library of Congress Cataloging-in-Publication Data

LaBadie, Horace W.
   Upgrade your computer printer and save a bundle / by Horace W.
 LaBadie, Jr.
       p.   cm.
      Includes index.
      ISBN 0-8306-3954-3 (hard)   ISBN 0-8306-3955-1 (paper)
      1. Printers (Data processing systems) — Upgrading.   I. Title.
TK7887.7.L34   1992
004.7′7—dc20   92-15640
                                        CIP

Book editor: Susan Bonthron
Supervising editor: Lori Flaherty
Designer: Jaclyn J. Boone
Cover: Sandra Blair Design and Brent Blair Photography, Harrisburg, Pa.   EL1-H

Contents

Acknowledgments *ix*

Precautions *x*

Introduction *xi*

Part 1   Compact Dot Matrix Printers

1   The generic printer 3
The power supply *3*
The platen *4*
The motor *5*
The electronics *5*
ROM and RAM *5*
The interface *6*

2   Expanding internal RAM 7
Download RAM *8*
Buffer RAM *8*
Adding RAM *9*
Seikosha SP-2000 *10*
Okidata Microline 192 *14*
Panasonic KX printer *16*
When not to upgrade *24*

Smith-Corona *26*
Epson FX-80 *29*
Assessing the upgrade *34*

3 Expanding internal ROM *37*
Okidata ROM *37*
Epson ROM *39*
Seikosha, Apple, and Epson *45*

4 Internal interfaces *49*
Serial interfaces *51*
Epson *52*
Panasonic *56*
Okidata *59*

5 Color as an option *63*
Color mechanics *64*
Citizen *65*
Panasonic *68*

6 Fonts *75*
Font cards *75*
ROM chips *76*

Part 2 Ink Jet Printers

7 The ink jet: a brief history *83*
The generic ink jet *84*

8 Adding RAM and ROM *87*
DeskJets *87*
RAM *87*
ROM *89*
The logical upgrades *91*
DeskJet to Plus or 500 *91*
DeskWriters *102*
Bubble Jets *109*

Part 3 Page Printers

9 Lasers and "lasers" *115*
The generic page printer *115*
Laser printers *115*
LED and LCS printers *118*

10   Expanding page printer RAM   121
Hewlett-Packard   *121*
Apple   *127*

11   Expanding page printer ROM   131
Apple   *131*
Cartridges—the other ROM   *134*
    Fixed-form font cartridges   *134*
    Custom font cartridges   *137*
    Scalable font cartridges   *139*
More than type   *140*
Hewlett-Packard PCL   *141*
Adobe PostScript   *141*
PostScript emulators   *142*
    Pacific Data's Pacific Page   *142*
    Adobe cartridges   *143*
    CPI's JetPage cartridge   *143*
    UDP's TurboScript cartridge   *143*
    Canon LPB-4   *145*
PostScript vs. the emulators   *145*
    Speed   *146*
    Compatibility   *148*
PostScript beyond the cartridge slot   *148*
    The Cannon CX engine   *148*
    The Cannon SX engine   *150*
PostScript beyond the 300 dpi horizon   *153*
    High-resolution controllers   *154*
    What the manufacturers don't want you to know   *155*

Part 4   Other Hardware

12   Daisy wheel and thermal printers   165
Daisy wheel: They ought to be called Sinclairs   *165*
Thermal transfer: just a note   *170*

13   Printer sharing   171
Switch boxes   *171*
    Manual   *171*
    Automatic   *173*
Buffers, converters, and low-level LANs   *175*
    Converters   *175*
    Data managers   *177*
    JetWay   *182*
    ServerJet   *187*

Macintosh users   *190*

LANs   *194*

Cabling   *194*

14   Paper handling   *197*

Bottom-feeding mechanism   *197*

Automatic sheet feeder   *198*

Cassettes   *200*

Part 5   Software: When Hardware Won't Do

15   Software: The substitute for hardware   *205*

Spooling buffers   *205*

Soft fonts   *211*

Dot matrix   *213*

Laser and ink jet   *215*

Page description languages   *225*

Hewlett-Packard PCL   *227*

Adobe PostScript   *227*

Appendix A   RAM chips, SIMMs, and SIPPs   *241*

Appendix B   Font samples   *265*

Index   *273*

Acknowledgments

I extend my gratitude to the following persons for their help in my research for this book: Teri VanderBoegh, Steve Rossow, Dodie Bump, Chuck Rogers, Darrell Ingold, Daniel Dresselhaus, Adriene Forester, James Lunning, Leslie Drohan, Don Lancaster, Don Thompson, Billi Lynch, and Rex Wickenkamp.

To the following companies that have provided products to be reviewed and photographed, I offer my thanks for their cooperation: Hewlett-Packard, Custom Applications, Inc., Citizen America, Dresselhaus Computer Products, UDP Computer Products, ASP Computer Products, and Pacific Data Products.

The following companies have provided photographs and/or data, for which I thank them: Pacific Data Products, Xänte Corporation, Okidata Company, Seiko-Epson America, Computer Peripherals, Inc., and Canon USA.

Precautions

✓ Always turn off the printer and unplug the power cord from the AC outlet before disassembly.

✓ Allow capacitors in power supply several minutes to discharge their stored current. Large capacitors can retain very high voltages for longer than you might expect.

✓ When using metal tools in the printer, never touch the pins of chips of short components together.

✓ Be extremely careful around high-voltage power supplies and high-voltage components of laser printers.

✓ Never open the laser scanning unit of a printer while the printer is operating. Laser beams can cause eye damage.

✓ Discharge static electricity by touching the metal frame of the printer before handling chips.

✓ Handle chips only as necessary. When not in your hand, chips should be either in their protective package or in the sockets.

✓ Double check orientation of newly inserted chips before reassembly and application of power.

Introduction

This book can show you how to expand the utility and prolong the useful life of your printer. It covers practically every printer made in recent years. It is not, however, a compilation of every printer ever sold. *PC magazine* estimated it tested more than 800 printers during the last 10 years and that more than 300 of them were still in production or in stock. And that number represents only a fraction of the total number of printer models actually produced in the last decade. Because it is clearly impossible to mention every printer without becoming a Dr. Johnson of printers, the intention is to follow Linnaeus and categorize.

To produce a text that is readable, reasonably priced, and submitted within a given time, requires that generalizations be the rule rather than the exception. Therefore, *Upgrade* is divided into dot matrix printers, ink jet printers, page printers, other hardware, and software alternatives. You may or may not find your own printer mentioned, but the printers represented are fairly representative members of those classes. In most cases, they were chosen because they were ready to hand, but some were chosen because their omission would have been inexcusable.

You'll learn how to add RAM, ROM, fonts, and other goodies to bring your printer closer to the newest and most-coveted printers without having to actually buy one. Naturally, some old printers just can't be brought up-to-date, and not every deficit can be fully compensated, but you will probably be surprised at what can be accomplished for some machines at the seeming ends of their evolutionary paths.

There are a couple of printer types that receive short shrift: daisy wheel and thermal transfer. The first is given a cursory treatment because daisy wheels are obsolete, and the second are barely mentioned because they tend to fall into two groups not particularly amenable to this type of book—the very cheap, and therefore disposable, and the very expensive, and therefore proprietarily supported. In any case, anything that could be said of them would be but an echo of the matter in the dot matrix section. There are only so many ways to say that the RAM chip goes into the open RAM socket.

As always, the procedures illustrated in this book are to be undertaken only by persons who feel comfortable around the insides of their electronic equipment.

If you are careful and read everything through thoroughly before opening your printer or computer, you will find that there isn't much that you can do that is mortal for either you or the machine. Still, it pays to look the territory over and identify the landmarks before setting to work. The best source of information when you are in a quandary is, surprisingly, the manufacturer of your printer. Many, if not all, will be happy to sell you the technical repair manual for just about any printer they have ever made. Sometimes a telephone call to their technical staffs will be all that is required. And not all repair technicians are averse to giving out a little free advice. Good luck.

Part 1

Impact
Dot Matrix Printers

Chapter 1

The generic printer

If computer stores were modelled after supermarkets, among all the dozens of national brand printers on the store shelves, you would find a section in which the cartons were stark white with simple black lettering. This section would be the generic printer section, and the items stocked in those unremarkable packages would be, like generic cereals or detergents, designed on certain basic principles to perform, in general, like other products in their category.

All printers are practically the same under the shells of their outer cases. Stripping a dozen printers from a dozen manufacturers down to their components would yield piles of very similar, in many instances, identical parts. Even the internal arrangements would have unsuspected consistency.

Because this book's purpose is to provide as much pertinent information about as many printers as possible, it is worthwhile to form some rough judgment of the applicability of the specific to the general. I work with individual printers that are representative of others in their classes.

Printers, whatever their origin, share many features in their design. A generalized description of the generic dot matrix printer would include the power section, the paper transport section, the print head and its transport mechanism, and the print logic circuitry.

These common landmarks of printer design are found in nearly the same locations in most printers. This results from necessity, much the same way all automobiles share certain design characteristics by necessity.

The power supply

The power supply is usually located in a rear corner of the unit, near the power cord receptacle or power cord entry point (Fig. 1-1). As a matter of simplicity, the power on/off switch can be found in the same area, reducing the number and length of any wires running between the switch and supply.

1-1 The landscape of the generic printer with power supply in foreground, ROM and RAM in middleground, interface connector in background, and tractor and platen at left.

If you are uncertain whether you are looking at the power supply, a further clue to its identification is provided by the transformer. The transformer, in older printers and in those of more recent manufacture that have been designed for business use, is usually the most massive single part of the printer. In some machines, notably those made by Seikosha, the transformer is normally small, accounting to a large degree for the lightness of that company's printers. As well as the transformer, you will find large capacitors and some form of heat dissipation as part of the power supply section.

The platen

The platen identifies the paper feed mechanism. In 99 out of 100 cases, a tractor or pin feed will also be part of the paper feed. This grouping is located near the center of the printer, front to back. The platen and paper transport are vestiges of the typewriter heritage of the modern printer. Innovation in this area is so rare that it might be considered eccentric. However, the Panasonic KXP-1124 shows that there is room for improvement; it uses a fixed semicircular platen, rather than a rotating cylindrical one, thereby conserving material and weight.

The motor

The pulse or stepper motor is the driving force of the paper feed mechanism. The motor is usually drum-shaped and sits behind one end of the platen. A series of gears that transfer the stepper motor energy move the platen and tractor. The stepper motor can produce discrete and minute movements under control of the logic circuitry, thereby making possible the small fractional line feed increments that dot matrix printers boast.

A carriage motor moves the print head laterally along a rail or rod. A timing belt governs the motor's movement. The timing belt is a notched plastic ribbon that interrupts a photooptical circuit as the print head traverses the paper. The number of interruptions translates into a measure of distance that the logic circuitry uses to position the head.

The electronics

The electronics of the printer are usually concentrated on one board. This board integrates both the input/output and the logic functions of the printer, and can be thought of as a simple one-board computer.

The CPU is usually of the older 8-bit generation, perhaps of the Intel 80xx or comparable series, because the computational and addressing functions of this type of computer are quite elementary. The 8-bit design limits to 64 kilobytes (64K) the amount of memory that the CPU can directly access, although bank switching can extend this range by shifting the set of addresses among different banks.

ROM and RAM

A separate chip or chips, sometimes called a *slave* or *coprocessor*, directs the input/output. The memory of the printer is about evenly divided between read only (ROM) and random access (RAM) memory. Both types of memory are usually socketed, although some designs solder the first RAM chip and leave an empty socket for the optional expansion.

The ROM is contained in one or two chips, selected from a group of programmable, read-only memory (PROM, EPROM, EEPROM) chips in an 8-bit-deep architecture. These chips hold the essential permanent instructions of the printer and control everything from resident character sets to the type of printer that the machine emulates. The most frequently used emulations fall into the Epson, IBM, and Apple ImageWriter families.

The RAM, like the ROM, is contained in one or two 8-bit-deep chips. These are static RAM, and the upper limit for expansion is usually 32K. Some RAM, between 128 bytes and 2K might be found in the CPU as well.

The interface

Generic printers are shipped with either a parallel or serial interface already installed. The Centronics standard parallel port is more common, while the serial port is offered as an option. If the serial interface is factory installed, the manufacturer sometimes produces two distinct versions of the printer. This is based on the same logic board, with the components soldered to the board as required for each interface.

Aftermarket installations are usually accomplished by plugging an auxiliary board into a multipin header provided for that purpose. The connectors are almost always at the back, although some printers place them in a recessed area under the printer.

Chapter 2

Expanding internal RAM

The user looking for an immediate improvement in printer performance can find it by expanding internal printer RAM. Added memory is first on every user's list of expansion items for the computer or high-end page printer, because its advantages are obvious: greater data capacity and more speed. But the low-end printer is often overlooked as a candidate for RAM expansion, probably because most people are not aware of the improvement in performance gained by even a small increment to the printer's standard memory. Indeed, if RAM expansion is thought of at all, it is often passed off as insignificant, because the usual amount of RAM that can be added (about 32K) is minute compared to the gargantuan expansions that are routinely made in computers and page printers, where the increments are measured nonchalantly in megabytes. The difference, of course, is a matter of degree.

Whereas the page printer or computer must manipulate huge amounts of data in nanoseconds, the dot matrix printer performs very simple tasks, and the data that it receives and prints are in a compact and finished format. Assuming that the file being printed contains only text and no graphics, each byte of the incoming data stream is roughly one printed character. Therefore, the dot matrix printer can process a large data file easily within the 32K limit of its memory. 32K is thirty-two thousand characters, perhaps six pages of double-spaced text.

Internal printer RAM serves as a temporary storage space for two species of incoming data. If the data consists of matter to be printed, the RAM in use is called a buffer. If the data consists of a predefined character set or set of printing parameters that have been sent down into the printer from the host computer, the RAM is regarded as a protected download area. Both types of data can reside simultaneously in the printer's RAM, although not in the same RAM addresses.

RAM sometimes can be partitioned by the user according to need, setting aside more or less space for one type of data or the other. Usually, a download area is relatively small in comparison to the buffer area, because the amount of data to be printed can be expected to be many times greater than the set of printing parameters. In any case, RAM is volatile, and the contents are lost when power to the printer is shut off or a flush command is received, thereby resetting all the bits to zeros.

Download RAM

The download area of the printer is a special reserved space where the user stores durable data to be used repeatedly by the printer. The most common use is for a typeface definition, which is discussed in the chapter covering font expansions. The download area is also used—primarily in page printers—for a set of printing extensions or interpolated commands. The resident command set is extended by combining commands and functions to provide a subset of complex page descriptors that are frequently needed. These serve as a shorthand to reduce the size of files containing the actual matter to be printed. Thus tedious repetitions can be shortened into a type of macro command that can be inserted as required. The increase in printing speed is the product of the smaller file size and the fact that the downloaded command subset has to be interpreted only once by the printer rather than at each occurrence.

The section of RAM assigned to receive downloaded data is normally written once and thereafter protected. That portion of printer memory is subtracted from all memory installed, and the buffer RAM size is adjusted accordingly. By assigning a smaller number of bytes to the download area, you can increase the buffer size without the physical addition of more RAM chips. Conversely, a larger download RAM cache removes more buffer RAM from use. Tradeoffs such as this are typical of all aspects of computer design and operation. It can only be obviated by increasing real memory.

RAM can be assigned in one of two ways: with software commands or from a menu or front panel button entry, as in the Okidata Microline 182. (The Microline 182 provides for varying amounts of download RAM according to the emulation and the expansion RAM installed.)

Buffer RAM

The data RAM buffer provides the printer with a continuous byte stream. This makes the printer's CPU more efficient, because time that would otherwise be consumed by the communications protocol and input port service can be devoted to internally processing data for printing. The buffer also frees the computer from the printer's data requests, allowing the computer to perform other tasks. Allocating a larger print buffer relative to the download area improves the performance of both the printer and the computer (within the other constraints of the printer, and dependent upon the type of data being printed). As I stated before, the printhead speed ultimately determines the printer's speed.

In practical terms, text or graphics that use one of the printer's built-in or downloaded character sets are processed and printed faster than text or graphics that originate in the host. For example, a file using the character set that is present in the printer's ROM can be printed quickly, because the file consists of ASCII standard codes that the printer compares to its internal equivalence tables. An ASCII code is located in the table and the dot pattern that has been assigned to that code is printed. The same process applies to downloaded typefaces, which are kept in a RAM equivalence table.

On the other hand, if the data to be printed are derived wholly from the host, as in the case of text files that use Macintosh or Windows typefaces, the printer is working entirely in bit-image mode. This mode requires that more dots be printed, and the buffer is filled not with simple ASCII codes but with bit patterns. As a comparison, one character in ASCII format will fill one byte (8 bits) of buffer RAM, but the same character in graphic format might fill twenty or thirty times as much RAM. Obviously, buffer RAM is rapidly used up by bitmapped graphics-based applications and that internal buffering is frequently ineffectual in reducing printing time.

Adding RAM

Printers manufactured since the early 1980s are provided with at least 2K of internal RAM. Early models were limited in the amount of RAM by the high cost of memory chips, and by the memory-addressing capabilities of their processors. Such processors could not effectively manage more than 64K of total memory, including the ROM that contained the printer's typefaces and command set. Since the majority of computers were operating comfortably with 64K RAM, an internal buffer of 2K was considered generous for printers. It was also adequate for the majority of printing jobs, since almost all files printed were in the form of simple text. Even a printer designed for business (for example, the Star Gemini 15—a wide carriage printer used for spreadsheets and forms) had only a 2K buffer. There were no empty sockets, and the sockets used for existing buffer RAM accepted 16-pin chips. Chips larger than 2K are made in packages with 18 or more pins and therefore cannot be used to replace the old chips.

You are likely to find that your printer is designed to accept either an $8K \times 8$-bit (64K) or $32K \times 8$-bit (256K) static RAM chip for expansion. An examination of the circuit diagrams or of the main printed circuit board itself can provide that information.

Chip denominations are idiosyncratic. Thus, the same 64K chip from different manufacturers can be rather sensibly labelled HM6264-12 (Hitachi) or UPD4464-12(NEC), or incomprehensibly designated TC5565P-12 (Toshiba) or AM99C88-12 (AMD). The density of the chip is usually listed at the end of the first "word," while the speed is abbreviated in the suffix after the dash (12 = 120 ns).

2-1 Seikosha SP-2000 9-pin dot matrix printer.

Ask for chips by their generic architectural arrangement 8K × 8 or 32K × 8.LP means low power. Low power RAM is not the same as static RAM.

Seikosha SP-2000

The easiest machine to demonstrate the basic technique of RAM upgrades is the Seikosha SP-2000 (Fig. 2-1). Seikosha brand printers, made by Seiko, are not the first computer peripherals produced by this company. They also own industry-leading Epson. Seikosha is a sister line that fills the lower price range for home and office printers.

Seikosha printers are all compactly built, lightweight, durable, and, it goes without saying, fully and legitimately Epson-compatible. Many of Radio Shack's printers are also manufactured by Seikosha under the Tandy label. The SP-2000 is the successor of the SP-1000, and like the 1000, is sold in three forms: the parallel 2000, serial 2000AS, and the serial 2000AP Apple ImageWriter clone. It is a 9-pin printer, but it produces an excellent near letter quality (NLQ) type almost indistinguishable from that of 24-pin printers. The parallel non-Apple serial printers can emulate either the Epson FX850 or the IBM Proprinter II, are rated at 192 characters per second (cps) in draft mode and 48 cps in NLQ, and weigh a slight 7.3 pounds. Indicative of their small mass is the power consumption figure: 24 watts while printing and just 9 watts when inactive. As with automobiles, a lighter machine requires less power to move it.

Since that time, however, RAM manufacturing technology has advanced by orders of magnitude, so that the density of memory chips has reached four megabits (4 million bits). Computer RAM is normally arranged in banks of eight or nine chips, since early chips were of such low density that it was necessary to spread an 8-bit byte across memory addresses on eight separate chips. This made sense, because RAM was not as reliable then as it is now, and a defective bit could be isolated to a certain chip and then worked around without replacing the chip. Since most memory was used for text, an error in one bit of one ASCII character merely resulted in a misspelled word. The ninth chip, used in machines where accuracy is critical, keeps a running check on the other eight chips in the bank. The chip stores the parity bit of each byte,and is called the *parity RAM.*

Except for page printers and special buffers, however, RAM in printers is rarely present in more than two chips and is usually contained in static RAM. Static RAM, as opposed to the more common dynamic RAM, is composed of low power or CMOS (complimentary metal oxide silicone) chips, which do not require the continual electrical refreshing of dynamic RAM. Static RAM is retentive in low-power situations, and more importantly for printer uses, it is often found in full 8-bit configurations. Thus, a chip that has 256K bits is not arranged in 1-bit ranks, to be used in bank width applications, but in 1-byte columns, wherein memory is arrayed in continuous addresses. Data are stored in full bytes, and can therefore be retrieved quickly. One static RAM chip with such an architecture constitutes a RAM bank in itself. This compact storage medium is well-suited to the rather cramped controller board landscape found in printers, where the larger portion of space inside the cabinet is occupied by mechanical components, leaving scant room for the electronics.

The SP-2000, unlike many other machines, is designed so that the end user can easily open and service the printer without becoming involved in a tangle of wires and connectors or losing a lot of screws. To add RAM to the 2000, you need only remove the top, pull out the ribbon cartridge, slide the print head carriage out of the way, and remove a rectangular plastic panel which snaps over a slot in

2-2 RAM access door of SP-2000 under printer's ribbon cartridge.

the bottom of the inner housing (Fig. 2-2). The cover slides to the right as you face the front of the printer.

The internal RAM supplied with the printer is an 8K static column chip. It may have the Sony name (as in Fig. 2-3), or Hyundai, Hitachi or some other maker's mark, but it will be in the chip socket as shown. You cannot confuse it with any other chip.

2-3 Native 8K RAM chip of SP-2000, indicated by tip of screwdriver. (Note: Do not probe inside of any electrical device with metallic objects.)

Because the factory-installed buffer is 8K, we have chosen a 32K replacement, which gives a fourfold increase in RAM for data reception. The 32K chip comes in a package identical to that of the 8K chip (Fig. 2-4), and the two are interchangeable. All you need to do is pull out the extant chip and push the new one into the socket.

The chip puller (also shown in Fig. 2-4) is a tong with thin, curved pincers that grasp the chip package under its ends. Remove the chip by securely hooking the prongs of the chip puller onto the chip and pulling upward with a gentle rocking motion, alternating the force between each end, so that the chip is lifted from the socket a little at a time (Fig. 2-5). Do not yank the chip as though you were pulling teeth; the pins of the chip can be bent or broken easily by a violent removal.

Put the replacement chip into the socket in the same orientation as the original; that is, with the indentation of the chip at the same end as the triangular index on the socket, which marks the location of pin socket 1. Some sockets have a notch rather than a triangle to show the correct positioning of the chip. In any case, if you are uncertain about the socket, insert the new chip so that its label is readable from the same direction as that of the adjacent chips (Fig. 2-6).

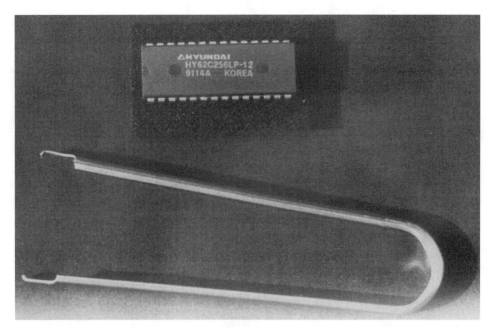

2-4   Typical 32K × 8-bit static RAM chip and chip puller.

2-5   Removal of old chip with chip puller.

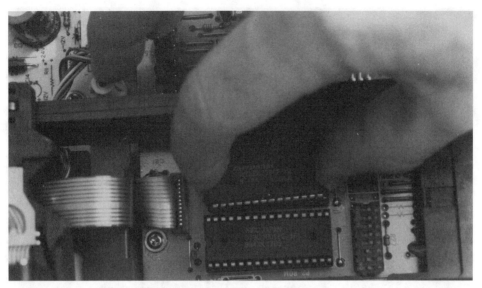

2-6 Insertion of new static RAM chip. Orientation is same as other chip.

Close the printer by reversing the process you used to open it, and the installation is complete.

Okidata Microline 192

The Okidata Microline 192 (Fig. 2-7), circa 1985, is another small 9-pin printer, indeed, one of the earliest of the compact printers. It is 14.17 inches wide, 10.83 inches deep (front to back), 3.15 inches high (about the size of the telephone directory for a large city), and weighs 9.9 lbs. It is smaller but heavier than the Seikosha SP-2000. The additional weight is due to the transformer and the metal plate om which the printing and carriage mechanisms are mounted in the plastic case. Although it feels more solid than the Seikosha, it is not appreciably more durable by reason of heft. The rated print speeds are 160 cps at 10,12, and 17.5 characters per inch (cpi), and 80 cps at 5,6 and 8.5 cpi in draft mode. There is no NLQ typeface as such, although the emphasized print serves that purpose.

To open the Okidata 192, you remove two Phillips head screws in the front of the machine. These screws are visible after the lid over the print head has been popped off. When you remove the platen knob, you can lift the top of the case upward and set it aside.

Approached from the rear, the power supply is on the left side, and the interface connector is in the right rear corner. The main circuit board covers the rear half of the printer, and is conveniently exposed to view and touch when the printer is open (Fig. 2-8).

The socket which is designed for reception of a RAM chip is directly to the right of the cluster of large capacitors, between the CPU and the RAM bank 0 chips that have been soldered to the board. The CPU is an Intel 8051 (under the

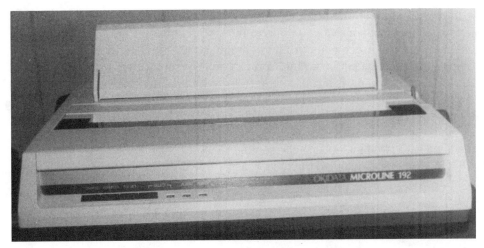

2-7 Okidata Microline 192, circa 1985, a capable, compact 9-pin printer.

shadow of the platen), and the RAM is a 4168 chip. The CPU has 128 bytes of RAM integrated into the chip, and the 4168 provides 8K of buffer area. The empty location between is assigned to RAM bank 1. There is an additional 4K RAM area which is used to store the start-up default parameters, such as the character set and typeface. This is dedicated and cannot be used by incoming data.

The maximum optional RAM capacity of the 192/193 printer is 8K. Therefore you need an $8K \times 8$ chip to expand the printer's total buffer RAM to 16K. Install the chip with the notch toward the interface connector (right of center in Fig. 2-8). If you feel uncomfortable installing the chip by hand, you can purchase

2-8 Inside the 192. Power supply is left, RAM and ROM are top and bottom center pairs of sockets respectively. One of each is empty.

a chip insertion tool that holds the chip in a friction-grip metal jaw. The tool has a plunger mechanism that you push to insert the chip into the socket. This tool ensures that the force is distributed equally across the length of the chip, and helps to protect against bent pins. You can buy the tool with an extractor in a set from Radio Shack, or as a separate item from almost any mail-order electronics supplier. The only problem with this type of tool is that, because of the depth of the jaws, it can be difficult to see whether the chip is correctly placed over the socket. It is easy to offset the chip by a pair of pins so that the chip is mistakenly installed with two pins outside the socket.

Once you have installed the chip, reassemble the case in the reverse order of disassembly.

Panasonic KX printers

The third representative dot matrix printer is the Panasonic KX-P1091. The KX-P1091 is not exceptional in its design. You must remove five screws to take off the cover. Three are in the front, along the top edge after the lid has been taken off. Two are in the rear, one at each corner of the cabinet. The interior is rather cramped (Fig. 2-9). Two-thirds of the main circuit board is covered by the printer mechanics. On the accessible portion of the board there is one open socket, so the opportunity to make a mistake is as small as the available workspace.Unfortunately, it is not RAM socket, but is reserved for ROM. If the potential for expansion is important, then this type of printer should be avoided.

2-9 Inside the Panasonic KX-P1191, familiar 9-pin printer.

Panasonic has since become more considerate, adopting designs with greater flexibility and clarity. The KX-P1180 is an example of this recent trend. The KX-P1180 is a 9-pin printer, about 16.75 inches wide, 13.4 inches deep, 5.2 inches high, and weighing 14.1 lbs. It is not a compact printer, and its design has not yet evolved to the level of some other printers, including some from Panasonic, but it does have an empty RAM socket.

You open the KX-P1180 by removing the top lids, inverting the printer, and using a flat-bladed screwdriver to disengage the case catches (Fig. 2-10). The catches are located in recesses on each front corner, adjacent to the rubber feet. Turn the printer right side up, take off the top of the case, and remove two screws located in the front (Fig. 2-11) in the area of the print head carriage. You can then lift up the printer mechanism, exposing the main circuit board. This is not a lovable arrangement. The location of the empty RAM socket is shown in Fig. 2-12. It will take a 32K static RAM chip. Insert it as indicated by the black semi-circle on the socket in the diagram.

The next step in Panasonic printer evolution is embodied in the KX-P1124 (Fig. 2-13). This 24-pin printer offers many more features than the 9-pin KX-P1180, to which it bears a strong resemblance. It is only slightly larger and heavier than the KX-P1180 (16.9 inches wide, 14.1 inches deep, 5.6 inches high, weighing 18.7 lbs.), but its features are much more advanced than is apparent at first glance. Aside from the higher density print obtained from the 24 pins, convenience of use and servicing are among its many improvements over earlier

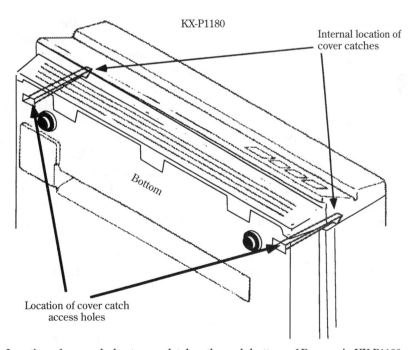

2-10 Location of access holes to case latches through bottom of Panasonic KX-P1180.

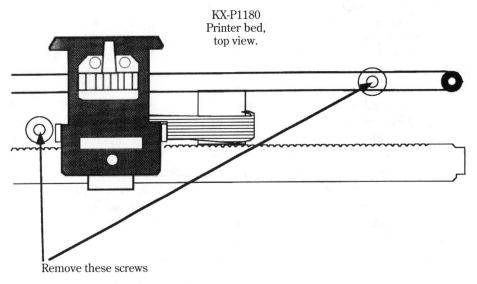

KX-P1180
Printer bed,
top view.

Remove these screws

2-11 Location of screws in 1180's bed.

models. The front panel (in the indented area below the controls) is a door that can flip down to open a path for single-sheet feeding. This innovation was included to make use of paper parking, once a luxury in paper handling that has now become a necessity.

You can remove the entire front panel by prying open the top edge and pulling forward (Fig. 2-14). When you have lowered the panel you can remove the three screws that fasten the top of the case to the lower portion, and lift off the top of the case. The front panel remains attached by the cabling for the control buttons and indicators.

The engineers at Panasonic obviously anticipated the addition of RAM by the user. They placed the main circuit board so that the RAM socket is in an uncluttered and unambiguous position (Fig. 2-15), making it easy to insert a 32K chip. Note that a Macintosh-compatible version of the 1124, called *WriteImpact,* is sold by GCC. References here and elsewhere in this text to the 1124 are applicable to that model as well. The path for RAM expansion in the 1124 is not as elegant as in the Seikosha SP-2000, but it is certainly a great deal easier than for many other printers, including the remaining two Panasonic printers to be discussed.

The KX-P1695 is a high-speed (330 cps) 9-pin printer, which looks very much like the 1180 and 1124, but is transitional in design, with characteristics of both siblings. The front panel is removable, as in the 1124 (although only the top portion is affected), and the top of the cabinet is fastened by three screws, also as in the 1124 (Fig. 2-14).

Unfortunately, the resemblance to the 1124 is only case deep, and to work on the main printed circuit board (PCB), you must follow the procedure for the 1180 model. As with the 1180, the printer mechanism must be removed before the cir-

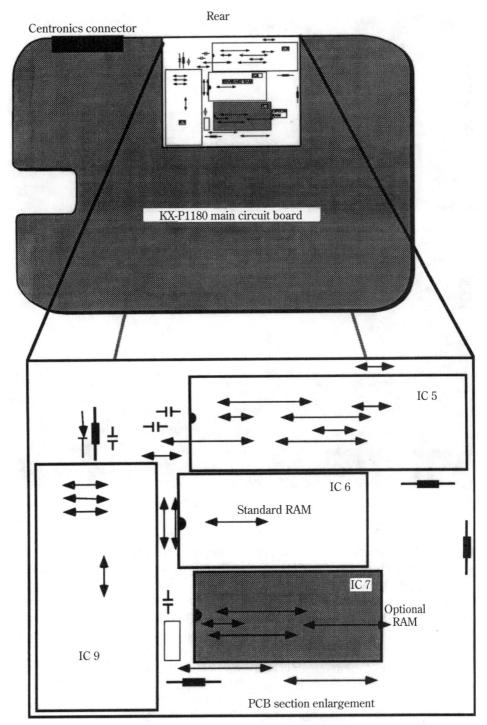

2-12 Relative location of socket for optional RAM on KX-P1180's main logic board.

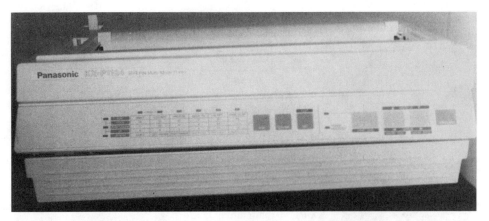

2-13 Panasonic KX-P1124, among the most successful 24-pin printers made.

2-14 Opening of 1124 begins with prying off of the front panel. Note partially removed case screws at each side and center.

cuit board can be reached. In this case, however, there are three times as many screws (six) to be located and taken out. Their positions are shown in Fig. 2-16. As you can see in the diagram, one of the screws is partially obscured by the tractor/friction paper feed selector. Depending on your work area, it may or may not be better to unplug the connectors from the PCB to the printing mechanism. If you can manage to lift the mechanism and stretch the cables, do so, because there are seven cables to disconnect and reconnection can be confusing.

The optional RAM in the 1695 is inserted in the IC 4 location, as shown in the diagram (Fig. 2-17), between IC 2 (ROM)and IC 5 (factory RAM). The CPU can access up to 64K, so a 32K chip is the largest that can be added. Its orientation is the same as that of its adjacent chips.

The KX-P1524 is a heavy-duty, high-speed, 24-pin printer. It is a wide-carriage

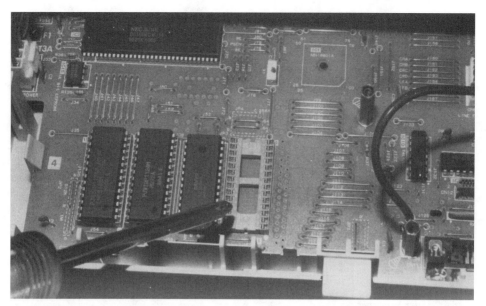

2-15 Inside the 1124: Open RAM socket on cleanly designed board.

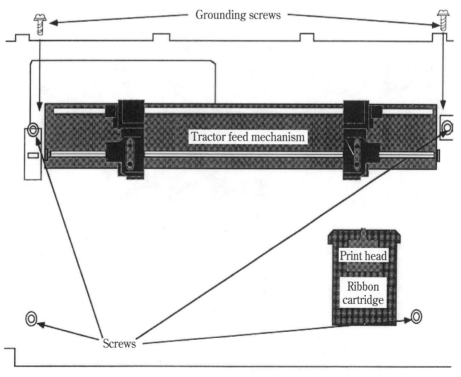

2-16 Screw positions inside Panasonic KX-P1695.

printer, weighs about twice as much as the 1124, and can be considered a business class machine. Its factory-installed RAM is contained in two 8K chips, and provision is made for the addition of a 32K chip.

The disassembly of the 1524 is rather more complicated than that of any other Panasonic discussed here. First, you must pry off the front panel by push-

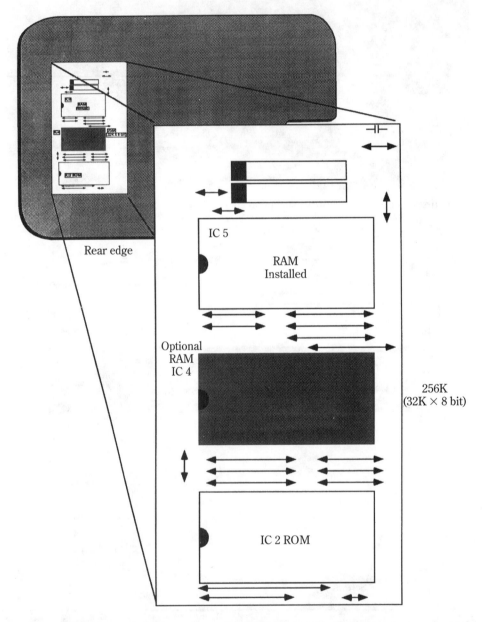

Rear edge

IC 5

RAM
Installed

Optional
RAM
IC 4

256K
(32K × 8 bit)

IC 2 ROM

2-17 Relative location of socket for optional RAM on 1695's circuit board.

ing three hooks on the inner surface of the upper cabinet. Next, unplug three connectors to disengage the front panel from the printer. Then invert the printer and take out the six cabinet screws. Finally, place the printer upright and pull off the platen knob. You can then lift off the top of the cabinet.

Inside, you must take out nine screws (Fig. 2-18). Then you must unplug all of the cable connectors except the rearmost, which is for the power cable. Next, disconnect the carriage cable to the print head from the special clamping connector (located in the front of the printer in Fig. 2-18). Be very careful, because reinstallation can be difficult if the cable end is deformed during removal. Remove the two cable clamp screws, and then pull up on the top of the clamp to open the connector before attemping to loosen the cable.

After lifting out the printing mechanism, you can locate the main logic board in the rear of the case. It is half-covered by a shield, which also must be removed before the RAM socket will be visible. You must remove all of the screws marked by arrows in Fig. 2-19. Following that procedure, you can finally do the simple task of adding the RAM chip.

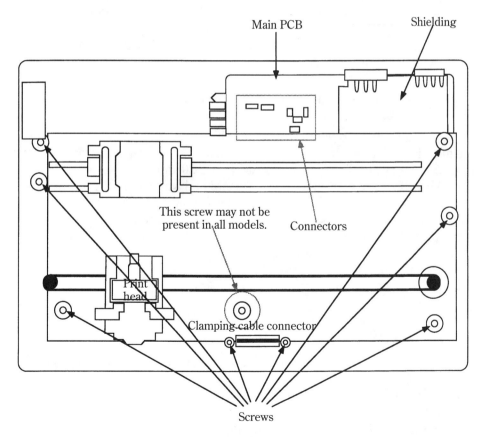

2-18 Layout of Panasonic KX-P1524. Remove all indicated screws to free printer mechanism.

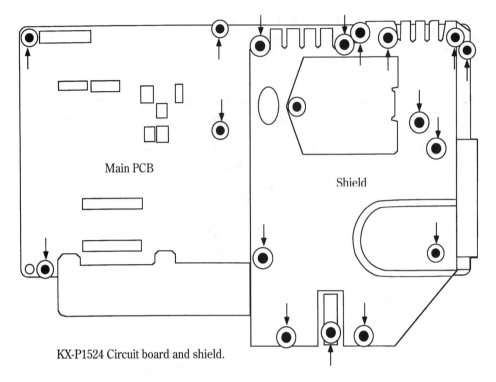

Main PCB

Shield

KX-P1524 Circuit board and shield.

2-19 After removal of printer mechanism, remove screws in shield to expose chips.

Looking from the rear, there are four chip positions on the left-hand side of the main PCB. The rearmost chip, IC 2, is ROM. The two most forward, IC 3 and IC 4, are factory-installed 8K × 8-bit RAM (Fig. 2-20 and 2-21). The empty socket, designated IC 5, is reserved for optional RAM and will hold a 32K × 8-bit chip.

Without the optional chip, the excess buffer capacity of the printer is either 152 bytes or 288 bytes, as selected by switch 7 on the third DIP switch at the rear of the printer. With the optional RAM installed, the receive buffer is expanded to 25.5K, so it is worthwhile to add the chip.

Now that you have learned what is involved in a typical RAM upgrade, you need to learn when to upgrade and when to pass.

When not to upgrade

The primary criterion on which to judge your printer's suitability for upgrade is the ratio of labor versus the benefits. Does the improvement in performance gained by installation of RAM justify the sometimes troublesome disassembly of the printer?

Consider the following two difficult cases, which serve as examples against which you can measure your own particular case.

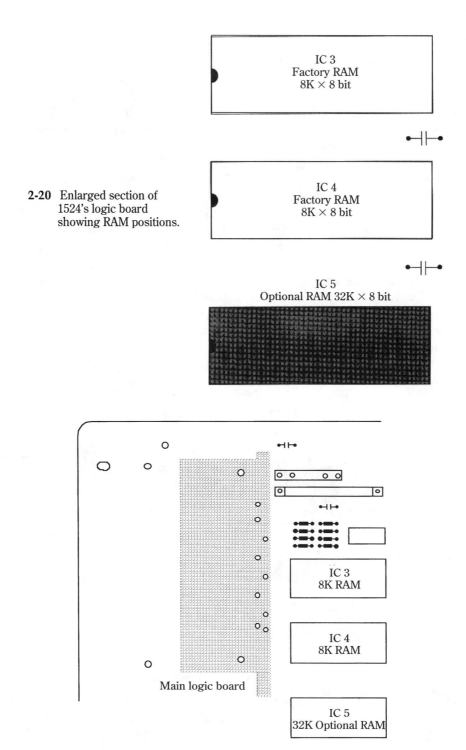

2-20 Enlarged section of 1524's logic board showing RAM positions.

IC 3
Factory RAM
8K × 8 bit

IC 4
Factory RAM
8K × 8 bit

IC 5
Optional RAM 32K × 8 bit

IC 3
8K RAM

IC 4
8K RAM

IC 5
32K Optional RAM

Main logic board

2-21 Area shown in 2-20 relative to other components on 1524's logic board.

Smith-Corona

The Smith-Corona name is so closely associated with the office equipment, especially typewriters, it is quite natural that the company should begin to sell printers as the computer's share of office space increased at the expense of the typewriter's share in the middle 80s. The Smith Corona D200–D300 series of dot matrix printers, manufactured by TEC for the Smith Corona label, consists of two machines, the narrow-carriage 200 and the wide-carriage 300. The machines were electronically and mechanically identical except for their paper width capacities.

The D200 was a versatile, dray horse of a printer. Its specifications were quite ordinary, and it fitted comfortably in the mid-range of printers manufactured in the period. One of its superior features was the standard inclusion of the serial RS-232C interface, which almost all other printer manufacturers made optional on their products (Fig. 2-22).

The D200, like the majority of printers of its time, was equipped with a 2K RAM buffer. Another advantage which the D200 had over competing printers was an open socket for a second 2K of RAM. Similar printers (for example, the Star Gemini models 10 and 15), had the same 2K buffer, but without an open socket and with the factory RAM soldered to the board (Fig. 2-23), preventing future expansion. The D200 was also inexpensive, making it quite a bargain, all things considered.

Opening the printer is not difficult. There are four screws, one at each corner, that attach the upper portion of the case to the lower. Once the top of the case is removed, however, things become more complicated.

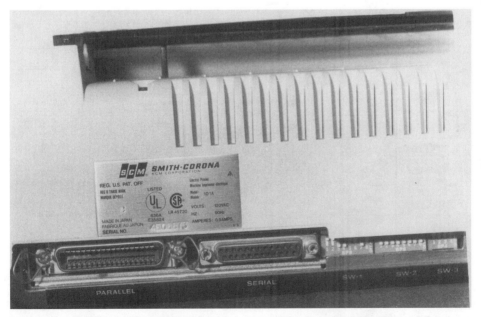

2-22 Rear of Smith-Corona D200 9-pin printer with dual ports and DIP switches.

2-23 Printed circuit board of Star Gemini 15.

First, the circuit board is covered by the printer mechanism (Fig. 2-24). There are four screws holding the mechanism to the case. Remove these and another problem presents itself. There are two open sockets on the circuit board, IC 34 and IC 35 (Fig. 2-25). We are interested in IC 35.

In most printers, it would now simply be a matter of inserting a 2K RAM chip in that socket, but the D200 requires some preliminary steps before that new chip can be used. There is a jumper location next to the socket for IC 35 (Fig. 2-26). This socket is a dual-purpose receptacle. If the jumper is across the P and

2-24 Inside the D200. Unfortunately, most chips are hidden by printer mechanism.

2-25 Removal of D200's printer mechanism reveals chips.

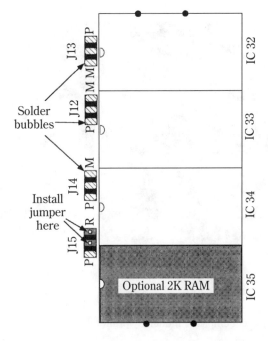

2-26 RAM and jumper positions identified on D200's circuit board.

center nodes, the socket is presumed to contain PROM. If the jumper links the R and center nodes, the printer logic recognizes the chip as RAM.

There is no shorting block, which means that one must be installed before the connections can be jumpered. Even if you are content to install a jumper wire as a permanent fixture on the board instead of a shorting block, you must still disassemble the printer and perform a radical operation on the circuit board in order to use the RAM.

First, mark and disconnect all the cables plugged into the board, after which the board must be removed from the printer. Next, you must heat the solder bubbles in the jumper position carefully and suck them into a desoldering pump or bulb. Then you must solder a jumper wire or shorting block in place. Finally, you replace the board in the printer and begin reassembly.

With all of that done, what have you gained? The buffer size has been doubled, but is the 2K of extra RAM enough bonus in return for the amount of labor and nervous energy expended? Anytime that you are forced to take a soldering iron to the main circuit board for such a small reward, you should pause and ask, Is it worth it? 2K is 2K, to be sure, but the actual utility of such a small block of memory in everyday printing is negligible. I do not think the upgrade worthwhile. When the labor is compounded by the risk of incurring permanent damage to the circuit board through a slip of the soldering iron, the possible addition of 2K becomes doubly unattractive. Reduce one of the negatives, or increase the positive, and the scales can tip in favor of the upgrade. If you figure that you have only your labor to lose, then the attempt might seem desirable. This is a borderline call, as the umpires put it.

Epson FX-80

Another printer for which the effort and expense to upgrade are considerable, but the benefits proportionately higher is the Epson FX-80 (Fig. 2-27). The Epson FX-80 (Fig. 2-27) is but one in an apparently interminable succession of dot matrix printers from the company that made dot matrix printers as ubiquitous as Elvis impersonators. You might consider the FX-80 hopelessly obsolete, because it can print only in draft mode, its paper handling can be wretched at times, and its speed is mediocre at best.

Adding RAM to the FX-80 seems impossible at first. There is nowhere on the circuit boards to add chips. The sockets provided for RAM (Fig. 2-28) are already filled to capacity. They are capable of supporting chips no more dense than 2K, either 4016 ($2K \times 8$ bits) static RAM or 6116 ($16K \times 1$ bit) dynamic RAM, amounting to a total of 4K RAM. Fortunately, because so many of the FX-80 and FX-100 Epsons were sold, and because Epson retained many design elements in later generations of printers, there are options.

There are four Phillips screws holding the case together: two in the top at the rear, set in deep wells, and two under the front cover, beneath either end of the cover's hinges. You must lift out the cover to allow insertion of the screwdriver into the recesses housing the screws. Disconnect from the main board

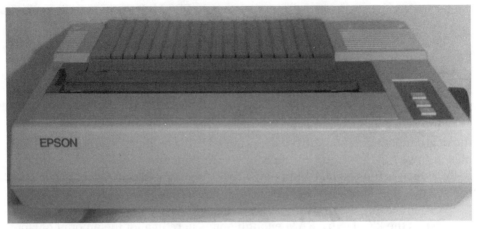

2-27 Epson FX-80, a very old reliable 9-pin printer.

the cable running from the control panel in the top of the cabinet and lay aside the case.

The best RAM upgrade for the Epson line is manufactured by Image Technology of Littleton, Colorado, and is called the Mega Buffer (Fig. 2-29). The Mega Buffer is an add-in board that can hold up to 4 megabytes of RAM. Amounts of memory in that range are often found in page printers, but such a prodigious buffer is unique in impact printers.

2-28 Epson FX-80 main logic board. CPU is top center, two 2K × 8-bit SRAMs are on right, and ROM chips are on left. Connector for optional interface is at extreme left.

2-29 Image Technology's Mega Buffer, Centronics interface and potential 4MB RAM buffer for older Epson printers. (Mega Buffer courtesy Image Technology)

The installation of the Mega Buffer into an Epson printer such as the FX-80 is very simple. There is a multipin connector (Fig. 2-30) on the main logic board that is normally used for the reception of an optional serial interface. This is not the same connector used by the FX EXT board found in some FX-80 machines, but is adjacent to the parallel interface connector. The Mega Buffer uses this connector, and takes control of data input. Note that the Mega Buffer board contains its own parallel connector; you plug the cable from the computer into this. The buffer itself is contained in a set of dynamic RAM chips installed by the user.

The chips are the rather uncommon 256K × 4 or 1Mb × 4 type, which are more frequently found in video memory. The buffer will function with as little as one chip, which yields a 128K RAM buffer. Chips are arranged in 4-bit nibbles, or half-byte banks, an arrangement that divides data into high and low nibbles.

Commonly, data are stored in RAM in a high and low bytes (sometimes called most significant and least significant bytes), in which a data element is deposited in what would normally be considered reverse order of precedence. A number greater than eight bits must be stored in two or more contiguous bytes, and the first portion of the number is stored in the second byte of RAM. Normally, this scheme is transparent to the computer user, who is ignorant of the shape and location of data.

In the Mega Buffer, the matter only arises because you must install RAM chips in accordance with the high and low byte (or nibble) convention. Therefore, if two chips are to be installed, you do not place them in consecutive board positions but in consecutive memory positions. Install the first chip in the first socket of the low nibble bank. Install the second chip in the fifth socket, which is

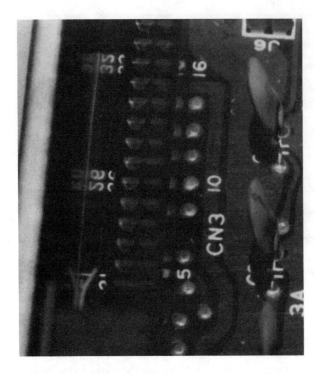

2-30 Connector for FX EXT board found in some FX printers.

the first socket of the high half of the bank (Fig. 2-31). More memory is added in that same alternating manner, two chips at a time, one high and one low.

Once the board has been plugged in, you need only connect the frame ground wire to a lug on the board (Fig. 2-32), and remove a shorting block on one set of jumper pins. This block enables the self test of the Mega Buffer board, and it is wise to allow the printer to cycle through this test once before connecting the printer to the computer.

The test verifies the RAM and prints out the result. Depending on the amount of memory you have installed, the test can run for 5–10 minutes. There is a string attached to the shorting block (Fig. 2-33) so that block can still be pulled after the self test has been successfully completed, even when the case has been closed and the screws tightened down.

Apart from the advantages of having a large buffer available for multiple downloading, as the memory expands above 128K in the Mega Buffer, the speed of its parallel interface doubles. At 128K, the data transmission speed is normal between computer and printer. Beginning at 256K on the buffer board, data transmission happens at twice the normal speed. So, the computer benefits from the whole file being downloaded into the printer in one continuous stream without pauses while the printer processes the data into printed matter. It also benefits from the super-speed transmittal rate of the surrogate interface built into the Mega Buffer.

High nibble bank   Low nibble bank

2-31 Mega Buffer in place. RAM banks are at bottom. String on lower right leads to self-test shorting block. (Mega Buffer courtesy Image Technology)

2-32 Grounding wire on right attaches to ground screw on logic board. (Mega Buffer courtesy Image Technology)

2-33 With case closed, top connector is active, bottom unused. Test jumper is still in place.
(Mega Buffer courtesy Image Technology)

Assessing the upgrade

What improvement can you expect to see in the printer's data-handling speed after a RAM upgrade has been performed? To give a meaningful answer is not possible without reference to particular facts. If, for example, you had upgraded a 2K or 4K buffer to 8K but the length of a typical document you print never exceeds 2K or 4K, then there would be no improvement! The same is true when an 8K buffer has been expanded to 32K or 40K. If the size of the files normally printed never exceeds 8K, there will be no difference to notice. In other words, why did you bother to make the upgrade?

Assuming you want to expand your printer's RAM buffer because the size of the files you ordinarily print are larger than the printer's factory RAM, what order of improvement can you expect in the printer's data reception? Table 2-1 gives some comparisons of the change as a result of RAM expansion. As an arbitrary benchmark, a plain ASCII text file of approximately 14K was selected as the test document to print on various machines. The times shown were measured from the moment of pressing the enter key until the computer was free to perform other tasks. Continuous fanfold paper was used. The data file was text only, single-spaced with a minimal amount of formatting. These parameters limit the interpretation of the times, which is my intention.

These figures indicate some very dramatic changes in the amount of time that the computer is tyrannized by the printer's monopoly. In draft mode there is little to be said because the printer has less actual work to do and can move at top speed. In near letter quality mode, the time savings are astonishing, beginning at better than 300 percent and rising to almost 5900 percent for the ancient Epson. In most cases, the upgrade results in draft and NLQ modes using roughly equivalent times to download the file. Considering that downloading a file when the printer is in NLQ mode ordinarily can take 3 to 18 times longer than in draft mode, this reduction is truly impressive. Even though the actual printing times are not reduced, the time that your computer (and you) have to waste waiting for the printer to complete the job is eliminated.

Table 2-1. Effects of internal printer buffer
on print data reception—ASCII file size 14K.

Printer	Print mode	Buffer size	Time
Seikosha SP-2000	Draft	8K	37 seconds
	Draft	32K	12–15 seconds
	NLQ proportional	8K	8 minutes 15 secs.
	NLQ proportional	32K	15–17 seconds
Panasonic KX-P1124	Draft	8K	1 minute 22 secs.
	Draft	40K	1 minute
	NLQ	8K	3 minutes 20 secs.
	NLQ	40K	55–60 seconds.
Epson FX-80	Draft	4K	2 minutes 2 secs.
with Mega Buffer	Draft	128K (half speed)	12 seconds
with Mega Buffer	Draft	256K (full speed)	10 seconds
with Dots-Perfect	NLQ[1]	4K	9 minutes 49 secs.
with Dots-Perfect	NLQ[1]	128K Mega Buffer	3 minutes 12 secs.
with Dots-Perfect	NLQ[1]	256K Mega Buffer	10 seconds
Okidata Microline 192	Draft	0K	3 minutes 52 secs.
	Draft	8K	2 minutes 2 secs.
	Draft	32K	19 seconds
	Emphasized	0K	4 minutes 13 secs.
	Emphasized	8K	4 minutes 6 secs.
	Emphasized	32K	40 seconds

[1] See chapter on ROM upgrades.

Chapter 3

Expanding internal ROM

A computer printer's "personality"—unlike a human's—is not a subject of debate between those who support the influence of "Nature" and those who argue the influence of "Society." For the printer, Nature and Society are the same. Printers are born and made. Contrary to what one might expect, the personalities of printers are not immutable, although they are fixed. This is not a paradox, merely an unfamiliar formulation of a simple fact. Printers are sent out from the factory with a specific set of internal instructions which are permanently "burned" into their read only memory. Under normal conditions, these internal instructions cannot be altered, but the silicon memories themselves can be replaced.

Nowadays, almost all dot matrix printers come with a split personality: an Epson instruction set and an IBM instruction set, standard in ROM. One is selected by the user and the other is dormant. It was not always thus. Indeed, many features which were once options are now but a flick of a switch or the touch of a button away. Near letter quality printing is another personality trait that was formerly something to be had only as a premium. In computer economics, at least, the trickle down theory does apply, for features once found only in the machines with the highest prices very quickly percolate down into the lower-priced strata. Alice, who found that she must run ever faster merely to remain in the same place, is the very model of the modern peripheral user. Fortunately, it is not necessary to fall behind merely by standing still.

Okidata ROM

Returning to Okidata, it was their practice to produce printers identical in all things except ROM signatures. There were Epson versions and IBM versions. If you purchased one, you were stuck with it, even if your needs changed, unless you went back to Okidata and bought the complementary ROM package for your model of printer. You can still change Microline 92/93 or 192/193 into its counterpart by pulling the old ROM switch.

Let's start with the Microline 92/93. To change the ROM so that IBM compatibility is the default, you must open the printer by removing the covers and the two Phillips screws inside the front. The top of the case is hinged on plastic projections in the rear and may be tilted back and off once the screws are out. At the rear of the M-92 there is a small circuit board which must be removed. In the M-93, the board need not be removed. Take out the two screws holding the board and disconnect the wiring harnesses, labelling them as you proceed so that they can be returned to their correct positions later.

With the board out, find chip socket locations Q4 and Q5, which should be on the right-hand side of the board, just below a set of six DIP switches. Take out any chips that might already be in the sockets. If there is one chip, take a quick look at the DIP switches above to the right. Set the first switch OFF (down), the second switch OFF, and the third and fourth switches ON (up). Leave the other switches as they were. If there are two chips already on the board, leave the entire set of switches at their factory settings. (Note: some models may not have a DIP switch array, only an empty spot on the PCB.)

If you are working on the M-92, insert the IBM ROM chip 31016303 into socket Q4 and IBM ROM chip 31016403 into socket Q5. For the M-93, put chip 31016503 into socket Q4 and chip 31016603 into socket Q5 (Fig. 3-1). Reassemble the printer.

Once the IBM ROM set is installed, the printer gains the IBM character set, including the graphics characters. It prints in Correspondence Quality (CQ) only in the 10 characters per inch mode. All other character settings cause the printer to revert to the data processing (draft) mode. Twelve characters per inch and its double wide derivative are not used.

3-1 ROM chips for Okidata Microline 92 transform Epson-compatible printer to IBM compatibility.

Similar ROM sets are available for the Microline 192/193 and for the older 82A/83A printers. The ROM positions of the 192 are shown in Fig. 2-28.

Epson ROM

The familiar Epson FX-80, to which we previously added an immense RAM buffer, is a printer badly in need of modernization in other areas as well. Until recently, Epson itself had sold its own upgrade kit for the FX-80 and FX-100 printers that contained a new set of ROM chips and a supplementary board that added Selectype features and an 8K RAM buffer. Since its discontinuance, Epson has been selling a competing third-party ROM upgrade which is applicable not only to the FX-80 and FX-100, but also to the 80+, 100+, 85, 185, and 286 members of the FX nuclear family, and to their color cousin, the JX-80. This upgrade is produced and marketed by Dresselhaus Computer Products and is called Dots-Perfect (Fig. 3-2).

The Dots-Perfect upgrade, when installed in an old FX-80 class of printer, teaches it several new tricks, first among them being near letter quality printing. It also adds the IBM character set and Proprinter emulation, as well as a buffer clear command. All of the new functions and most normal printer commands can be selected with the control panel buttons. You can choose NLQ merely by tapping the FF (form feed) button once, and return to Draft quality by tapping the LF (line feed) button once. For other functions, a menu system is activated when the ON-LINE and FF buttons are pressed simultaneously. Thereafter, the FF and LF buttons are used to rotate through the menu items and to select or de-select items. There are fifteen separate functions which may be toggled on or off in various combinations. These are listed in Table 3-1.

Each tap of the FF button causes the printer to move to the next function, which you can then select (or cancel if already selected) by tapping the LF button. The printer emits a beep each time the FF button is tapped, giving audible feedback to the user. You can reset all menu items to their default values by two rapid taps of the LF button. The number of FF button taps represents a fixed location in the menu cycle, making FF button taps additive. Therefore, to select both emphasized and underline requires five taps of the FF button and one tap of the LF button to select the emphasized function, followed by five more FF taps to move to the underline function, and one LF tap to select it. Pushing the ON-LINE button returns the printer to its on-line condition, ready to print in emphasized underline mode.

Activation of a menu item is signalled by a short beep from the printer, and deactivation is signalled by a long beep. The blinking of the ON-LINE indicator light gives visible feedback: it remains on longer during the blink when an item has been toggled on and remains off longer during the blink when an item has been switched off.

There are numerous other functions buried in the ROMs, such as a hexadecimal dump mode, useful to programmers, which can be called at power-up by holding down the FF and LF buttons. You can software-control all functions

3-2 Dresselhaus Dots-Perfect ROM kit for Epson FX/KX printers adds NLQ type to standard draft. Similar kits are available for MX and RX models. (Equipment courtesy Dresselhaus Computer Products)

through Escape sequences, making the upgrade compatible with existing Epson drivers, and allowing the user to write custom routines, for example, in BASIC.

This method of menu itemization and selection is logical, but it is also sufficiently complex to induce confusion. Anticipating this human frailty, Dresselhaus includes a metallized label (Fig. 3-3) to put on the printer that summarizes the options and their corresponding number of button taps.

Installation of the Dots-Perfect ROMs begins with opening the case as described in chapter 2 for the addition of the Mega Buffer. Inside, at the rear (looking from the front) there might be an auxiliary board of the type shown at the center of Fig. 3-4, with a cable trailing to a plug that is attached to a socket on the main board, or there might be another board labelled FX EXT without the connecting multiconductor cable, or there might be no board at all. If there is a

**Table 3-1. Dresselhaus
Dots-Perfect function selection.**

Function	FF button taps
Condensed print	1
Elite (12 CPI)	2
Proportional	3
Double wide print	4
Emphasized print	5
Double-strike print	6
Perforation skip	7
0.5 inch left margin	8
Italicized print	9
Underlining	10
Fine printing	11
8 lines per inch	12
Quiet	13
Slashed zero	14
8 inch paper width	15

3-3 Label showing menu choices with Dots-Perfect ROM upgrade. (Equipment courtesy Dresselhaus Computer Products)

board, you must remove it in order to reveal the ROM sockets. The board is held in place by two or three screws, and is plugged into a multipin socket beneath it on the main logic board. When you lift the board from the socket, you can lay it aside. If it is connected to the logic board by a cable, simply fold the cable back and lay the board down within the printer shell.

The three chips in the Dots-Perfect kit, labelled 4A, 4B, and 5A, are substitutes for the chips already in the printer (Fig. 3-5) and relate to similarly named locations

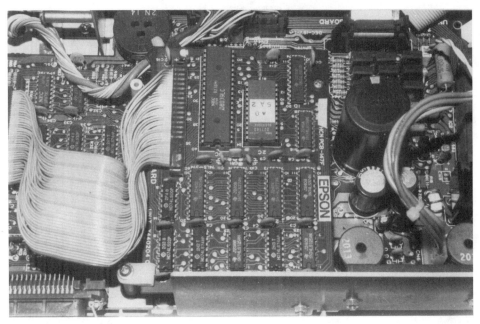

3-4 FX EXT auxiliary board found in some FX printers must be removed to expose ROMs on main logic board.

on the logic board (Fig. 2-28). Socket 4A might not contain a chip, but you should be able to identify the socket for the new chip. You will note that there is a thin wire leading from the small chip, 4B, to one of the larger chips, 5A. Be very careful not to break this wire or its solder joints on either of the chips. Follow the procedures discussed in chapter 2 to remove old chips and prepare new chips prior to insertion. If the socket for chip 4A did not previously contain a chip, it would be a good idea to check the pin receptacles for dirt that might have accumulated over the years, and to clean out the socket with compressed air or a photographic blower brush before continuing.

Once the board and chips are prepared, insert the chips into their relevant sockets, taking care that the chips are oriented correctly in the sockets; that is, with their notched ends facing the rear of the printer and all legs in their corresponding receptacles. Press each chip firmly into its socket and check again for bent or misaligned pins.

On those printers that did not have a chip in socket 4A, you must remove a jumper wire or resistor from the main logic board before you can operate the printer. The jumper or resistor location (near the CPU on the logic board) is called J1, which is silk-screened on the board (Fig. 3-6). Identify this jumper location and if a jumper wire or resistor is present, cut it at one end with a pair of nipping pliers (a set of fingernail clippers will work in the absence of pliers). You need cut only one lead or end of the wire or resistor. Push the wire or resistor slightly aside to ensure that the connection is broken, but be certain that it touches no other connection or component on the board.

3-5 Dots-Perfect ROM chips. Note wire connecting chip 5A to smaller chip. (Equipment courtesy Dresselhaus Computer Products)

3-6 Location of jumper wire J1. Position might be filled with a resistor on some boards, empty on others (as here). Remove if present.

The last board-level modification you must make before reassembly is to move the shorting block on the jumper pins at J7 to the pins at J6. The jumper pins are located just above chip 5A, looking toward the back of the printer (Figs. 2-28 and 3-7). The J6 jumper pins are on the left. If the shorting block is on J7, simply pull it up and off and push it down onto J6.

Finally, you must reset some of the printer's DIP switches. They will look something like those pictured in Fig. 3-8. The eight-switch array is switch one, and the four-switch array is switch two. The switches should be reconfigured to reflect the changes as tabulated in Tables 3-2 and 3-3.

Reassemble the printer, peel the Dots-Perfect label from its backing and affix it to the printer near the control panel, and you will have recycled some valuable

3-7 Shorting block above chip 5A must be placed in position J6 of jumper pins as shown.

3-8 DIP switches which must be reconfigured after installation of Dots-Perfect.

Table 3-2. Epson DIP switch functions
as redefined by Dots-Perfect.

Switch 1

Switch	Function	OFF	ON
1-1	Paper width	Narrow	Wide
1-2	Slashed zero	No	Yes
1-3	Paper out	Yes	No
1-4	Emulation	IBM	Epson
1-5	Extended characters (ASCII 28-255)	Italic	IBM graphic
1-6	Language set	Table 3-3	Table 3-3
1-7	Language set	Table 3-3	Table 3-3
1-8	Language set	Table 3-3	Table 3-3

Switch 2

Switch	Function	OFF	ON
2-1	Printer select recognized	No	Yes
2-2	Auto sheet feeder	No	Yes
2-3	Perforation skip	No	Yes
2-4	Carriage return + line feed	No	Yes

Table 3-3. Language set selection by DIP switch.

1-6	1-7	1-8	Epson language set	IBM language set
❑	❑	❑	SPANISH	INTERNATIONAL
❑	■	❑	SWEDISH	INTERNATIONAL
❑	❑	■	ITALIAN	INTERNATIONAL
❑	■	■	DANISH	INTERNATIONAL
■	■	❑	FRENCH	INTERNATIONAL
■	❑	❑	UK	INTERNATIONAL
■	❑	■	GERMAN	INTERNATIONAL
■	■	■	USA	STANDARD

Legend ■ ON
❑ OFF

resources. How good is the improvement? Figure 3-9 shows actual FX-80 output in its newly acquired near-letter-quality mode. The NLQ of the 9-pin head is surprisingly good, almost as good as that of a 24-pin printer (Fig. 3-10), and certainly the equal of any other more recently manufactured 9-pin printer. A scanned reproduction shows the comparison more clearly (Fig. 3-11).

Seikosha, Apple, and Epson

One last ROM change that might not be sanctioned by the printer's maker is the transformation of a Seikosha serial Epson-compatible printer into an Apple Im-

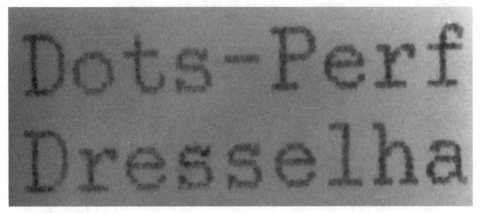

3-9 Highly magnified NLQ output of FX-80 with Dots-Perfect installed. Compare to Fig. 3-10.

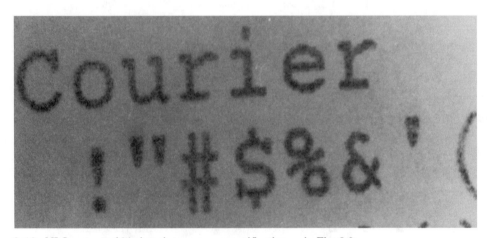

3-10 NLQ output of 24-pin printer, same magnification as in Fig. 3-9.

```
!"#$%&'()*+,-./0123456789
!"#$%&'()*+,-./0123456789:

!"#$%&'()*+,-./0123456789
!"#$%&'()*+,-./0123456789:
```

3-11 Epson 9-pin with Dots-Perfect in side-by-side comparison to Panasonic 24-pin NLQ, scanned and magnified.

ageWriter compatible. The price of an ImageWriter, a C.Itoh-Toshiba product, has always been Apple-high in the sky. Even used, ImageWriters sell at prices that are stratospheric compared to newer, more fully-featured printers. Seikosha SP-1000AS and Seikosha SP-2000AS serial printers, however, sell at sea-level prices, and they are only a sea change away from being ImageWriter workalikes.

The Seikosha 1000AS and 2000AS are the serial interface versions of the standard parallel interface Epson-compatible printers, the 1000 and 2000. Seikosha also produced ImageWriter-compatible versions of those serial printers, with an AP suffix, which are virtually identical to the AS printers except in their ROMs. It is, therefore, quite easy to transplant an Apple-like ROM into a Seiko-Epson body without fear of rejection. Naturally, you can perform the reverse operation with equal ease, turning the AP into the AS if you wish.

The Seikosha 1000 has a cluster of three chips on the logic board. The ROM is the third from the front edge (Fig. 3-12). The Epson ROM is part number 10407-BAS21 in the Seikosha catalog, and the Apple chip is part number 10410-BAP21. Because the Epson chip is 128K and the Apple chip is 256K, you must set a jumper on the logic board to permit the board to recognize which chip is resident. If the Epson chip is used, the shorting block should be placed on jumper J5. To use the Apple chip, remove the shorting block from J5 and place it on jumper J6.

If you have been reading carefully, you will have noted that a small qualification crept into the description of the conversion with the word "virtually." It was introduced to convey that, even with the exception allowed for the ROM chips, the machines are not 100 percent interchangeable. There are some small differ-

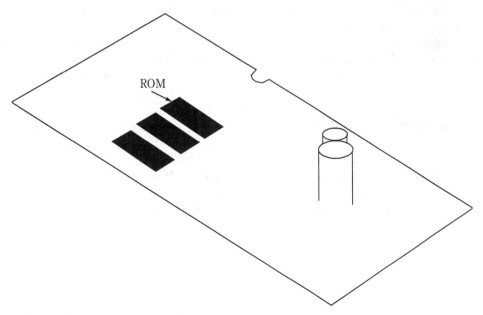

3-12 Location of ROM in Seikosha SP-1000 serial printers.

ences in mechanical gear ratios that can affect the shape of the printed output. For instance, in the SP-1000AP, the carriage return motor has a 15-tooth gear, while the AS version uses a more finely pitched 17-tooth gear. There are similar differences in the ribbon drive-reduction gearing and in the drive pulley. Does that add up to a major problem? If you think so, the necessary parts can be changed. The Epson-for-Apple-version part number substitutions of the affected parts are summarized in Table 3-4. Be aware, however, that Seikosha does not stock any of the Apple-model parts and they can only be purchased on special order from Japan, which might result in a three month or longer wait. The ROM chip is normally only sold with the entire PCB assembly, which lists for $249.95, about $100 more than either the 1000AP or 2000AP series printers cost new at discounted retail outlets. The good folks at Seikosha Parts, however, will burn an EPROM on request for about $30–35, which tilts the $100 savings over a new printer back in your favor.

Table 3-4. Seikosha 1000A serial printers parts substitutions.

Part	Epson AS P/N	Apple AP P/N
ROM	10407-BAS21	10410-BAP21
CR Motor Gear	84300-1080	84308-1080
Ribbon Reduction Gear 1	84300-1671	84308-1671
Drive Pulley	84300-1043	84308-1043

There remains one small difference that is not especially significant: The serial interface connectors are not the same on both printers. However, because it is simpler to change the printer cable than to replace a soldered connector, it is mentioned only so that the proper cable can be purchased or made.

One very common ROM change, that has yet to be mentioned, occurs every day in thousands of homes and businesses, and that is accomplished with the font cartridges. Cartridges are merely small printed circuit cards bearing ROMs with additional typefaces. The cartridges plug into a card edge connector or other bus connector, giving the printer extra ROM area. In its ALQ series of printers, Alps is just one company that has used this idea to expand the selection of typefaces in a simple impact dot matrix printer. If your printer can use font cards or cartridges, and you think that you need additional typefaces, cartridges can be a good way to extend the utility and life of your printer.

Chapter 4

Internal interfaces

There are two types of printer interfaces: parallel and serial.

Centronics parallel interface

Nearly every dot matrix printer is equipped with a Centronics-compatible parallel interface. Centronics was a pioneer in the development of peripheral interfaces, and the term *Centronics interface* was, for a long time, synonymous with the term *parallel interface*. (For an idea of the time frame that defines the term *pioneer* in microcomputer matters, take a look at the Atari 825 printer in Figs. 4-1 and 4-2. This antique is really a Centronics 737 in Atari's clothing, circa 1980. Note that the "Centronics Parallel" interface uses an edge card connector (Fig. 4-3), which can be adapted to the more recent 36-pin AMP shell with the custom cable shown in Fig. 4-4.

Today, Centronics has been absorbed into the Genicom company, and the term *parallel interface* is heard almost exclusively. With the exception of Apple computers, a parallel interface is universally included as standard equipment on modern computers. It would seem, then, that there is no reason to bother about interfaces, yet they remain one of the most perplexing and frustrating problems for computer users. You never seem to have exactly what you need to facilitate connecting this to that: You have only one parallel port and you need two printers, or you have only serial ports, but the best deal you can get is on a printer with a parallel interface.

Fortunately, printer manufacturers are companies of people who use printers and computers, and who know that it is necessary to be flexible. In general, printers can use an interface other than the one sold as standard. Usually, by adding a serial port, although, as we saw in the case of the Mega Buffer, it can also mean adding a parallel port.

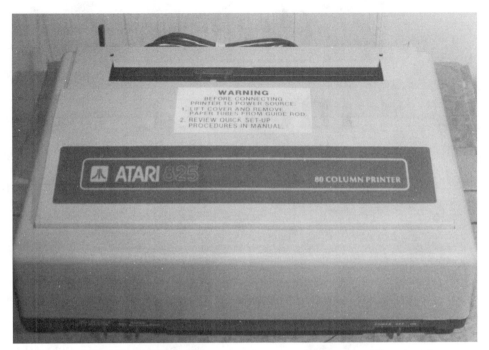

4-1 Antique Atari 825 9-pin draft printer is OEM version of Centronics 737.

4-2 Inside the 825 (aka 737). Design is eccentric by current standards.

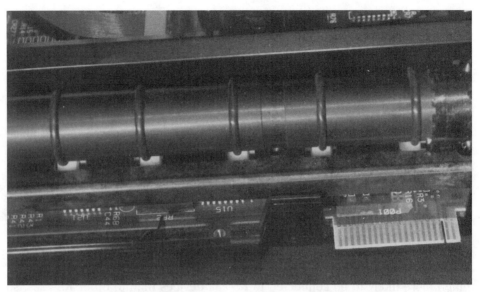

4-3 Atari implementation of "standard" Centronics parallel interface is edge card connector.

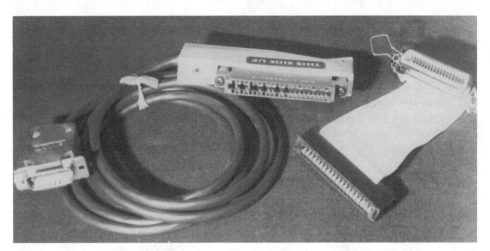

4-4 Atari cable. Adapter on right allows use of now-standard parallel printer cable.

Serial interfaces

Until about 1984, serial communications were considered chaotic enough not to need further complication. The RS-232C "standard" had been implemented in sufficiently numerous and incompatible ways so that none but the most inventive minds at Apple had even considered throwing yet another standard at the public.

The Lisa, Apple's first attempt to break into the office environment with a business computer, used a common 25-pin D connector, but its serial communications chip was covertly faking standard RS-232C. It was, in truth, an RS-422 device in disguise. The Macintosh, Lisa's little brother who grew like Topsy, brought RS-422 out into the open with a 9-pin D-sub connector. Then IBM weighed in with its own revision of RS-232 shrunk down into the selfsame 9-pin D-sub form. Apple then upped the ante to RS-423 format with a mini-DIN 8 connector. Apple didn't invent the 422 and 423, but it did comprehend the advantages of those underappreciated conventions. To the user, this change means only that a new cable is needed to connect an old device, but to hardware designers and software authors it means a great simplification of serial communications.

RS-232 can be implemented with as few as two wires, but it is more often found as a tangle of crossed and shorted lines. RS-422, by contrast, insists on matched pairs of positive and negative lines, one pair for transmitted data and the other for received data. As these pairs go alternately high and low, the transmission of data is signalled and acknowledged. There is no ambiguity when two RS-422 devices are connected to each other. Unfortunately, RS-422 devices are much more likely to be connected to RS-232 devices than to other RS-422s, so that a good deal of user pain is the result. Add the IBM AT and XT serial connectors and there are now three fairly confusing serial communications standards from which manufacturers can choose.

Epson

The foregoing digression explains the availability of two serial interfaces for Epsons. Image Technology, maker of the Mega Buffer, also sells RS-232C and RS-422 serial interfaces with optional buffers for the Epson FX series printers. For the normal printer and computer combination, either the RS-232 interface or the RS-422 will do equally well. Any difference noticeable to the user will be largely a matter of cabling, as mentioned above. If, however, the computer is itself an RS-422 device, specifically a Macintosh, then the like interface for the printer will simplify matters. Although the Mac can fall back to RS-232 conventions as necessary, the RS-422 is easier to work with for the user, since the matched pairs of lines eliminate any timing or signal complications between the computer and printer. A second reason to choose the RS-422 over the RS-232 is the extended range—as much as 5000 feet—which the RS-422 makes possible should the computer and printer be placed apart in distant sites. For our purposes, the RS-232 interface will illustrate the installation.

Having already mentioned the FX-80 and demonstrated that it is a simple matter to add a buffered parallel interface, I'll once again use it as an example, this time for the addition of a serial interface. The procedures for opening the printer and identifying the major landmarks are set out in chapter 2. Figure 4-5 shows the location of the connector into which you can plug optional interfaces. If an FX EXT board or auxiliary board is present, it might be necessary to remove it temporarily in order to locate the connector properly, but the serial interface board and the native board should both reside in the printer without

4-5 Enlargement of section of Epson FX-80 logic board showing connector for optional interfaces. See also Fig. 2-28.

crowding or mutual interference. If the multistranded cable obscures the connector, it can be tucked to one side to clear the way for the interface card.

On the bottom of the board are two rows of closely spaced header pins embedded in a plastic foam strip (Fig. 4-6). Remove the strip. To insert the pins into the connector on the logic board, simply push the interface board down on the connector until the pins are completely and firmly seated in their respective

4-6 Image Technology's serial interface and buffer for older Epsons. RAM buffer is in two chips at upper left. (Interface courtesy Image Technology)

sockets. Take care to align the pins precisely before pushing the board home. Make certain that all of the pins are in the connector, and that none will be bent or broken during the installation. If the holes on the corners of the board line up with the screw holes in the plastic mounting posts that rise up from the logic board, then the interface has been correctly installed. Use the screws provided with the kit to secure the interface to the posts.

The interface board has an 8-position DIP switch on the rear edge, mounted to the left of the DB-25 connector (Figs. 4-6 and 4-7). The switches are used to set the default parameters for operating of the board. The first three switches, numbers 1, 2, and 3, from the left, are used together in various combinations to select the baud rate at which data are to be received by the printer. For communication to be possible, the baud rate selected must be the same as that at which the computer is transmitting. If the computer is transmitting at 300 baud, then the printer must be set up to receive at 300 baud. The higher the baud rate used, the faster the transmission rate of data from computer to printer, and the sooner the computer will be free to go on to other tasks.

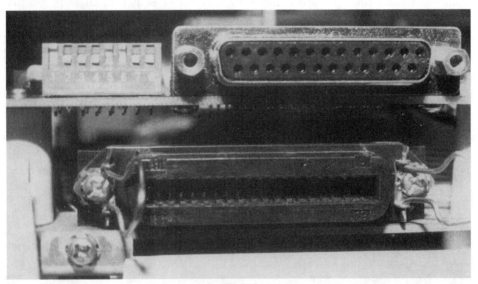

4-7 Interface installed. DIP switches set serial communication parameters. (Interface courtesy Image Technology)

Baud rate is roughly equivalent to bits per second (bps); thus, 300 baud can be approximately construed to mean that 300 bps are being sent. Although that might sound fast, remember that there are 8 data bits to one byte or data word, so that 300 baud is actually only 37.5 bytes of data per second. Because it takes one byte for a single ASCII character in a word, 300 baud can translate into as few as six or seven English words per second. The real transmission rate drops even further when you add to that rate the overhead in clock cycles that the computer and its software consume in transmitting the data over the interface, and the printer uses up in receiving.

The fastest speed permitted by the printer's interface is 19,200 baud, but many computers or software packages can only transmit at 9600 baud. Check the manuals for the computer, the computer's serial interface, and the computer software to determine the appropriate rate. The printer DIP switch settings for the possible baud rates are tabulated in Table 4-1.

**Table 4-1. Image Technology RS-232C
interface baud rate DIP switch settings.**

Baud Rate	Switch 1	Switch 2	Switch 3
150	❑	❑	❑
300	■	❑	❑
600	❑	■	❑
1200	■	■	❑
2400	❑	❑	■
4800	■	❑	■
9600	❑	■	■
19,200	■	■	■
Legend	■ ON		
	❑ OFF		

The next four switches are used to select the length of the data word, parity or no parity, odd or even parity, and type of handshaking. Switch 8 places the printer on-line or in the self-test mode. Switch positions and functions are shown in Table 4-2.

Table 4-2. DIP switch 4 to 8 functions and settings.

Switch	Function	ON	OFF
4	Data word length	8 bits	7 bits
5	Parity used	Yes	No
6	Parity type	Even	Odd
7	Handshaking	RTS	XON/XOFF
8	On line/local	Self-test	On line

Again, the computer settings for the communications parameters must be the same as those for the printer. Usually, the printer device driver will permit the setting of all parameters for the computer to match those already set in the printer. Typically, the settings selected will be 9600 baud, 8 bits, no parity, and XON/XOFF handshaking.

The serial interfaces also offer an optional data buffer. The buffer is contained in two chips that can be installed in the sockets shown in Fig. 4-6. They are in the area just behind the DIP switches. As in the Mega Buffer, they are arranged in high and low nibbles, so that either one or two 256K × 4-bit or 1Mb × 4-bit chips can be used. If one chip is used, it is placed in the low nibble, and memory is 128K or 512K. Two chips produce 256K or 1Mb of buffer RAM. Even 128K is far in excess of the optional buffer ordinarily found in impact printers. With no RAM installed, there is an 80-byte buffer integrated into the CPU.

All that remains is to remove the small cutout panel at the rear of the printer to leave an opening for the DB-25 connector. Purchase or make a suitable cable to connect the printer to the computer. Cables for an IBM-type machine terminate in a DB-9 or a DB-25 connector. Note: The original interface must not be used while the serial board is installed in the printer. So, you cannot alternate between the interfaces, to serve, for instance, two computers.

Panasonic

Panasonic printers offer a serial interface as an option. The same model serial interface, KX-PS10 (Fig. 4-8), is used in several printers, including the KX-P1124, which will serve as an example for the expansion. The interface can also be installed in the KX-P1180, 1191, 1123, 1624, and 1695. Because Panasonic's manual for the interface includes machine-specific instructions for installation, and the same principal points apply to all, I will only describe installation in the 1124.

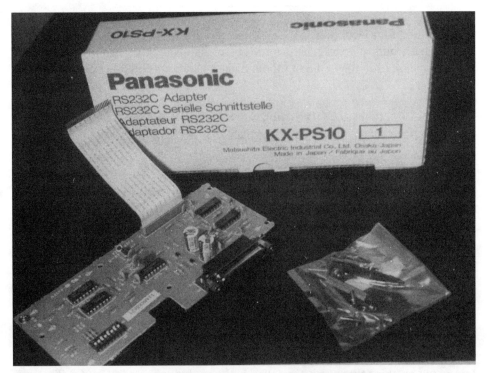

4-8 Panasonic KX-PS10 optional serial interface for several Panasonic printers.

You open the printer to install the serial interface in the same manner as for RAM expansion, described in chapter 2. Unplug the power cord, pull off the platen knob, pull down the front panel, remove the three screws, and take off the top of the case. There is a cutout panel in the rear of the case (Fig. 4-9) that must be taken out to allow the DB-25 connector to protrude. Inside the rear of the printer the connector for the ribbon cable from the interface is located on the right-hand side, looking from back to front (Fig. 4-10).

4-9 Cutout in rear of printer's case for optional interface connector.

Before the board can be put into the printer, however, two hexagonal posts must be screwed into holes in the bottom of the printer to act as supports for the board and to receive the screws that fasten through the board.

The hexagonal posts are supplied with the interface. Bend the ribbon cable back over the front edge of the interface board, and press it firmly into the connector on the logic board as shown in Fig. 4-11. Properly seat the cable by making sure it is evenly and tightly grasped in the connector. Lower the board into the printer and insert the screws to fasten it to the plastic and metal posts. The installation is complete.

Reassemble the case and reconnect the power cord. Set the serial communications parameters for the 1124 and 1124i from the front panel as explained in the printer's user manual. Ignore the DIP switch settings. For the 1124, 1124i, 1123, 1624, and 1695, the factory default settings are 9600 baud, 8 bits, with parity. For the 1180 and 1191, the defaults are 1200 baud, 8 bits, no parity, all of which are set with the DIP switches on the interface board (Fig. 4-12). Special

4-10 Location of connector for serial interface board on KX-P1124 logic board.

setup instructions for the 1123, 1624, and 1695 are in the operator's manuals supplied with the respective printers. Tables 4-3 and 4-4 contain the switch combinations for the KX-PS10 interface for the KX-P1180 and 1191.

It is interesting that just five lines are used in the DB-25 connector: Pin 1 for the frame ground, Pin 2 for transmitted data, Pin 3 for received data, Pin 7 for the signal ground (a reference), and Pin 20 for the data terminal ready (DTR) hard-

4-11 Ribbon cable from interface plugs into logic board connector.

4-12 Serial configuration DIP switches on KX-PS10 interface board.

wired handshaking. It is also curious, but of no importance, that the DIP switches are set in a pattern exactly the reverse of that used by the Image Technology board.

Okidata

Most Okidata printers have, as an option, either a high-speed or super-speed serial interface. The Okidata Microline 192 and 193, discussed in earlier chapters,

Table 4-3.
KX-P1180 and 1191 KX-PS10
serial interface baud rate DIP switch settings.

Baud Rate	Switch 1	Switch 2	Switch 3
150	■	■	■
300	❏	■	■
600	■	❏	■
1200	❏	❏	■
2400	■	■	❏
4800	❏	■	❏
9600	■	❏	❏
Legend	■ ON		
	❏ OFF		

Table 4-4. DIP switch 4 to 8 functions and settings.

Switch	Function	ON	OFF
4	Data word length	7 bits	8 bits
5	Parity used	No	Yes
6	Parity type	Odd	Even
7	PRINTER	Mark	Space
	BUSY signal	(–12V)	(+12V)
8	Handshaking	XON/XOFF	DTR

have the necessary connector for serial interface expansion (Fig. 4-13). As with the Panasonic and Epson, it is a very simple matter to plug in the Super Serial board and set the parameters by DIP switch (Fig. 4-14). Okidata is one of very few companies that offer an RS-422 version of the serial interface option.

As easy as it is to add a board to most printers, some companies have postulated that many users, if given the preference, would prefer not to have any contact whatsoever with a PC board and have enclosed their serial interface options in a plastic case. Alps and Citizen have adopted this modular cartridge design for some of their printers. All you have to do to add the interface is snap open a panel or door on the printer (Fig. 4-15) and pop in a sealed box. There is a connector in the printer that mates with a connector on the cartridge, and that is that. Close

4-13 Okidata Microline 192 logic board. Connector for Super Serial board is comb-like structure at top right.

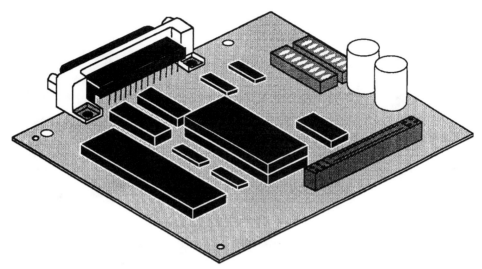

4-14 Okidata Super Serial interface board (RS-232C). DIP switches are on right, next to capacitors.

the hatch and the printer is ready for serial setup. If serial interfaces are going to remain options, this is certainly the way that they ought to be handled in all future designs.

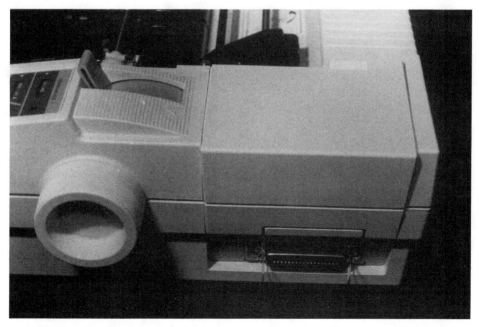

4-15 Hatch for installation of serial interface in Citizen printer. See also Fig. 5-5. (Printer courtesy Citizen America)

Chapter 5

Color as an option

RAM, ROM, and interfaces are the big three of printer expansion. Those are the areas in which there is the greatest need for upgrading, and usually by intention, they are the areas most amenable to upgrading in the great majority of printers. There is another option that recently has become more popular, if not actually more important, and that is color.

The mechanics of color impact printing have been around in much the same form for some time. Contemporary color 9-pin printers adhere to Epson JX-80 compatibility as their standard, which is a commentary on how little color-printing technology has advanced in comparison to color-display technology. The JX-80 standard, based on 1970s technology, places serious restrictions on the number of colors that can be mixed, and thus reduces the utility of color printers, since fidelity to the displayed image is the touchstone of computer printing.

There is no good, inexpensive color impact printer that can produce accurate paper printouts of complex color computer images. Color is fine when used in broad blocks of the primary hues, for instance in a bar graph, but a portrait captured on a color monitor and printed by any dot matrix impact printer adorns the subject with a blotchy, pimpled complexion. Resolution must suffer, because colors that cannot be directly mixed—say all but a dozen of the 16 million commonly available—must be printed by a dithering process which groups adjoining color dots to fool the eye into seeing a single color. While this may work on the illuminated screen of a television or color computer monitor, on paper it fails. Still, used with discrimination, color from an impact printer can add life to the page.

To be perfectly clear, either your printer is born to be colorful or it is not. If a printer is meant only for black printing, then the only way to make it print in color is to have a selection of solid primary color ribbons and to switch them in and out of the printer, printing one color at a time. This method has the advantage of perfect simplicity, but it also has the disqualifying disadvantage of perfect tedium. It is time-consuming, messy, and tends to wear not only on the nerves but on the printer and on the printed page as well. In order to print in shades or to print in more than one primary color, you must run the same page through the printer many times, once for every color that makes a shade or for every primary used. Altogether, it is better to abstain.

If your printer is capable of printing color, you probably already know that, or you should. Look in the operator's manual: manufacturers are not shy about advertising the capabilities of their printers. If you are looking for a color printer, here are some to consider: the Apple ImageWriter II, the ALPS ALQ series, the Epson JX-80, EX-800, and LQ-2500, the Star Rainbow 1000 and 1020. All of these are color capable right out of the box. All they require is the appropriate color ribbon. Why are these printers color capable while others from the same makers are not? Look at a color ribbon and the answer is obvious.

Color mechanics

Color ribbons are created when separate bands of color ink, usually red, yellow, blue, and black, (or yellow, cyan, magenta, and black) are laid down along the length of the fabric of a ribbon. But getting the color on in separate bands is a lot easier than getting it off in the same separate bands or in the right order if colors are to be mixed. The printer needs three things before color can be printed: (1) the color lookup table must be present in ROM so that the printer logic will recognize the color requested and be able to direct the print head and ribbon to print it; (2) the ribbon carriage must be upwardly mobile; and (3) there must be a mechanism to synchronize the motions of the print head with those of the ribbon to find and print the correct colors.

The ROM either contains the color information or it doesn't. It is that simple. Between similar machines within a product line, you might be able to extract the ROM from a color model, such as the Star NX1000 Rainbow, and place it into the monochrome NX1000, but that would not convert the black-only printer into a color printer. For this to happen, the printer would have to be able to move the color ribbon up and down in precise increments, so that only one band of color falls beneath the pins of the print head.

Ordinarily, the ribbon in a black-only printer simply goes from one side to the other: lateral movement is all that is required of it. In color printing, vertical motion is also required, which means that the designers of the printer must make modifications to the basic printer design, allowing movement of the ribbon in two dimensions. A typewriter with a correcting or two-color ribbon has the essential mechanics, but they are refined in the color-capable printer, due to the more exacting tolerances involved in computer-driven printing. Finally, there must be a means of linking this vertical ribbon motion to the main power train of the printer. Therefore, if a printer is not designed with the requisite ribbon carriage and motor linkage, even if it has the required ROM routines, it cannot be adapted to color printing—with one or two exceptions.

Citizen

Citizen dot matrix impact printers are almost unique in that, while they cannot print color in their standard configuration, they can add that capability as an option. The printers do not have the basic mechanism that makes compound movement of the ribbon possible, relying instead on a separate motor to make it color capable. The motor is the option that drives color printing in the Citizen printers. The ROM is already color aware.

The color kit for Citizen printers therefore consists of a motor and a color ribbon cassette (Fig. 5-1). The printer has a reserved bracket on the right-hand side of the print head well (Fig. 5-2) into which the color motor fits. The ribbon carriage is spring-loaded and can be elevated and depressed with the fingers.

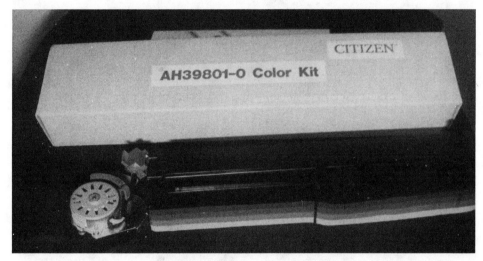

5-1 Citizen color option kit for many Citizen printers. (Some Tandy printers are also made by Citizen.) (Equipment courtesy Citizen America)

The motor receives signals and power from the logic board circuitry through a connecting cable, which plugs into the printer housing just above the motor bracket (Fig. 5-3). One end of the color cassette fits into the gearing (Fig. 5-4) attached to the motor, which then raises or lowers the ribbon cassette to bring the required color band under the print head pins.

Installation of the motor and ribbon is the same across all color-capable printers in the line. This is an excellent example of the advantages of standardization of parts within a product line. To notify the printer that it has been converted from black to color printing, you must set a single DIP switch (Fig. 5-5) in the 200 GX or you must invoke a menu option from the LCD panel in the GSX-140 Plus. The 200's DIP switches are in a cavity on the end of the printer, into which the optional serial interface module is placed. The Citizen 200 emulates either an Ep-

5-2 Color motor mounted in bracket at right-hand end of print head well in Citizen 200 GX. (Equipment courtesy Citizen America)

5-3 Connector on color motor plugs into printer to transmit color signals to motor. (Equipment courtesy Citizen America)

5-4 Both sides of Citizen color motor. Gears engage ribbon cassette to shift color bands. (Equipment courtesy Citizen America)

5-5 Location of DIP switches in Citizen 200 GX. Connector at left is for serial interface. (Equipment courtesy Citizen America)

son JX-80 or EX-800 when in color mode. The 140 Plus emulates the Epson LQ-2500 with color.

In the event that there is some color fringing due to incorrect shifting of the ribbon, there is a detent-stopped lever (Fig. 5-6) on the color motor that adjusts the degree of shift. Running through each color one at a time, the lever is moved up or down a notch until all colors print clearly and without edge mixing. A problem which can simulate such fringing results from failing to seat the ribbon cartridge fully in the GSX-140. Because the ribbon carriage is spring-loaded, it tends to stop pushing on the cartridge when the spring begins offering resistance, leading you to believe that the cassette has been inserted satisfactorily. However, it must be pushed until it clicks solidly in place or the colors will not print correctly. This is not a problem with the 200-GX, although the 200 and 140 are practically identical in their mechanical construction.

5-6 Detent-stopped lever on color motor to adjust color band purity. (Equipment courtesy Citizen America)

Panasonic

The Panasonic MP-1300AI is another printer which is adaptable to color. It solves the same problems as the Citizen printers, but in a less elegant manner. A color kit, the MP-10 (P/N MP-13005), contains a color ribbon, a snap-in printed circuit board module, and a large ribbon drive (Figs. 5-7 and 5-8) to convert the black printer. The PCB is housed in a slim case and holds the color ROM, RAM used as a color buffer, and the print head driver circuitry. The PCB is inserted through an aperture in the top of the printer case at the rear, and fits into a large connector on the main logic board located just forward of the serial interface connector

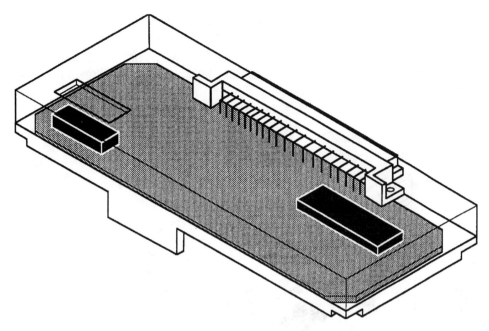

5-7 Seikosha MP-1300AI color option printed circuit board, cutaway view.

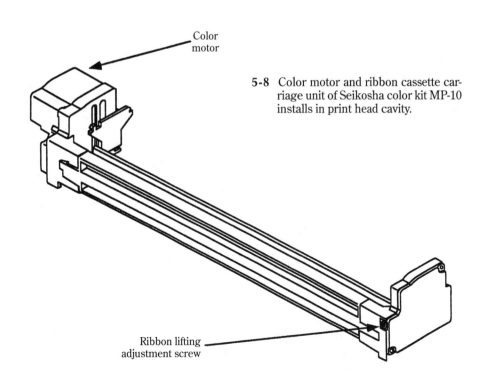

Color
motor

5-8 Color motor and ribbon cassette carriage unit of Seikosha color kit MP-10
installs in print head cavity.

Ribbon lifting
adjustment screw

(Fig. 5-9). Part of the information contained in the color ROM is the color lookup table, from which the colors are designated for printing (Table 5-1). Digital values generated by the color board CPU are fed into two signal lines, called *CCP1* and *CCP2,* which are used to select among the four colors (yellow, cyan, magenta, and black).

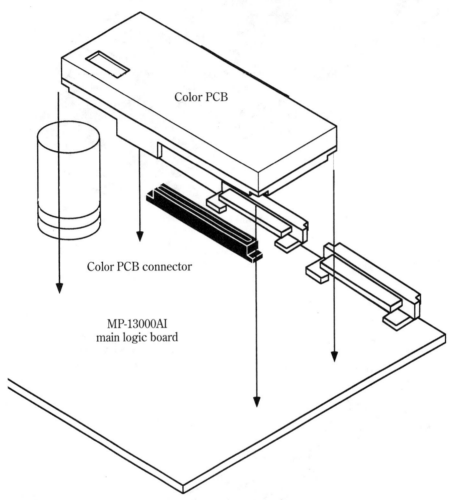

Color PCB

Color PCB connector

MP-13000AI
main logic board

5-9 Color PCB assembly installs on logic board through door on Seikosha MP-1300AI's case.

The color unit houses a motor on its left end, which is integrated with a ribbon carriage that slips into the front of the printer. The unit is used to shift the striped ribbon up and down as directed by the signals received from the color PCB. Adjustment screws on the motor housing (Fig. 5-10) and on the ribbon carriage (Fig. 5-11) allow tuning of the ribbon shift to correct any color fringing.

Table 5-1. Seikosha MP-1300AI color lookup table.

Color	CCP1 digital value	CCP2 digital value
Yellow	0	0
Cyan	0	1
Magenta	1	0
Black	1	1

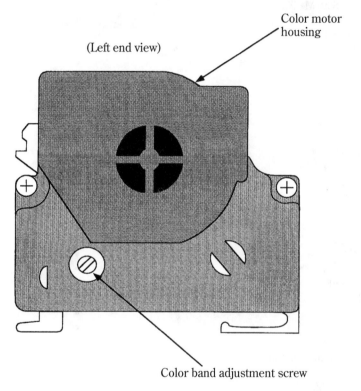

Color motor housing

(Left end view)

Color band adjustment screw

5-10 MP-10 color motor housing with color band adjustment screw.

Table 5-2 shows some of the impact dot matrix printers that are either color capable out of the box or can be upgraded to color with optional accessories.

As you can see, color runs in families. Star Micronics is the leader in standard, inexpensive color capability and Citizen has the most printer models, past and present, that can be upgraded to color.

Table 5-2. Color-capable dot matrix impact printers.

Printer	Color standard	Color optional
AEG-Olympia NPC 136-24	•	
Alps ALQ 218/224	•	
Alps ALQ 318/324	•	
Alps ALQ 224e, 224gx	•	
Alps ALQ 324gx	•	
Apple ImageWriter IIs	•	
Brother M-1809, M-1909		•
Brother M-1824L, M1924L		•
Brother M-2518	•	
Brother M-4018	•	
Citizen GSX-130		•
Citizen GSX-140, GSX-140 Plus		•
Citizen GSX-145		•
Citizen 200-GX		•
Citizen HSP-500/550		•
Citizen MSP-50		•
Citizen 224D		•
Citizen Swift 24, 24e		•
Citizen Swift 9		•
DCS/Fortis 4215		•
Epson LQ-860	•	
Epson LQ-2550	•	
Fujitsu DX2300, DX2400		•
Fujitsu DL3300		•
Fujitsu DL3400		•
Fujitsu DL4400		•
Fujitsu DL4600		•
Fujitsu DL5600		•
Genicom		•
Okidata Microline 293	•	
Okidata Microline 393 Plus	•	
Olivetti 1055	•	
Seikosha MP-1300AI		•
Seikosha SK-3000AI		•
Seikosha SK-3005 Plus		•
Star Micronics NX-1000 Rainbow	•	
Star Micronics NX-1020 Rainbow	•	
Star Micronics NX-2420 Rainbow	•	
Star Micronics XR-1000		•
Star Micronics XR-1500		•

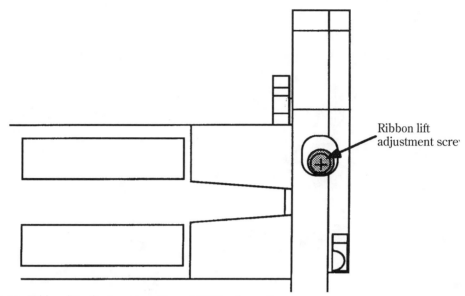

Ribbon lift
adjustment scre

5-11 Ribbon lift adjustment screw on MP-10 color unit.

Chapter 6

Fonts

The multitude of typefaces that laser printing and PostScript have provided to computer users have whetted the appetite for fonts in the general impact printer public. The days when a serif and a nonserif typeface in 10 and 12 pitch would satisfy the demands of almost everyone are gone forever. There are a number of ways in which the demand for more typefaces has been met. For the moment, I will discuss only the hardware solution for impact dot matrix printers.

The number of type families added to the standard complement in modern impact printers is quite large in comparison to the standard set available in the middle 1980s. A draft and NLQ Courier typeface in roman, bold, and italic styles, with proportional and nonproportional widths, at 10 and 12 characters per inch formed practically the entire font library of perhaps 90 percent of the dot matrix printers sold. As manufacturers strove to fight off the assault of laser printers, more typefaces found their way into the ROMs of more and more printers, but still, in comparison to the wealth of type at the top of the line; less-expensive impact printers languished in font envy. The problem with dot matrix printers, from the manufacturer's point of view, was the limited amount of circuit board real estate and the limited amount of memory that that small space imposed. The bitmapped typefaces used by dot matrix printers in near letter quality mode can consume a lot of ROM, and the need to keep printers inexpensive dictated that only so much could be done within price and space constraints. The solution adopted by many companies was to keep circuit boards as simple as possible and the price of printers as low as possible while adding typefaces as an option at extra cost. The user could then decide exactly how much money to spend on fonts and on which fonts.

Font cards

The cleanest method of adding fonts is a font card. This is typically a slim, rectangular board in a plastic case about the size of a playing card, and perhaps as thick as a couple of stacked, 3½-inch floppy disks. The card contains a ROM chip and is inserted into a slot provided in the printer's case. The slot feeds into a connector on the printer's logic board. The user thus has a choice of, say, Letter Gothic or Times Roman, in addition to the typefaces already in the printer. This is the approach used by Alps and Okidata. Shown in Fig. 6-1 is the Okidata Microline 390/391 arrangement. (Some printers, such as the Microline 393, have the card slot on the right.) The principal advantage of the font card is its simplicity. The font card is fully protected from incorrect installation and most static electricity discharges by its plastic case, reassuring for many users.

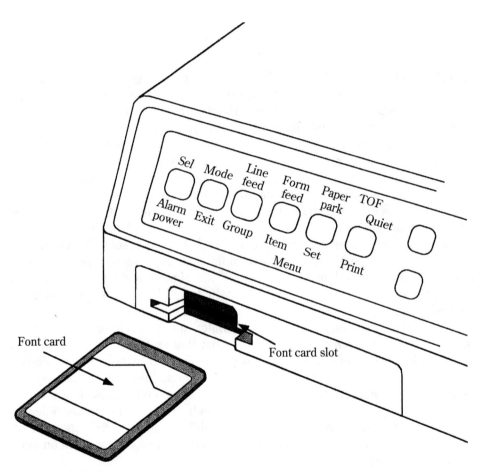

6-1 Okidata font card ROM and card slot in Okidata printers.

ROM chips

Another method of internal hardware expansion involves adding the ROM chip physically to a socket on the printer's motherboard, rather than using an extension such as a card. This method requires that you open the printer's case and handle the ROMs. Unlike the font card, ROM chips are not protected from static electricity and are subject to installation in the wrong socket or reversal in the right socket, leaving them vulnerable to user error. The advantage here is price. A naked ROM chip is much cheaper to produce than a complete ROM card package. Seikosha uses this approach for its SL90/92 printers. A section of the SL90 main logic board is shown in Fig. 6-2, with its two font-ROM sockets indicated as P9 and P10.

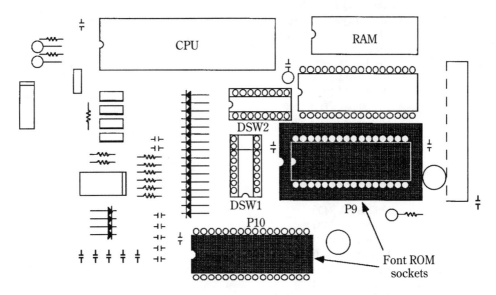

6-2 Seikosha font ROM sockets P9 and P10 on SL90 logic board.

The Panasonic KX-P1524 uses a method somewhere between the two, requiring the insertion of a font card into a connector on the main logic board. The font card is necessary to generate letter quality type from the printer. Figure 6-3 shows the location of the logic board connector.

Table 6-1 lists some of the printers that accept font cards or font-ROMs.

Table 6-1. Printers that accept font card/cartridges.

Printer	Card/Cart	Font-ROM
AEG Olympia NP 80SE	•	
AEG Olympia NP 136SE	•	
AEG Olympia NP 80-24E	•	
AEG Olympia NP 136-24E	•	
AEG Olympia NPC 124	•	
Alps ALQ 218/318	•	
Alps ALQ 224e/324e	•	
Alps ALQ 224gx/324gx	•	
Brother M-1809	•	
Brother M-1909	•	
Brother M-1824L	•	
Brother M-1924L	•	
DCS/Fortis DM 2210	•	
DCS/Fortis DM 2215	•	
DCS/Fortis DM 3215	•	
DCS/Fortis DQ 4110	•	
DCS/Fortis DQ 4210	•	
DCS/Fortis DQ 4215	•	
Fujitsu DX 2300	•	
Fujitsu DX 2400	•	
Fujitsu DL 3300	•	
Fujitsu DL 3400	•	
Fujitsu DL 4400	•	
Fujitsu DL 4600	•	
Fujitsu DL 5400	⋆	
Okidata Microline 390 Plus	•	
Okidata Microline 391 Plus	•	
Okidata Microline 393 Plus	•	
Panasonic KX-P1524	•	
Seikosha SL-90/92		•
Star Micronics NX-2410	•	
Star Micronics NX-2415	•	
Star Micronics NX-2420	•	
Star Micronics NX-2420R	•	
Star Micronics XB-2410	•	
Star Micronics XB-2415	•	
Star Micronics XR-1000	•	
Star Micronics XR-1500	•	
Toshiba P-321 SL	•	

⋆Standard

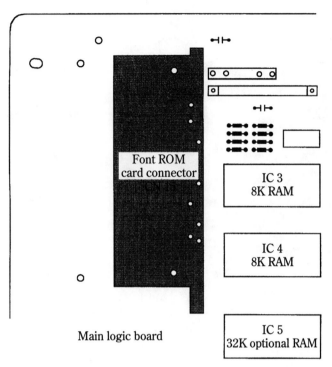

Font ROM
card connector

IC 3
8K RAM

IC 4
8K RAM

Main logic board

IC 5
32K optional RAM

6-3 Panasonic KX-P1524 font ROM connector.

Part 2

Ink Jet Printers

Chapter 7

The ink jet
a brief history

Ink jet printing has been around for more than a decade. The first ink jet printers were manufactured by companies such as Xerox and were intended for high-volume business users who needed exceptionally clean-looking printed output on mass distribution items. Of course, the prices were exceptionally high.

The first noncommercial ink jet printers suitable for individual home and office use were from Hewlett-Packard (HP). The Thinkjets were quiet, produced very attractive pages, and were priced competitively with impact printers. They had the disadvantage of requiring clay-coated or other specially formulated paper to produce their best looking output, and the inks were subject to smearing. Printing on ordinary paper was possible, but the resolution advantage was lost as the image degraded. They also could not print forms using carbon paper to make multiple copies. Personal use of ink jet printers came and went.

In February 1988, Hewlett-Packard revived the almost comatose ink jet market by introducing the first DeskJet (Fig. 7-1). The DeskJet was the product of feedback from the users of previous ink jet printers, and it addressed many if not all of the faults that had turned away many disappointed users.

The DeskJet could print on ordinary bond paper at 300 dpi with practically no bleeding. It gave a very sharp type image even at 5 points, not quite equalling the clarity of a laser printer but certainly excelling that of the best impact dot matrix printer. The inks were still not smudge-proof, and areas of black fill could and would emerge wet from the printer, and were subject to running if dampened. At two pages per minute, the DeskJet was faster than a dot matrix impact printer, although laser printers routinely printed at three to four times that rate. It had room for font expansion and memory for downloaded typefaces, rivalling the flexibility of LaserJets. The only unequivocally negative aspect of the DeskJet was the price per page, which was higher than impact or laser printers. Still, in price, speed, versatility, and quality of printing, the DeskJet was nicely fashioned to assume a secure niche above the dot matrix and below the laser, which it did.

7-1   Hewlett-Packard DeskJet 300 dpi thermal ink jet printer.

Successive revisions of the design led to the DeskJet Plus, the DeskJet 500, and the DeskJet 500C, solving many of the remaining objections to the original DeskJet with greater economy of ink usage, stable, run-resistant inks, greater speed, greater memory capacity, and (with the 500C) color printing.

While Hewlett-Packard was making and keeping the desktop ink jet printer market, Kodak and Canon, which had cornered the market for page printer engines, began selling compact ink jet printers.

The Kodak Diconix was lightweight, could run on batteries, printed on plain paper, and was obviously intended to capture the growing market for portable printers to accompany the burgeoning laptop computer market. It has a maximum resolution of 192 dpi and uses the same basic technology as the HP and Canon printers.

The Canon series of ink jet printers is called the Bubble Jets (Fig. 7-2), and includes both portable and desktop printers. As with their laser printer engines, Canon sold the basic Bubble Jet printer to many other companies for repackaging under company trade names such as Brother and Star.

The generic ink jet

As with the impact printer, there is a generic ink jet technology. In this case, the resemblance is not coincidental, since the two major vendors of ink jet printers HP and Canon, are the joint developers of the current ink jet printing process. Only the specific implementation of this shared technology differs.

The ink jet printing head has no mechanical or moving parts. The head is a cluster of minute nozzles, through which the ink is propelled onto the paper

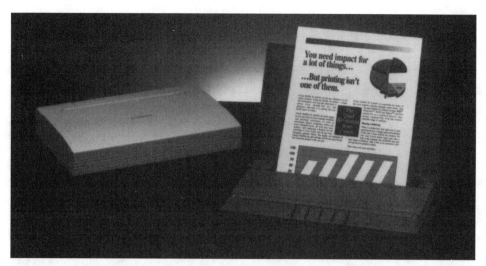

7-2 Canon BJ10ex Bubble Jet 360 dpi thermal ink jet printer. (Photograph courtesy Canon USA)

(Figs. 7-3 and 7-4). Hewlett-Packard uses 50 nozzles in its DeskJet printers (48 in the color DeskJet 500C), while Canon uses 64 in the print heads of its Bubble Jets. Behind each nozzle is a reservoir of ink called the firing chamber. The rear wall of the chamber is a thin film resistor, which acts as a heating element when

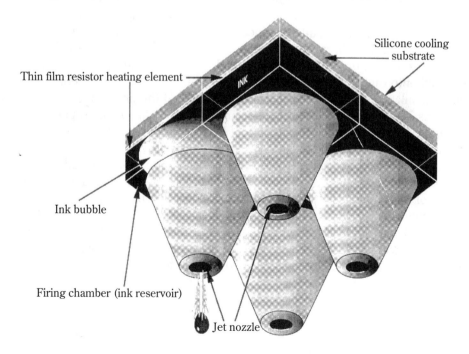

7-3 Common design of Canon/Hewlett-Packard-developed thermal ink jet technology.

7-4 Actual HP ink jet print head cartridge showing ink jet nozzles.

an electric current is applied. The heating of the element at the rear of the ink reservoir causes the ink in contact with the resistor to vaporize, forming a bubble in the surrounding liquid ink. Since the ink as a vapor occupies a greater volume than as a fluid, it expands rapidly and violently, forcing the still-liquid ink nearer the nozzle out of the reservoir and into the nozzle orifice, whence it is sprayed onto the paper. The electric current then turns off, completing one cycle. The ink reservoir refills, the resistor cools, and the process is repeated, as many as 5,000 times per second. Such brief cycles and so many repetitions per second cause a residual accumulation of heat in the resistor that must be dissipated, lest ink be boiled by the resistor even when there is no current. A wafer of silicon is applied to the rear surface of the resistor to act as a heat sink. This permits the continuous operation of the jet without overheating. Following the example of the Canon laser printer in which the printing process is self-contained in a disposable cartridge, the ink jet print head itself is integrated into the disposable ink cartridge and is replaced whenever the ink is expended. As with the laser toner cartridge, this expense can be lessened by refilling and reusing the ink jet cartridge, a process discouraged by Hewlett-Packard and Canon.

Chapter 8

Adding RAM and ROM

Adding RAM to the Hewlett-Packard DeskJet or Canon Bubble Jet is not the same as adding RAM to an impact printer. The impact printer divides its RAM into two segments; the majority of RAM functions as a data buffer to receive data for printing, and a much smaller area is reserved for a downloaded character set.

DeskJets

RAM

The DeskJet also has two areas of RAM, one to buffer incoming data and one to store downloaded fonts, but their proportions are reversed from those of the impact printer. The DeskJets have a fixed data buffer of 16K in the models preceding the 500C, which has a 48K buffer; none can be expanded. As purchased, the DeskJet has no download RAM, but it was meant to use a wide variety of downloaded typefaces, so-called "soft fonts," and expansion of RAM for that purpose was anticipated.

All DeskJets have two cartridge expansion slots located on the right side of the printer, next to the control panel and indicator lights (Fig. 8-1). The plastic cover strips can be pried up and taken off to open the slots for use. In the bottom of each slot is a card edge connector into which the card contained in every cartridge fits.

Each cartridge can contain 256K as either RAM or ROM (Fig. 8-2). Cartridges contain either 128K or 256K, and are self-configuring at start-up. This is significant because there is a difference in RAM capacity between the DeskJet and later models in the family. The original DeskJet can access up to 128K per slot, giving a total of 256K RAM for downloaded character sets. If a cartridge containing 256K is used in the original DeskJet, only the first 128K is recognized,·

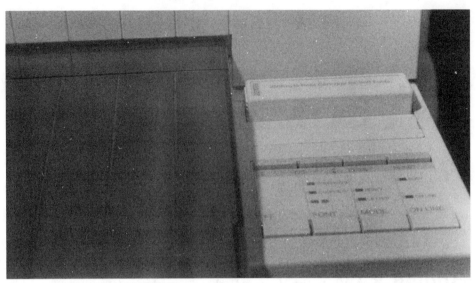

8-1 One of two cartridge RAM/ROM slots behind keypad control panel of DeskJets.

and the total for the machine remains 256K. The DeskJet Plus and its successors, the 500 and 500C, can access a total of 512K of expansion RAM, or two 256K cartridges simultaneously. At present there does not seem to be a way to use cartridge RAM for data buffering. The DeskJets allow for great flexibility in typeface selection, but they are deficient in RAM buffer. With text this is not especially

8-2 HP DeskJet RAM cartridge, left, and font ROM cartridge, right.

hobbling because the data are in their raw ASCII state and occupy a minimum of space. However, the speed of graphics printing could be greatly enhanced by the enlargement of buffer RAM, since graphics data can swell into millions of bytes.

ROM

ROM expansion in the DeskJets is used primarily to increase the typefaces resident in the printers and has been accomplished in two ways: through improved factory-installed ROMs and through external cartridges. The first DeskJet model 2276A had only a Courier typeface built into ROM. This typeface set was incomplete; the Italic face was absent, and no landscape fonts at all were included. The 2276A was capable of printing Courier in two point sizes, 6 and 12, or four pitches, 5, 10, 16.67, and 20 characters per inch, and could print each size in bold, single and double underline, subscript and superscript, and in portrait orientation. The 2277A (DeskJet Plus) added Italic printing in the 5, 10, and 20 characters per inch pitches, as well as landscape faces for 10, 16.67, and 20 characters per inch in normal and bold styles. The C2106A (DeskJet 500) added Letter Gothic and proportionally spaced Compugraphic Times in portrait mode. Table 8-1 summarizes the internal fonts of the four DeskJets.

Table 8-1. DeskJet internal fonts.

Font	DeskJet	DeskJet Plus	DeskJet 500	DeskJet 500C
Courier Roman Portrait	•	•	•	•
Courier Bold Portrait	•	•	•	•
Courier Italic Portrait		•	•	•
Letter Gothic Portrait			•	•
Letter Gothic Bold Portrait			•	•
Compugraphic Times PS			•	•
Compugraphic Times Bold PS			•	•
Courier Roman Landscape		•	•	•
Courier Bold Landscape		•	•	•

The ROM font cartridges are the same size and shape as the RAM cartridges, but have a row of LEDs along the upper edge that show which typefaces are selected. Hewlett-Packard has marketed a number of such cartridges, and many more are sold by Pacific Data, AGT, and other companies, many of which had already produced cartridges for the Hewlett-Packard LaserJets. There are some incompatibility problems with the Deskjet 2276A for cartridges introduced with and after the DeskJet Plus. Table 8-2 lists the Hewlett-Packard cartridges and their compatibility with the various DeskJets. In general, cartridges made for the DeskJet 2276A are, with one exception, forward compatible, while most are not backward compatible to the DeskJet.

Table 8-2. DeskJet cartridge compatibility.

Cartridge	DeskJet	DeskJet Plus	DeskJet 500	DeskJet 500C
22706A	•	•	•	•
22706B	•	•	•	•
22706C	•	•	•	•
22706D	•	•	•	•
22706E	•	•	•	•
22706F	•	•	•	•
22706G	•	•	•	•
22706H	•	•	•	•
22706J	•	•	•	•
22706M	•	•	•	•
22706P	•	•	•	•
22706Q	•	•	•	•
22706R		•	•	•
22706T		•	•	•
22706U		•	•	•
22706V		•	•	•
22706W		•	•	•
22707A	•	•	•	•
22707B	•	•	•	•
22707E	•			
22707F		•	•	
22707K	•			
22707L	•	•	•	•
22707P		•	•	
22708A	•	•	•	•
22708C	•	•	•	•
22708D	•	•	•	•
C21209B			•	•
C21209C			•	•
C21209D			•	•
C21209E			•	•

The DeskJet 2276A could use an Epson FX emulation cartridge, sold by Hewlett-Packard, to allow use of the DeskJet with software that had no support for the new machine. Usually, if a LaserJet driver were available among the software's printer selections, it would work well with the DeskJet. But Hewlett-Packard, wishing the DeskJet to compete successfully against high-priced 24-dot impact printers, understood that the assurance that users could move to the ink jet without sacrificing their old software was an important consideration. To ensure this same continuity with the DeskJet Plus, a new cartridge for Epson emulation and an IBM Proprinter cartridge emulator were introduced for the Plus. By the time the 500C was unveiled, however, Hewlett-Packard felt sufficiently secure with the breadth of specific software support for the DeskJet family that it deemed further cartridge emulation neither warranted nor needed.

The logical upgrades

Internal ROM upgrades were offered by Hewlett-Packard in the form of printer conversions or exchanges. After the introduction of the DeskJet Plus, no upgrade was initially announced, a decision for which Hewlett-Packard received considerable negative criticism. When the DeskJet 500 was introduced, therefore, Hewlett-Packard had ready a plan by which owners of previous models could receive an upgrade to the newest model through a local Hewlett-Packard dealer. The conversion replaced the logic board of the DeskJet and modified the engine and cabinet cover. This upgrade was discontinued when the 500C was brought to market. Hewlett-Packard then offered to take older DeskJets in exchange for the 500C, if a fee were paid and the printer shipped to HP. However, since the fee ranged from $450 for 500 owners to $550 for DeskJet Plus and DeskJet owners, persons wishing to move up to the 500C probably could have done better by selling their old printer and applying the money to the purchase price of the color printer, which cost slightly less than $700 at discounted retail.

DeskJet to Plus or 500

For those who wish to upgrade their DeskJets manually, replacement parts can be obtained through Hewlett-Packard's Corporate Parts Division. The upgrade from a DeskJet 2276A to a DeskJet Plus (2277A) is accomplished as follows.

The changes made in the DeskJet Plus from the DeskJet included the addition of fonts (see Table 8-1); support for landscape printing; some increase in printing speed (especially during graphics printing); and a refinement of the paper movement mechanism to eliminate excessive paper skewing (accomplished by altering the paper feed motor and paper pickup). The changes were adopted in the Plus and were carried over into the 500. The DeskJet Plus and DeskJet 500 are identical, therefore, except for their logic printed circuit boards (PCA). They share some common parts with the original printer, and most of its features. The DeskJet Plus and 500 use a different CPU chip than the DeskJet 2276A, which explains their larger memory capacity. Table 8-2 shows the cartridge capabilities for four different DeskJet models.

The DeskJet must be completely disassembled to perform any upgrade. First, you must flip up and lift off the access door from the printer. Open the printer case by inserting a flat-blade screwdriver into the latches on the bottom

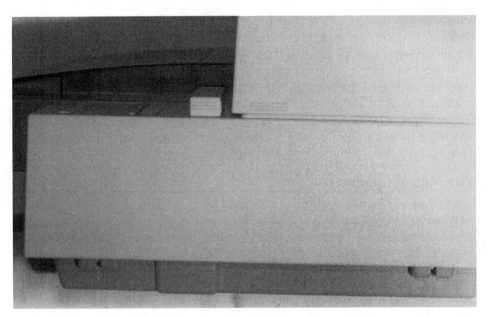

8-3 Lateral locations of DeskJet case latches on bottom edges of upper case. Insert a flat blade screwdriver to disengage.

edges of the printer ends (Fig. 8-3), freeing them while lifting up gently on the cover. The printer must be in an upright position during the unlatching, because the printing mechanism is held in place by the locked cover alone. The printing mechanism can drop out of the base should the printer be inverted or tipped after the latches have been loosened. There are four latches, two on either end, and they should be loosed in pairs. Free all four latches before you attempt to lift the cover from one end.

Once all of the latches have been disengaged, you can lift the cover enough to allow disconnection of the cable that runs between the keypad and the logic board (Fig 8-4). You can then remove the cover. Note: With the cover removed, the paper width lever (in the front just under the input paper tray) is exposed and subject to breakage. If the paper width lever is broken, it cannot be repaired; the entire printing mechanism must be replaced.

Behind the connector for the keypad cable is the cardboard shield over the cartridge slot connectors (Fig. 8-5). Pull the shield straight up and lay it aside. Next, disconnect the grounding strap from the ground plane. Not all printers have the grounding strap, but if it is present, you will find it attached to the paper motor on the left end of the printing mechanism (Fig. 8-6). Looking at the printer from the front, right to left, find and unplug from the logic board the carriage motor cable, located on the right, front-end behind the cartridge connectors; the Logic PCA cable front and center (this passes back beneath the mechanism and attaches to the head driver PCA, and is shown in Fig. 8-7; and the paper motor cable, left end, which passes forward from the paper motor be-

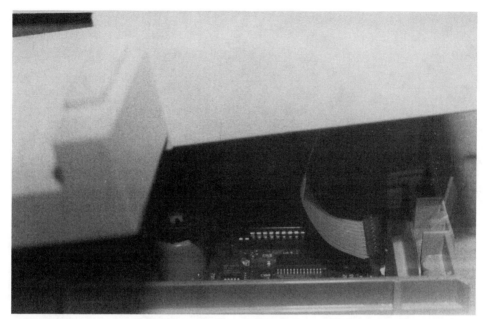

8-4 Keypad cable and connector on right end of DeskJet's logic board.

8-5 Cardboard shield around cartridge slot connectors.

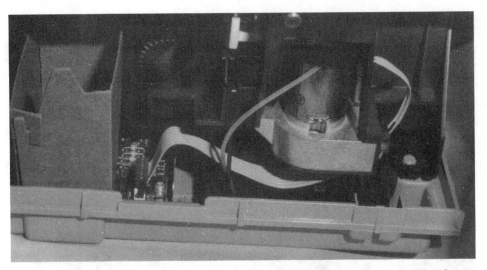

8-6 Cartridge edge connectors. Cable must be disconnected. Tubing is from old style cartridge priming pump.

hind the electrostatic discharge (ESD) clip and under the paper tray lever (Fig. 8-8). Finally, lift the printing mechanism out of the bottom of the case and set it safely out of the way.

The logic PCA is fastened to the ground plane by seven screws (Fig. 8-9). Remove the screws and unplug the cable which connects the power supply PCA to the logic board (Fig. 8-10). Remove the logic board from the ground plane.

The logic board used in the DeskJet Plus carries the HP part number 02277-60112 if purchased separately, and costs $270. If you purchase it as an exchange item, order it by the part number 02277-69001. In either case, the part contains

8-7 Disconnect cable beneath center of paper tray.

8-8 Disconnect paper motor cable from logic board near paper width lever in front of printer.

the upgraded DeskJet Plus ROMs. For those who might be able to find a board lacking the ROM, the ROM chips themselves can be bought as part number 1818-4619, described as 2277A firmware. For those who prefer to upgrade to the DeskJet 500, the logic PCA is part number C2106-60001 new ($280) or C2106-

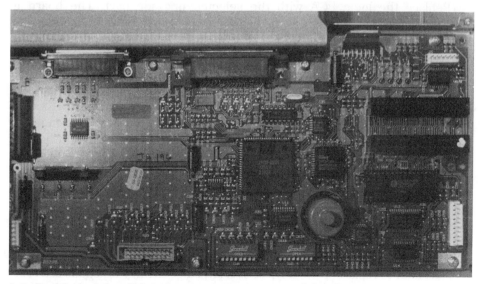

8-9 DeskJet logic board. Interface connectors are at rear left and rear center.

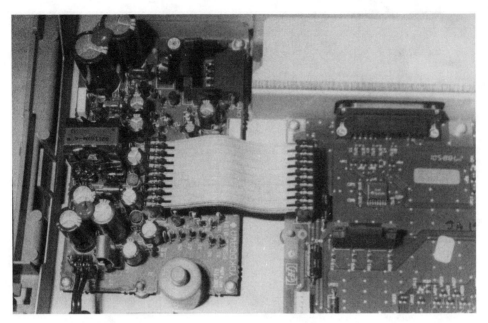

8-10 DeskJet power transformer module (left) and its cable to logic board.

69001 for an exchange ($190). The DeskJet 500 firmware is part number 1818-4793. Considering that the logic PCA for the 500 is only $10 more than the corresponding board for the Plus, it makes sense to go directly to the newer model. If you can persuade HP to accept the 2276A logic PCA in exchange, then you can actually save $80.

Replace the logic PCA with the selected upgrade part. The board is mounted in the same manner as the old one it replaces. The winged connector clips on the parallel interface connector must be through the opening in the case before the Logic board is secured by the screws. All cables should be reconnected except the paper motor cable. The paper motor used in the original 2276A model printer is incompatible with the model 2277A and C2106 printer logic boards, and must be replaced. If the 2276A paper motor is connected to one of the later logic PCAs, the motor will run in reverse. The paper motor is held to the printing mechanism by two screws (Fig. 8-11). You might have to remove the metal ESD clip to free the motor cable. You can pry the finger of the clip from the base with the flat-bladed screwdriver you used to open the case. The new paper motor is part number 02277-60100, priced at $23. It is mounted in the same manner as the old motor. Plug the cable into the logic PCA and put the ESD clip back. Don't forget to connect the power supply cable.

With the addition of the new paper motor, you can reassemble the printer. The last item to replace is the keypad overlay, since the key functions are redefined by the new logic board. The overlay is part number 0227-80069.

8-11 Paper transport motor (circular object) electrostatic discharge clip (ESD) and braided grounding strap on left side of DeskJet.

Testing Test the printer for proper operation before restoring the cabling to the computer. The flashing of the keypad control lights will signal any anomalies discovered during the power-up sequence self-test. The various error conditions and their LED control panel combinations are shown in Table 8-3. The possible causes listed assume that the obvious error is not present; for instance, when a paper out error is detected and there is paper in the input tray, or a paper jam is indicated, but the page has been ejected. The likelihood is great that any error reported is caused by a loose or misconnected cable.

A problem not readily recognized at the time of reassembly is the binding of the carriage against the cover. When snapping down the cover, it is easy to catch the rear edge of the ink cartridge carriage and to trap it under the cover. This binding will cause a carriage stall and be diagnosed as such on start-up (see Table 8-3 for errors and their LED indices). Because the carriage pivots front to back, the descending cover will not be prevented from closing on its latches. The carriage presents no detectable resistance, actually bending over backward as you push down the cover.

While tilted back, the carriage can also be pushed too far to the right, causing it to overrun the sled. The prominence on the sled will then be inside the carriage's right end, instead of outside, and will act as an impediment to the carriage's motion. When the carriage moves left during the start-up self-test, it will drag the sled to the rail stops and will itself be arrested as the sled encoun-

Table 8-3. DeskJet Plus and DeskJet 500 self-test & operational errors.

LEDs flashing	Error detected	Type	Possible Cause
On line	Paper out	OP/S-T	Head driver PCA or cable; logic PCA or cable
Busy & on line	Paper jam	OP/S-T	Paper motor or cable; logic PCA or cable
All	Faulty plug-in cartridge	S-T	Bad RAM or ROM cartridge
All in alternating pattern with grouping of:			
On line & Cour 10/20	Carriage stall	OP/S-T	Obstruction
Mode & landscape	Firmware failure	S-T	Logic PCA or cable
Font LEDs	PCA component failure	S-T	Logic PCA or cable
Busy & on line	PCA component failure	S-T	Logic PCA or cable
Double pitch, mode, & on line	Cartridge connector failure	S-T	Cartridge connector or cartridge

Legends OP—Operating error, S-T—Self-test error

ters the stops. This too, will appear as a carriage stall in the keypad LEDs. Therefore, while the cover is still up, check the position of the carriage and for unobstructed movement of the print head.

Two other error states not readily apparent from the LED's keypad should be mentioned here, because they might arise as a consequence of disassembly. If no LEDs are lighted, there is a power problem. Harking back to the advice given above, that a loose or misconnected cable is the usual suspect, I would in this case advise you first to check that the power cord to the power module is in the ac outlet, and that the line from the module is plugged into the printer. This doesn't involve taking the printer apart again. If this does not yield positive results, test the power module with a volt-ohmmeter to verify that it is producing the needed voltages at the printer's end of the cord. There should be 20 volts ac coming from the first and third contacts in the power cord, counting from the inside bend of the power cord plug (Fig. 8-12).

Alternatively, before you do any work on the printer, you can purchase a fuse module from HP (part number 02227-60030), which contains a series of fuses and LEDs to confirm the power integrity. This unit fits between the power module and the printer, and the LEDs light if there is power. It has the consequential function of protecting the printer's power module from damage if there is a printer fault that could cause a catastrophic short in the power supply. The power supply has irreplaceable fusing, and therefore a blown fuse in the supply unit forces its disposal. Each fuse in the fuse module is represented by one of the LEDs, and if a short in the printer occurs, a fuse in the fuse module will blow and its associated LED will go out as an index of the failure. The power supply is fully protected.

If there is power from the power supply module, then you must open the printer. Check the cable from the dc power PCA to the logic PCA and the logic PCA cable. Very likely one of these cables will indeed be loose. If the printer fin-

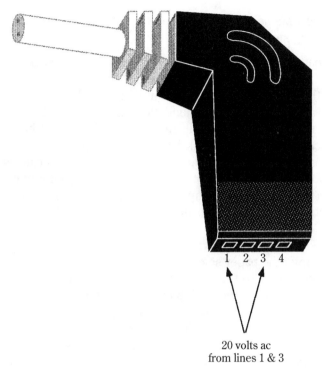

1 2 3 4

20 volts ac
from lines 1 & 3

8-12 DeskJet power cord voltages at printer end.

ishes the self-test without declaring a fault, execute a printing test to verify the operation of the new logic board and paper motor.

Paper skew   One further note is needed. If you have converted the DeskJet according to the preceding instructions, you have not created a DeskJet Plus or DeskJet 500. There were changes made to the printing mechanisms of the latter two machines to correct a print skewing problem in some of the older DeskJets. The changes were made to the pressure plate, which elevates the paper stack to contact the paper drive rollers, and the paper width lever, of which the left wall of the input paper tray is a part. The pressure plate was hinged to ensure uniform elevation of the paper, and the left wall of the paper tray was altered to push the paper stack more evenly against the right wall. Because these parts are inseparable from the printing mechanism itself, neither of these changes can be introduced to the older printing mechanism found in the DeskJets 2276A.

Hewlett-Packard has determined that printing skew for all models of the DeskJet should not exceed ±0.006 per inch on 95 percent of all pages. Thus, if a block of text one inch from the paper's edge has a skew of more than 6/1000 of inch, the page is out of specification. Frankly, skew must probably exceed this amount by one or two magnitudes, this is to say 10- or 100-fold, to be noticeable. (Skewing of ⁵⁄₀ inch would most certainly be noticeable.) If your particular

DeskJet is showing an unacceptable amount of paper skewing, you can attempt to correct it with the following steps.

1. Ascertain that the paper is within Hewlett-Packard's specifications for the DeskJet. Although the DeskJets have been designed to print on a variety of papers found in the office and home environments, not all papers may be suitable for your printer. HP recommendations are contained in the user's manual. Briefly, paper should be in the 16 lb–24 lb. weight class, long grain, and uncoated. Do not use ink jet or ThinkJet papers. Papers made for copying machines, cotton typing bond, and standard letterheads are all generally suitable for the DeskJets. However, even though the paper does fall within these guidelines, any one particular paper may have undesirable characteristics that make it unacceptable. Try another brand of paper.

2. Check the squareness of the paper. Print some pages, restack them and return them to the top of the paper stack, printed side up. Print the same matter over again, and compare the two sides. If one side exhibits skewing in one direction, while the other exhibits skewing in an opposite direction, then the paper may not be within the accepted tolerances for squareness established by the paper manufacturers.

3. Confirm that the paper is loaded into the input tray correctly. The input paper stack should contain no more than 100 sheets and never fewer than 10. Paper should be manually tamped to produce squared edges and should be placed in the tray so that its right edge is tightly against the right wall of the tray. If using U.S. letter or legal size paper, the paper width lever is used to make the left edges of the stack flush, but it should be moved back to the left after squaring. There should be no more than 25 sheets in the output tray at any one time.

4. If changing papers and reloading the paper stack, do not reduce the print skewing, print 20 pages and measure the skew on each as accurately as possible. Skew is calculated by measuring the distance from an edge of the paper to the column or row of text nearest that edge in two separate locations of the page and dividing the difference by the distance between those locations. Let the first measurement be called a, the second measurement b, and the distance between locations A and B be called C (Fig. 8-13). Subtract the smaller of a and b from the larger of b and a, and divide the result by C, a–b\C or b–a\C, which should yield a number within the skew specifications established by Hewlett-Packard (±0.006 inches per inch) for 19 of the 20 pages.

5. As a last resort, clean the carriage guide, the pivoting platen, the paper drive rollers, and the pinch rollers (Fig. 8-14). To clean these parts requires delicacy, and improper cleaning can cause damage or abnormal wear to the affected parts. The carriage guide is the only part of the printer which can be cleaned with a solvent other than water. This is

Paper edge

a
A
a
A
B
b
B
b
C

Paper stack should contain no more than 100 sheets and never fewer than 10, should be manually tamped to produce squared edges, and should be placed in the tray so that its right edge is tightly against the right wall of the tray. If using U.S. letter or legal size paper, the paper width (C) is used to make the left edges of the stack flush, but it should be moved back to the left after squaring. There should be no more than 25 sheets in the output tray at any one time.

4) If changing papers and re-loading the paper stack do not reduce the print skewing, print 20 pages and measure the skew on each as accurately as possible. Skew is calculated by measuring the distance from an edge of the paper to the column or row of text nearest that edge in two separate locations of the page, and dividing the difference by the distance between those locations. Let the first measurement be called **a**, the second measurement **b**, and the distance between these locations **A** and **B** be called **C** (Figure 8-). Subtract the smaller of **a** & **b** from **b** or **a**, and divide the result by **C**, $\frac{a-b}{C}$ or $\frac{b-a}{C}$, which should yield a number within the skew specifications established by H-P for 19 of the 20 pages. (See above.)

8-13 Measuring paper skew of DeskJet pages.

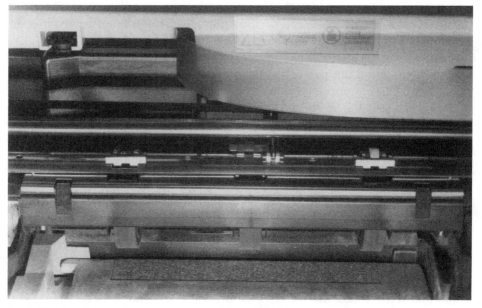

8-14 Pinch rollers and paper transport rollers of DeskJet.

where ink can build up over time and usage, and a solution of water and alcohol can be used to dissolve the ink. To clean the carriage guide, use a tissue moistened (not wet) with the solution, and very gently and carefully clean away ink deposits. Avoid contact with any of the drive or pinch rollers, as alcohol can damage them. The drive rollers should be cleaned with a tissue moistened with water only. The pinch rollers should be cleaned with a cotton swab moistened with water only. Note: Never use platen cleaner or alcohol. The pivoting platen should be cleaned with a dry cloth. Paper dust should be brushed away or vacuumed from the printer.

If none of the above steps, either singularly or in combination, succeed in preventing skew, then, regrettably, the entire printing mechanism must be replaced. In this case you should not go ahead with the conversion, since it would be a waste of money.

DeskWriters

It is possible, by substituting the appropriate logic PCA, to change a DeskJet into a DeskWriter for use with a Macintosh or, should you so desire, to change a DeskWriter into a DeskJet. Because the interface connectors are different, the bottom of the case would also need to be changed to accept the new cabling.

Extending print cartridge life One further upgrade has been distributed free of charge to DeskJet, DeskJet Plus, and DeskWriter owners whose printers have been printing fewer than 200 pages per cartridge. If you purchased a new HP ink cartridge during 1991 or 1992, you have seen the brochure enclosed with the cartridge. One side details the handling and installation of the print cartridge, and the reverse offers the upgrade. The free offer expires in September, 1992, but can be purchased after that date from HP.

The upgrade is a small kit (Fig. 8-15) that contains three plastic parts: the bracket, sled, and drain pan of the print cartridge station, situated on the extreme right side of the printer when the cover has been elevated. (This is the "home" position of the print head when it is at rest) The bracket contains a rubber wiper to clean the print head nozzles and a "spittoon" to catch the ink ejected during the regular spitting, which keeps the jets free of dried ink. As part of its design, the sled contains a cap to cover the jets when the print head is idle in the home position. The drain pan reaches the old system in which primed ink was evacuated to an absorber in the base of the printer. To determine if your printer needs this upgrade, follow these steps:

1. Turn off the printer, and disconnect the ac cord from the wall outlet.
2. Remove the smoked plastic cover, the output paper tray, and any paper in the printer.
3. Turn the printer on its end so that you can view the small plate on the bottom of the printer that displays the printer model and serial numbers. The

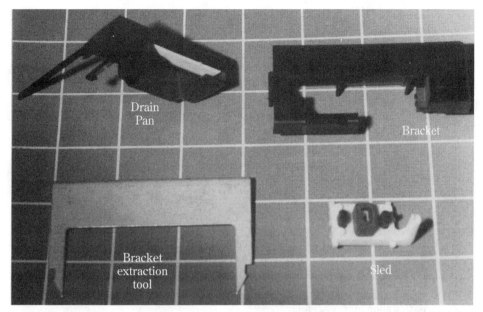

8-15 Print cartridge station upgrade kit contains new drain pan, sled, bracket, and bracket extraction tool.

plate is in the recessed well where the cable and power cord connectors are located.

4. Check the serial number. If it begins with 2937 or a higher number, the printer has already been fitted with the new parts and no further modification is needed. If the number begins with 2936 or a lower number, then proceed to the next step.

5. Turn the printer upright again and open the cover. Slide the print head left to the middle of the printer. Look at the home station and sled. If the color of the sled is white or off-white, the parts have already been installed. If the sled is black or dark gray, the upgrade applies to your printer. Order the Print Station Upgrade Kit, part number 02276-60106 from Hewlett-Packard.

Installation instructions in seven languages are included with the kit, but I include the procedure here so that you can know in advance how it is performed.

After disconnecting the power cord and interface cables, remove the output paper tray and its cover. Open the lid and slide the print head to the left, exposing the print cartridge station (Fig. 8-16). Take the tool provided in the kit and place its tines in the grooves of the bracket which covers the station (Fig. 8-17). One set of grooves is located on the right end of the bracket, while the second set is on the inner wall of a rectangular aperture near the left end. The grooves actually form the sides of an eyelet, one at either end of the bracket, which engages a projection and holds fast the bracket. Push the tool slowly and firmly down un-

8-16 Print head cartridge is "parked" in cartridge service station. Move it left to expose station for replacement.

til it clicks into place over the bracket. The tool spreads the eyelets away from the pins, and the flanged areas of the tool's tines grip the bottom edges of the eyelets. Pull the tool up and out of the printer, extracting the bracket as you draw the tool upward (Fig. 8-18). You can discard the tool and bracket or disengage the tool from the bracket and save it against the possibility that the new bracket might need to be extracted sometime in the future.

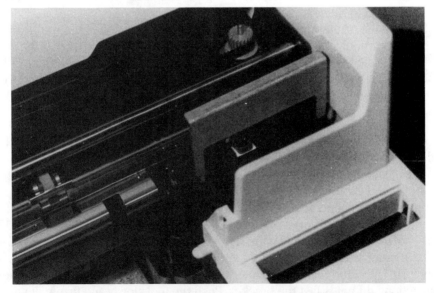

8-17 Bracket removal tool in place. Push it down until it clicks into bracket.

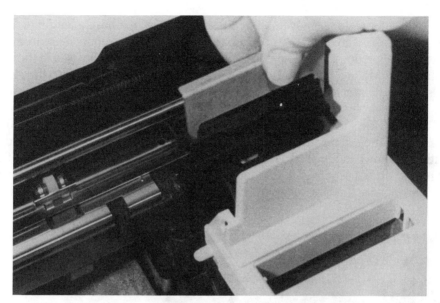

8-18 Lift up tool to remove bracket. Both can be discarded.

8-19 Old style sled with priming tube attached sucked ink from cartridge for cleaning, wasting ink.

With the bracket removed, lift out the old sled. It will have a length of flexible plastic tubing attached to its bottom (Fig. 8-19). Pull the tubing loose from the sled and tuck it down into the printer out of the way. It will not be used in the new installation. Make certain that the tubing is not in the cavity beneath the sled's rails, or it will interfere with the installation of the drain pan. The tubing can be pushed forward in the printer and down toward the logic board below.

Discard the old sled. If your printer has a serial number lower than 304A 17929, take the drain pan from the upgrade kit and place it in the print cartridge station as shown in Fig. 8-20. (Note: Printers with a serial number of 3040A 17929 or higher do not require the drain pan.) The drain pan fits between the rails of the station, with the long tail to the right. Push it down until it clicks into place.

8-20 New drain pan installed between rails of station.

Place the new sled from the kit on the rails of the station (Fig. 8-21). The rails have a slight curving rise on the right end. There are two rectangular projections about midway along the rails that act as stops. The sled has four white pegs on its sides. The sled is correctly positioned when it straddles the rails and the pegs on the left end of the sled are on the left side of the rail stops (Figs. 8-21 and 8-22). Slide the sled down to the left on the rails until the pegs on the right end of the sled encounter the rail stops.

Place the new bracket over the station (Fig. 8-23) so that the ribs on the un-

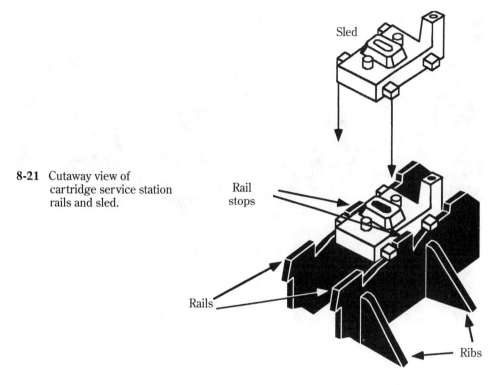

8-21 Cutaway view of cartridge service station rails and sled.

Sled

Rail stops

Rails

Ribs

derside of the bracket align next to the ribs on the front side of the station. The ribs are located in front of the forward rail and have the appearance of buttresses (Fig. 8-21). The bracket will surround the sled. Push the bracket down until it clicks into place (Fig. 8-24).

8-22 New sled in place.

8-23 Lowering new bracket around sled.

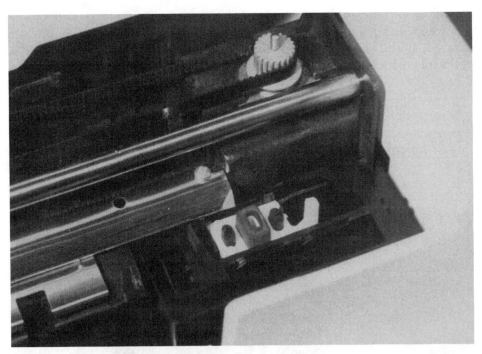

8-24 New bracket and sled installed.

Placing the bracket completes the installation of the station upgrade. Slide the print head back to the right into the home position. Verify that it has free movement from side to side. Close the lid and put the paper tray and its cover back on the printer. Reconnect the power cord and cables, and execute a self-test of the printer. If the test prints normally, the installation has been successful. Failure to print suggests that an obstruction of the print head occurred. Open the lid and carefully attempt to move the print head. Check the station to see if the bracket is fully pressed down into position and make sure the tubing from the old sled is not obstructing the movement of the print head. If the tubing is in the cavity beneath the sled, it can prevent the drain pan from being properly seated, which can, in turn, interfere with the movement of the sled.

This upgrade improves the printer's performance in several ways. Primarily the change affects the life of the cartridge. HP observed that the priming of the cartridge to clear the print head nozzles of blockages or bubbles wasted ink and thereby reduced the number of pages that could be printed. Priming occurred regularly and could be induced by the user from the control panel with the Prime button. The tubing attached to the old sled was looped about the priming pump at its nether end and terminated on an absorbent pad in the printer's base. The priming action was carried out in the home position while the sled was capping the printhead nozzles. The priming pump squeezed the tubing, partially evacuating the tubing. When the pump released the tubing, the vacuum sucked air and ink through the print nozzles, priming the firing chambers and clearing any debris or air bubbles that might have been present. The ink was drawn down the tubing and expended on the absorber. This entire process was found to be superfluous and wasteful. Cartridges could be kept clean merely by the spitting action and wiping of the nozzles, sparing ink. Later machines omitted the pump. The new station design was retrofitted to the older machines, eliminating the pump's action by disconnecting the tubing, thereby giving them the benefit of ink conservation. Another improvement made by the upgrade is in the rubber wiper on the station bracket. The old design was factory calibrated for each machine, and if the wiper became misaligned, the entire bracket had to be replaced with a newly calibrated unit. The revised design allows field replacement of the wiper. A third improvement was the addition of the drain pan, used to catch the ink splashed from the print head by the wiper and by priming. The absorber in the bottom of the machines was also changed, since it had less volume of ink to catch.

Bubble Jets

Canon Bubble Jets are less amenable to upgrading than are Hewlett-Packard DeskJets. The portable machines such as the BJ-5, BJ-10 or 10ex cannot accept interface, RAM, or ROM accessories or expansion. In fact, the only option offered for the portable machines is the 30-sheet capacity Automatic Sheet Feeder, priced at $90 list (shown attached to the BJ-10ex in Fig. 8-25). The BJ-10ex is ca-

8-25 Canon Bubble Jet with optional cut sheet feeder. (Photograph courtesy Canon USA)

pable of three emulations, the Canon BJ-130e, the Epson LQ, and the IBM Pro-printer. The Epson LQ emulation is acknowledged by most reviewers to be superior to the IBM emulation for both text and graphic printing. One advantage of the IBM as compared to the Epson mode, however, is the larger font download partition that makes it available for "soft" character sets. The maximum RAM of

8-26 Canon Bubble Jet 300 family. (Photograph courtesy Canon USA)

the BJ-10ex is 37K, but it can be configured into two sections, one of 34K for downloaded typefaces and the remaining 3K for input data buffer. In the Epson mode, 20K of RAM is automatically set aside for the input buffer, while the other RAM is reserved for fonts. The 300-series printers are more adaptable.

The Bubble Jet 300 (Fig. 8-26) and its wide-carriage sibling, the 330, both have 30K RAM buffers. But each can accept a maximum of 128K in the form of RAM cards, which are inserted into slots on the top of the printers at the right rear. ROM cards containing optional bitmapped fonts also use those slots. There are three font cards available from Canon for $99 each, the General (Script, Press Roman, Boldface, Thesis), the OCR (OCR-A, OCR-B, Olde World, Prestige Symbol), and the Modern (Presentor, Orator, Essay, Gothic Symbol). The printers have parallel interfaces, but an optional RS-232C/422A serial card is offered for $119. Sheet feeders with either one or two bins holding up to 100 sheets can be attached ($150 for the one-bin model; the second bin can be added later for $129). Unlike the DeskJet family of desktop printers, the 300 series is unique in that its members can accept pin-feed continuous forms, which is much more convenient for high-speed printing than the single sheet feeding used by Hewlett-Packard.

For color, aside from the obvious method of refilling empty ink cartridges with color inks, one must purchase the new BJ-800 or 820 printers (Fig. 8-27). Both use four separate color ink cartridges, have 7K data buffers, and emulate the Epson LQ-2550. Each has a built-in cut sheet feeder. The 820 has an SCSI interface in addition to the parallel interface that is standard on the model 800.

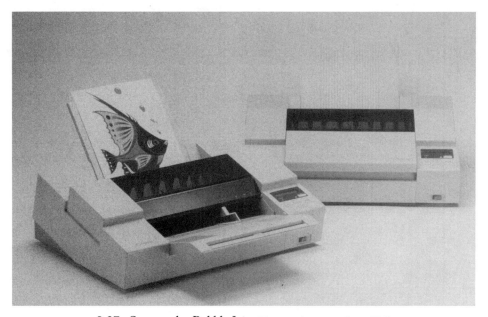

8-27 Canon color Bubble Jets. (Photograph courtesy Canon USA)

Part 3

Page Printers

Chapter 9

Lasers and "lasers"

In general usage, the term *laser printer* has acquired a generic meaning more properly belonging to the term *page printer*. It is likely that this misuse shall continue and spread as the laser printer and its kin become the standard printers of the office and home. Even now, journalists refer to light emitting diode (LED) and liquid crystal shutter (LCS) printers as *lasers,* and then proceed to show that they are not laser-based at all. In the future, any belated attempt to make the distinction will more than likely be dropped, and all page printers, whatever their source of illumination, will be termed *lasers*. Here, I remain a stick in the mud, and lasers will be lasers, LEDs will be LEDs, and LCSs will be LCSs.

The generic page printer

There are three building blocks for a page printer: the scanning mechanism and its controlling electronics, the paper movement mechanism, and the photosensitive printing system. Add a few incidentals such as interfaces and some high-level computer intelligence, and you have a page printer.

Laser printers

Using a laser printer as the primary reference, a page printer consists of some fundamental units whose coordinated actions add up to a modified form of the xerographic process used in copy machines. Indeed, the first Canon laser engines were assembled from the same basic parts used in their personal copier products. Reduced to their components, then, laser printers are merely copy machines that use a digital original instead of a paper one.

The laser scanning unit is the core technology of the printer. In its simplest form, it is a laser diode, a silicon miniaturization of laboratory lasers, coupled to a precise high-speed system of mirrors by which pulses of the laser light are

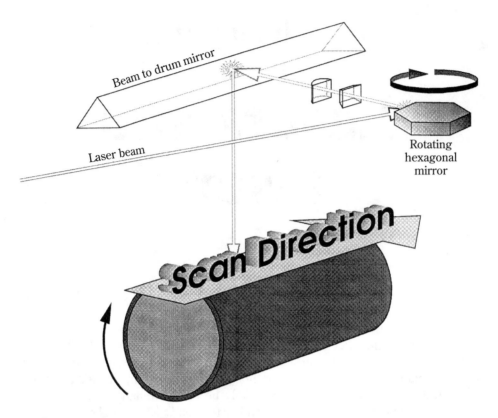

9-1 Laser scanning system diagram.

flashed onto a photosensitive surface (Fig. 9-1). The laser beam reflects from a hexagonally faced mirror spinning at about 33,000 revolutions per minute. Each face of the mirror creates one scan line of the finished page. The scanning beam passes through a focusing lens and a curvature compensation lens. The latter adjusts the beam to allow for the difference of travel that exists between the ends and center of the image. The beam next encounters a prismatically shaped beam-to-drum mirror which bends the light downward and onto the photosensitive surface of the drum. Except for the aperture through which the laser beam is emitted, it is a closed system. The laser and mirrors are in a sealed, heart-shaped box.

The laser beam is directed or modulated by the dc controller, which determines the rate at which the beam is turned on and off, therefore determining the dot resolution of the printer. The laser diode scanning unit used by most laser printers is capable of much higher dot resolutions, up to 2500 dpi, than the currently standard 300 dpi. The cost of building a controller and exposure system capable of such exactitude over an extended term is the only prohibitive factor in the production of typesetter quality printers for everyday purposes. Modifications have been successfully made to printers already being produced to raise resolutions to 800×800 dpi and even 1200 dpi, but they are not "cheap" by any normal use of the word. Frankly, without a magnifier, it is almost impossible to distinguish 300 dpi from 800 dpi in a text comparison. Graphics are another matter, and higher resolution makes a great difference in the clarity and shading of scanned pictures and in the purity of line from vector-generated drawings.

Besides putting more and smaller dots on the page, the other means of increasing the perceived resolution of a laser printer is to overlap the dots in such a way that the interstices are covered, thereby reducing the scalloping effect created when round dots are placed together tangentially (Fig. 9-2). Hewlett-Packard has used this method, called resolution enhancement technology (RET), to smooth the edges of curves in both text characters and graphic figures. Other companies have developed similar techniques to place dots in dithered patterns that minimize the jaggies or aliasing of curved or oblique shapes. These schemes are cheaper to effect in hardware, as is reflected in the continuing downward trend in laser printer prices, even with the added technol-

Normal laser printer dot placement

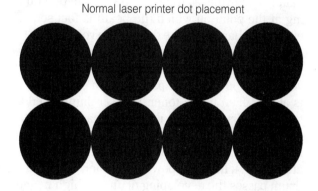

9-2 The effect of resolution enhancement technology.

Resolution-enhanced dot placement

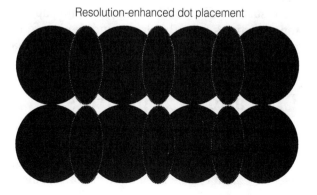

ogy. But all of these methods must be regarded as temporary measures, substitutes for the real enhancement of low-priced higher resolution, which can be expected to arrive very soon.

The laser beam's pulses fall upon the photosensitive surface where the whole image of the page is painted in electrically charged points. The surface is usually made from a photoconductor such as selenium, which has the property of increasing or decreasing its electrical conductivity or resistance as it is exposed to or shaded from light. The drum is prepared for writing by a primary corona, a thin wire stretched the length of the drum through which a high-voltage electric current is passed. The corona effect produces an ionization of the atmosphere around the wire and a 600-volt negative electrical charge is imparted to the surface of the darkened drum. Thus, as the drum rotates, the entire drum is charged. A side effect of the corona effect is the production of ozone, which is absorbed by a filter in the printer.

The action of the laser beam on the negatively charged drum is to disperse the charge wherever it illuminates a spot. The charge is reduced to approximately −100 volts as the light lowers the potential resistance of the drum's coating at the point on which the beam is focused. Thus, an image is delineated in electrical charges on the drum. The rotation of the drum carries the charged image past a developing drum on which toner has been spread. A magnet in the developing drum attracts the iron-based toner particles, and a uniform negative voltage is applied to the particles. An extra 1600-volt point-to-point repulsive bias is also applied to the toner. In laser-illuminated areas, the combined charges of the image drum and the repulsive charge of the toner particles is higher than the combined attractive forces of the developing drum and its magnet, and the toner is projected from the developing drum onto the surface of the image drum, creating a black image of powdered toner. When an unilluminated area of the image drum passes the developing drum, its high negative charge lowers the electrical bias, and the toner particles cannot overcome the magnetic attraction of the developing drum. Thus, unilluminated areas of the image remain white.

Continuing its rotation, the image drum carries the toner image to the printing station where it contacts the paper. The paper has already passed over a secondary corona from which it has acquired a high-voltage positive charge on its back surface. The positive charge of the paper attracts the negatively charged toner particles from the drum, and the image is transferred to the paper. The powdery black toner is then melted and fused to the paper by the fusion rollers, finishing the printing process.

LED and LCS printers

The principle of laser printing, that light produces changes in the electrical conductivity of a photoconductor, can be applied with equal validity to page printer engines whose sources of illumination are not lasers. While most page printers use the Canon engine in some form, or an engine of similar design, companies such as Okidata have designed their own engines based upon light emitting diodes, or LEDs.

LED engines, unlike laser engines, have no scanning mechanism; in fact, they have no moving parts at all in the illuminating portion of the engine, and are therefore much simpler to design and much cheaper to build than laser-based engines. The reduction in moving parts also contributes to a lowered probability of failure. In contrast to laser diodes, LEDs consume less power, are not sensitive to environmental variables such as temperature, and cannot be injurious. On the other hand, there are practical limits to the resolution at which LED-driven engines can currently be built.

LED engines are composed of arrays of LEDs, 300 to the inch, which are individually turned on or off to provide discrete spots of light on the long axis of the image drum (Fig. 9-3). As in the laser engine, the switching on and off of the LEDs creates a charged pattern on the drum, one raster line at a time. From that point, the developing and printing processes are essentially the same as in a laser engine.

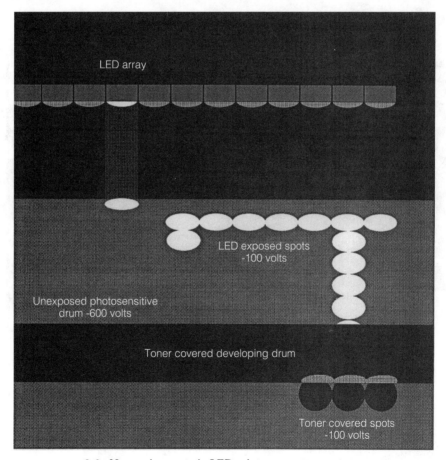

LED array

LED exposed spots
-100 volts

Unexposed photosensitive
drum -600 volts

Toner covered developing drum

Toner covered spots
-100 volts

9-3 No moving parts in LED printer exposure system.

Liquid crystal shutter engines are similar to LED engines in their lack of moving parts, and are similarly inexpensive. Unlike the LED engines, there is only one source of illumination, a lamp. The spots of light which dispel the charge on the surface of the image drum are formed by minute shutters which are placed between the lamp and the drum. The shutters are not mechanical, but are made of liquid crystals, very much like those in a liquid crystal display, whose opacity can be regulated by electrical currents. The action of a liquid crystal shutter is analogous to that of a venetian blind (Fig. 9-4). If the crystals within the shutter are aligned transverse to the light, their flat surfaces are contiguous to each other and the shutter is closed, blocking the light from reaching the drum. If they are aligned on edge, the shutter is open, passing light through to the drum. Some very advanced camera shutters are of this same design. Such a shutter never sticks and can attain very short exposure times. Eventually, however, the shutter becomes unresponsive, even as liquid crystal displays lose their contrast.

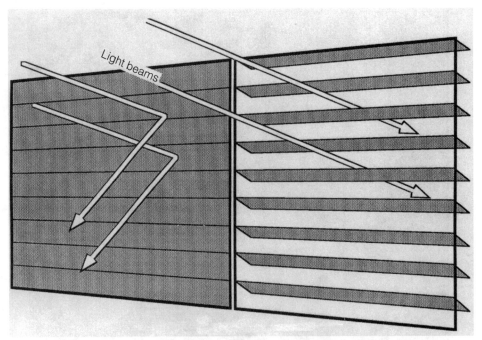

9-4 LCS printers "open" and "close" opaque liquid crystal shutters like venetian blinds.

Chapter 10

Expanding page printer RAM

RAM expansion in page printers is an either/or matter: Either it can be done very simply or it simply cannot be done. Older Apple LaserWriters, such as the LaserWriter Plus, came with a fixed 1.5Mb of RAM soldered to the logic board (Fig. 10-1), and there was no provision made for additional RAM. Granted that 1.5Mb is generally sufficient for daily printing jobs, and it is about 1Mb more than the factory-installed RAM of many other printers manufactured after the Plus, but additional RAM can speed printing of complex PostScript images and can permit more fonts to be downloaded at any one time. Apple built more flexibility into some subsequent printers, but others, like the LaserWriters II NT, were given fixed RAM amounts (albeit twice that of the original LaserWriters).

Hewlett-Packard

Hewlett-Packard, has endowed its laser printers with RAM expansion capabilities. The design of the LaserJet Series II is typical with respect to the expansion path taken by HP and most of its competitors. The logic board of the Series II has a connector which gives the CPU access to as much as 4Mb of optional memory. The connector is reached through a hatchway located on the left side of the printer (Fig. 10-2).

Once you remove the access door, the connector is visible. Expansion memory boards must conform to the specifications set up by HP, but individual boards can vary greatly in their features and in their RAM capacities. Hewlett-Packard itself makes the standard for RAM boards, containing 1, 2, or 4Mb of RAM in fixed amounts (Figs. 10-3 and 10-4).

The advantages of HP boards are that they are from HP (with all that implies for quality and ensured compatibility); that the chips are soldered securely to the boards; and that each board can be inexpensively laid out for its unique configuration.

10-1 LaserWriter One logic board. ROM banks are at center, fixed RAM is left, input/output connectors lower right.

The disadvantage is inherent in the last advantage: more memory cannot be added without replacing the existing board bodily, a needlessly wasteful act. Buying a single-size RAM board generally means buying the largest size you can afford, even though you might be absolutely certain that you will never need greater memory in the future. With memory, as with speed, it seems that too much is never enough. If possible, then, either buy the largest fixed-size board or buy an expandable board.

10-2 Hewlett-Packard RAM expansion slot accepts card with memory. (RAM card courtesy Hewlett-Packard)

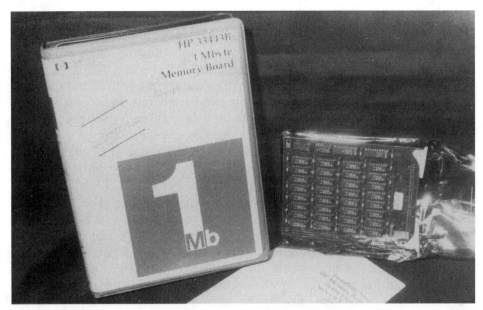

10-3 Hewlett-Packard fixed-amount RAM card for LaserJet II. (RAM card courtesy Hewlett-Packard)

10-4 Soldered memory of Hewlett-Packard RAM card. Soldering assures quality. (RAM card courtesy Hewlett-Packard)

Expansion RAM boards of either fixed or expandable design plug into the connector on the logic board. Replace the access cover and that is all that there is to the job. You never have to touch the fixed size boards again, unless you economized and later find the board insufficient.

Expandable boards, however, are, by their nature, made to be removed and upgraded. Pacific Data, JDR, AGT, Computer Peripherals, Inc. (CPI), and numerous smaller companies market expandable boards, each taking slightly different views of the best method to add RAM to their respective boards. The JDR type of board for the HP Series II and IID uses ordinary slow (120 ns), 1-megabit dynamic RAM chips.

Banks are filled with 8 chips to create 1Mb: four banks are available. You need only insert the chips into the sockets to expand memory. The JDR boards for the HP IIP, IIIP, III and all of the CPI type of boards (Fig. 10-5) use the rather more unusual 4-bit dynamic RAM chips that are favored by video RAM board makers and some interface buffer makers, such as Image Technology. One megabyte of 256K × 4 chips would also require 8 chips. CPI sells sets of 8 Oki chips, but similar chips can be purchased from most RAM vendors for less.

Expandable boards are filled by the bank in a definite order. The board in Fig. 10-5 has been configured for 2Mb using the 4-bit chips. The two outer banks (those nearest the connector) are filled first. Further expansion will require that two more megabytes be added, filling the remaining two banks. The DIP switch

10-5 Third-party Hewlett-Packard compatible expandable RAM card. Memory banks are filled in right to left.

is used to set the amount of memory installed and the type of printer into which the board is to be inserted. (You can fit this board into either a Canon LPB8-II R/T or the Hewlett-Packard LaserJets II and IID. The engines of all HP laser printers are manufactured by Canon, and most of the printer parts based on the same engines are interchangeable.) The legend above the DIP switch shows the permutations of settings relevant to the possible memory and printer combinations. Boards using 1-bit chips sometimes have a set of jumper pins and shorting blocks instead of a DIP switch.

Does it really matter which type of expandable board you choose? The price of a set of the 4-bit chips is usually disproportionately higher than the price of a set of 1-bit chips, but, if a board will accept high-density 4-bit chips, then the price disadvantage shrinks. Generally, the fewer chips the better, although memory failure rates have declined almost to the vanishing point due to the improved manufacturing and fault-detection techniques used by RAM makers. However, socketed chips do tend to move about in reaction to the thermal stress cycles of warming and cooling as the power is turned on and off.

In addition to the heat generated on the board by the chips themselves, there is considerable heat created by the printer's other electronics and by the printing processes. If a chip loosens in its socket, the pin contacts can become intermittent as the board expands and contracts, and dirt can collect between the pins and their sockets, further degrading the circuit. As a rule, chips should be pushed down into their sockets periodically as a preventative, and the fewer chips there are, the less chance there will be for a problem to develop. At this point, however, if there is a choice, the lower price of 1-bit chips will probably be the determining factor in deciding which expandable board to purchase.

RAM expansion for most page printers that are capable of accepting additional RAM is accomplished in a similar manner. Table 10-1 lists some of the printers for which RAM expansion boards are available.

As you can see from the table, another incentive to purchase the largest-capacity, fixed-memory board available is that the price per megabyte of RAM

Table 10-1. Page printer RAM expansion comparisons.

Printer	Mb RAM	P/N	Price/Mb
Hewlett-Packard			
II,IID	1	33443B	95
	2	33444B	63
	4	33445B	45
IIP,III,IIIP,IIID	1	33474A/B	70
	2	33475A/B	60
	4		47
IIsi	1	C2063A	55
	4	C2065A	55
Apple LWII NTX	1	M6005	89
	4	M6006	55

Table 10-1. Continued.

Printer	Mb RAM	P/N	Price/Mb
IBM			
4019,4019E	1	1039136	99
	2	1039137	69
	3.5	1038675	57
4029	2	1183334	89
	4	1183335	89
Panasonic			
KX-P4420,4450I	1	KX-P443	95
	2	KX-P441	73
	4		61
KX-P4450	1	KX-P440	159
KX-P4455	1	KX-P442	185
Okidata			
OKI400	1	70014701	99
	2	70015801	70
OKI800,820	1		135
	2		97
Epson*			
EPL-6000	1		99
	2	IBS401	80
	4		61
EPL-7100	2	C822011	85
NEC 90/290	2	4892	95
T.I. MICROLASER	1	2555739-0001	60
	2		60
	3		60
	4		60
Toshiba*P'LASER 6	2	LS6-NB0090	80
	4	LS6-NB0100	62
QMS			
PS-410	2	2600900-902	70
	4	2600900-901	65
PS-815/825	2		95
	4		70
Brother			
HL-4	1	Mb-410	99
	2	Mb-420	90
	4	Mb-440	67
HL-8/8E	1	Mb-810	149
	2	Mb-820	97
Sharp JX9500PS**	1	JX95MJ	89
Star LSO4	1		129
	2		90

Printer	Mb RAM	P/N	Price/Mb
	4		75
Canon			
LPB-8II,IIR,IIT	2	S63-1880	48
	4		52
LPB-IV	1	S63-2230	189
	2		122
LBP-8III	1	S63-2340	175
	2	S63-2350	150
	3	S63-2360	155

*Epson EPL-6000, Toshiba PageLaser 6, Mannesman Tally 905, Facit 6060, and Packard Bell 9600 use the same memory boards.

**Sharp, Dataproducts, and Tandy lasers are based on the same Sharp engine.

varies inversely to the capacity of the board, the cost decreasing as the capacity increases. In other words, the cost of manufacturing the board is absorbed in the price of the first megabyte. The manufacturer or vendor can add additional megabytes more cheaply than the end user, who does not have the advantage of purchasing RAM in quantity.

Apple

Another, less-frequent memory expansion is Apple's LaserWriter II NTX and its immediate successors. The NTX's motherboard can be loaded with 12Mb of RAM through the installation of single inline memory modules, or SIMMs (Fig. 10-6). Although the SIMMs used by the NTX are peculiar, they are similar in form and function to the SIMMs used in other Apple machines, being eight 1-bit chips mounted on an edge connector card.

NTX's and Macintosh IIfx's use the same SIMMs, supporting simultaneous input and output. They are distinguished visibly by a notch in the bottom of the board. (SIMMs for the NTX must be specified when ordering, while SIMMs for the IIf and IIg are Macintosh-compatible standard units. SIMMs designed for the IBM and its clones use nine chips and are not adaptable to either the Macintoshes or the LaserWriters.) The LaserWriters IIf and IIg have 32Mb of RAM addresses available when 4Mb SIMMs are used.

SIMMs are installed in the edge card sockets on the motherboard (Fig. 10-7). This method of expansion has the advantage of both fixed and expandable memory because, while the chips themselves are soldered securely to their own circuit board, the amount of RAM that can be added is limited only by the CPU's ability to address it and the user's ability to afford it. Furthermore, if one chip fails, you need only replace the affected SIMM bank of memory in which the faulty chip resides, whereas if a chip fails on a fixed-capacity board, you might have to discard the entire board.

LaserWriter II NTX SIMM

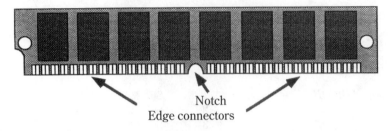

Notch
Edge connectors

SIMM installed in socket, front view

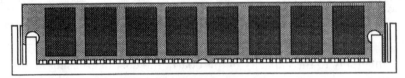

SIMM socket, top view

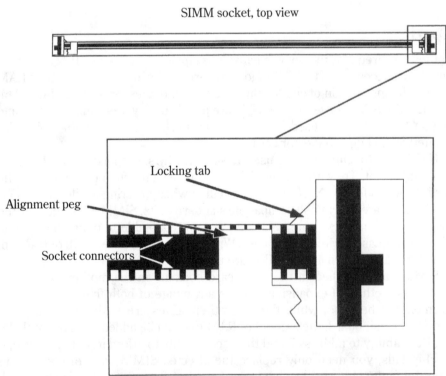

Locking tab

Alignment peg

Socket connectors

Enlarged view of SIMM socket locking tab and alignment peg

10-6 Peculiar SIMM for Apple LaserWriter II NTX and typical SIMM socket.

10-7 SIMMs installed in sockets on LaserWriter II SC logic board.

SIMMs have the disadvantage of being somewhat more breakable than larger boards, and the tabs of their sockets can be broken by careless installation. Also, dirt can accumulate in unpopulated sockets and cause contact interruptions if the sockets are not cleaned before installation.

10-8 SIMMs are installed from rear of socket. Note how locking tabs at end of socket engage module.

The SIMM edge connector has plastic tabs on either end (Figs. 10-6, 10-7, and 10-8) that flex to admit the SIMM and then snap back against the card's ends to hold the module in place. There are also two horns or projections that engage two complementary holes in the tops of the module's ends to ensure correct alignment of the SIMM in the socket. The plastic tabs are pliable within reasonable limits, but they can be broken. A broken tab will lead to a loose SIMM, which can lead, in the end, to memory errors.

The SIMM is inserted from the rear of the socket, with the chips facing away from you (Fig. 10-8). The metallic connectors should be at the bottom, and the two alignment holes should be at the top. The bottom of the SIMM is placed into the connector first, with the top of the SIMM at an angle of about 30 degrees from the perpendicular (Fig. 10-9). When the module is fully seated in the socket, push the top forward while maintaining a downward pressure. The module should swivel into position past the plastic tabs, which should click tightly over the ends of the board. The eyelets should slip over the horns, and the face of the board should be flush against the socket. If the SIMM is slightly elevated in the socket, it will not make good contact with the socket connectors, and the horns will hold the board away from a 90 degree upright position. If you have to remove a SIMM, you must spread the plastic tabs gently to allow the board to slip out, one end at a time. Do not force a SIMM in or out of its socket, or you could break the tabs.

10-9 Proper angle for installation of SIMM.

Chapter 11

Expanding page printer ROM

Upgrading the ROM of a laser or laserlike printer is possible in very few machines. If you consider the additional ROM that most printers can access through their cartridge slots, however, then the field of discussion becomes rather wider.

Apple

Only in PostScript LaserWriters from Apple Computer can actual ROM be exchanged to create an upgraded machine. The original LaserWriter contained a ROM set that delivered 17 fonts in three type families: Hevetica, Times, and Courier. The LaserWriter Plus was a nearly identical machine with the exception of the ROM set, which extended the internal fonts to the now standard 35, adding New Century Schoolbook, Palatino, Avant Garde, Zapf Chancery, Zapf Dingbats and Bookman type families to those in the previous set. (Symbol, a collection of Dingbats, was in both machines. Helvetica Narrow, a typeface interpolated on demand from Helvetica, was also added. This was a simulated form of the real PostScript typeface.)

Owners of older machines were given the option to purchase an upgrade from Apple at a typically outrageous price. Apple dealers would extract and retain the old logic board and install a new one. A 10-minute operation cost something like $1,000. Users who had paid nearly a thousand dollars to upgrade their original 128K Macintoshes to 512K were, perhaps, inured to such demands upon their funds, but others who had purchased third-party RAM upgrades held on to their wallets and waited. Eventually, enough newer ROM sets became available in the aftermarket that users could buy the chips for about $200 and make the ROM switch themselves.

Before replacing the chips, turn off the machine and unplug the electrical cord. If the printer has been running, allow it to cool before opening the case.

You should unplug the logic board from its power source before doing any work on the board itself. (This is standard practice when you work on any electrical device). The power connector is located in the left rear corner. The connector for the LED indicator lights, right front, should also be unplugged (see Fig. 10-1 for the locations of the connectors). Unplug the Video I/O and Serial I/O cable connectors by spreading the locking wings of the sockets. This will loosen the connectors, permitting them to be unplugged.

The LaserWriter logic board (Fig. 10-1) has 16 ROM sockets. These contain the Adobe PostScript language and the other instructions necessary to control the printer. The original LaserWriter had a set of 256K chips, while the LaserWriter Plus had a chip set consisting of denser 512K chips. That was the only difference between the two.

A LaserWriter ROM chip set is shown in Fig. 11-1. The chips are in two banks, HI and LO, and are arranged in two rows of eight. The first seven chips in each row are numbered consecutively, 111 to 117 and 118 to 126, with the last two chips numbered 139 and 140 in the LaserWriter. You need only pull the chips and replace them with their LaserWriter Plus counterparts. If you pull two chips at a time and fill the sockets with the appropriate substitutes before moving on to the next pair, you will be better able to maintain the correct order.

Ascertain that each new chip is facing in the same direction as the chip it replaces and that all pins are in their respective sockets (not bent under the chip

11-1 LaserWriter ROM chip set.

package or outside of the socket) before moving on to the next chip. Inspect the old chips before putting them on the foam mat and the mat is returned to its static-resistant bag. If any of the pins became bent during removal, you can manually straighten them. Use great care not to twist and break them. You can purchase pin-straightening tools for a few dollars should any pins appear to be too bent for manual straightening.

Once you have installed all the chips, there is one more step to take. You must remove a jumper wire and install a new wire so that the printer can recognize the higher-density chips. The jumper positions are directly above the ROM section, toward the rear edge of the logic board (Figs. 11-1 and 11-2). Cut or desolder the wire in the 256K position, and solder a shorting wire into the 512K position. If you desolder the wire you can reuse it.

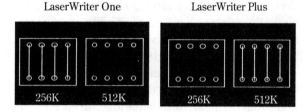

LaserWriter One   LaserWriter Plus

11-2 Jumper JM17 positions for LaserWriter and Laser-Writer Plus ROM sets.

A combination desoldering iron and bulb, or a bulb and small wattage iron, are better than an iron and desoldering braid. With a separate bulb and iron, you apply the bulb's tip to the solder side of the board and the tip of the iron to the component side of the joint. In this way, you can anchor the bulb on the wire where it protrudes through the board. Melt the solder and suck it through into the bulb. Then pull the wire free with needle nose pliers, and clean any remaining solder out of the holes.

Use a 15-watt or smaller soldering iron and thin-wire electronic solder to add the shorting wire to the 512K position. Be extremely careful not to drop solder onto any of the board's components. If you cut out the old wire instead of desoldering, you can fashion a new wire from a section of insulated solid copper wire, or from a portion of uninsulated wire snipped off a resistor lead. Heat the connection with the tip of the iron. Do not allow the iron to touch any other portion of the board; it should touch only the metallic ring to which the wire is to be soldered. Inspect the joints when cool to make sure there are no gaps or solder bridges. You can then return the board to the printer and plug in the connectors again. Make certain that the video and serial cables are plugged into their corresponding sockets and are locked in by the tabs.

After you turn the printer on and it has passed through its warm-up cycle, the LaserWriter Plus test page should print. Should the warm-up not proceed as normal, or the test page not print, turn off the printer and go back over your work.

Are all the chips in their proper sockets and facing in the right direction? Are any pins not making contact? Are the video and serial cables in their correct sockets and are they right side up? Is the power connector firmly in place? Are the LEDs connected? Is the jumper wire installed in the right position and well-soldered?

If the printer still will not work, return the old ROM chips to their former sockets, move the jumper wire, and try the printer. If it works with the old chips, then the new set is defective. If it does not work, then you might have been careless during the upgrade and damaged the board. Such damage can be very difficult to track and expensive to repair, so always be extremely careful when working on the logic board.

Cartridges—the other ROM

The majority of page printers are not LaserWriters, and do not "speak PostScript." The majority are Hewlett-Packard or HP compatibles and use PCL. As such, they do not have the flexibility of Adobe-type fonts built into their ROMs, and to achieve the type variety of which PostScript is inherently capable, they must make use of the external ROM that cartridges supply.

The cartridge market, as with other laser printer accessory markets, is defined by Hewlett -Packard itself. The number and contents of almost all the type and emulation cartridges manufactured and sold are determined by reference to the cartridges sold by Hewlett-Packard since the introduction of the LaserJet Series II.

Fixed-form font cartridges

HP produced 25 font cartridges with alphabetic suffixes. Each cartridge contained a group of stylistically or functionally related bitmapped typefaces. Thus, if you wish to have a Times typeface in a particular point size, you could conveniently plug a Times cartridge into one of the two cartridge slots in the lower front of the printer (Fig. 11-3). You then use a software printer driver that recognizes that cartridge, and the typeface is then treated as a native to the printer.

The advantages of such a system are that it makes an infinite number of typefaces accessible, those typefaces are in the printer at all times, and their use is transparent. The disadvantages are that the number of cartridges allowed in the printer is limited to two, and the number of typefaces and sizes is limited to those bitmaps specifically written in the cartridge ROM. And there is considerable disadvantage of cost: multiply the price of one cartridge by 25 and, to paraphrase Everett Dirksen, it can add up to real money.

Pacific Data Products was the first company to overcome some of those disadvantages by exploiting the advantages of cartridges. Instead of one grouping per cartridge, Pacific Data took all the contents of the 25 HP cartridges and put them into one cartridge, the 25 in One! (Fig. 11-4). The cost and inconvenience of font cartridges was immediately reduced to $\frac{1}{25}$. Since then, other companies such as Computer Peripherals, Inc. and UDP Data Products have compiled sin-

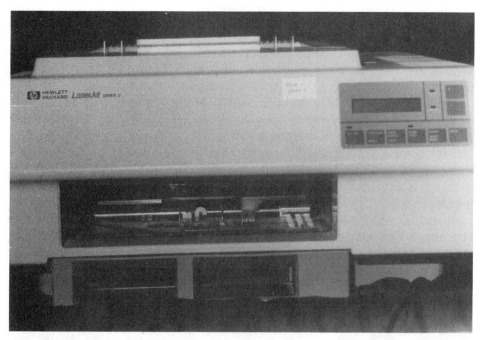

11-3 Two cartridge ROM slots of Hewlett-Packard LaserJet Series II are in front below the paper cassette aperture.

11-4 Pacific Data Products' pioneering 25 in One! font cartridge for LaserJets.
(Equipment courtesy Pacific Data Products)

gle-cartridge collections of typefaces to compete with both HP and Pacific Data. New collections are being added every other month, it seems.

The challenge has become not to copy the Pacific Data cartridge, but to create new selections for niche markets, such as collections of decorative or headline fonts that will effectively monopolize those particular markets.

Pacific Data, Computer Peripherals, UDP Data Products, and others have formulated competing cartridge lines with many overlapping or superimposable characteristics. Headlines, word processing, spreadsheets, tax forms, science, and mathematics are among the specialized typeface groupings for LaserJets and compatibles. UDP's TurboGold cartridge (Fig. 11-5) brings 167 fonts together in a single cartridge. These include a typical mixture of large point size bitmapped fonts (Helvetica, Park-A, and Presentation in sizes up to 48 points), fonts appropriate for body text (proportionally spaced Times Roman and Helvetica, and monospaced Courier, Prestige Elite, and Letter Gothic in sizes from 3.6 up to 14 points), very small fonts suitable for printing 132-column spreadsheets (3.6 point Letter Gothic and 4.8 point Lineprinter), very specialized forms-generating fonts (TaxLine Draw), and fonts with scientific and mathematical

11-5 UDP's TurboGold font cartridge duplicates contents of 25 in One! and adds more fonts. (Equipment courtesy UDP Data Products)

symbols and formulae (Math 7, 8, 8A, 8B, and PiFonts in both proportional and monospaced faces, as well as PC-8 in Lineprinter for computer applications). A sample printout appears in appendix B.

Computer Peripheral's ActionSet! and SuperSet+ cartridges are multipurpose typeface bundles. The ActionSet! cartridge contains 102 bitmapped fonts ranging from 6 to 18 points. It includes Helvetica, Times Bold, and Presentation Bold for headlines; Lotica for spreadsheets; Prestige Elite for science and math; PC Line and Tax LineDraw for taxes and other forms; and Times, Letter Gothic, Prestige Elite, Courier, and Helvetica for word processing.

The SuperSet+ cartridge is a compendium of other cartridges, a superset which subsumes the ActionSet! and Pacific Data's 25 in One! cartridge, plus the contents of Hewlett-Packard's ProCollection and Microsoft cartridges—425 fonts in all. Unfortunately for owners of HP LaserJet II printers, only the lower 168 fonts are addressable by the printer logic.

Custom font cartridges

The move toward greater specialization in font cartridges has reached perhaps its ultimate level in the user-programmable cartridges that have recently been brought to market. Pacific Data has led the pack in this field as well. Its Font-Bank cartridge is built around the newer "flash" memory, a type of memory that has qualities of both RAM and EPROM. Data can be written to flash memory by the user, as with ordinary RAM, but it can retain that data after power has been turned off as with EPROM. And, like EPROM, the data can be erased and the memory rewritten with new data as required. Thus, a cartridge containing flash RAM can be customized to fit the needs of individual users, and it can be altered as those needs change. If the user needs Times in 10- and 12-point sizes, Helvetica in three sizes, dingbats in one size, and a cursive typeface in one very large point size, then cartridges for each typeface (each of which contains a dozen point sizes) would be largely wasted. With a FontBank cartridge, the user can write to the cartridge only those point sizes needed, a much more efficient use of memory and cartridge slots. The sources of the fonts must be purchased, of course, but fonts on disk are comparatively inexpensive, so that the combined price of the one cartridge with its custom selection of typefaces remains much lower than the combined price of all the cartridges it replaces.

The other major advantage of a FontBank is realized by the user who is accustomed to downloading fonts to the printer on a regular basis. With the Font-Bank, all of the commonly downloaded fonts can be stored permanently in flash memory, saving both the user's time and the printer's RAM. The latter can be used far more productively by the printer for page production. The cartridge can hold not only typefaces, but frequently used PCL macros. Items such as letterheads and other boilerplates which are normally transmitted in full from the computer to the printer, can be invoked from the cartridge as if they were characters in a font. You can purchase the cartridge with either .75Mb or 1.5Mb of flash RAM.

The FontBank cartridge is similar to other cartridges except for the DIP switches on one side which are used to place the cartridge in the program or print modes. In the program mode, the cartridge can receive downloaded fonts and macros. The software supplied with the cartridge allows users to select fonts from supported applications (WordPerfect 5.0/5.1, Microsoft Word 5/5.5 Windows 2.x and 3.0) to enter into the flash memory. The FontBank can store any Hewlett-Packard or compatible format font.

Scalable fonts can be programmed for Series III printers. Adobe PostScript fonts cannot be used unless first converted to PCL format. The support software sets up drivers automatically. Once all the fonts have been chosen for inclusion in the FontBank, the computer downloads them to the cartridge, along with a catalog of the fonts. Assuming that the average "soft" font occupies between 20K and 30K of space, the .75Mb cartridge could hold approximately 25–30 fonts.

Once the downloading is complete, turn the printer off, remove the cartridge, and set the DIP switches in the print mode. You can then use the cartridge as you would any standard cartridge. You can reprogram the cartridge at any time on any HP printer except the IIsi. You must program the entire cartridge at one time, however. Fonts cannot be added or subtracted individually.

To make a change in the flash RAM's contents, you must rewrite the entire memory. This is a necessary inconvenience because flash memory is not like a disk, on which files can exist in fragmented form with an extant directory to thread them together. Deleting or adding fonts from the flash memory would result in "holes," or gaps in the catalog, with no guarantee that new fonts would fit into the spaces vacated by those subtracted. Therefore, alterations can only be wholesale.

Bitstream, a vendor of HP- and PostScript-compatible typefaces, sells a customizable font cartridge called Font City. Unlike FontBank, Font City is primarily a vehicle for Bitstream type. It is programmed with a basic set of faces: Swiss 721 (a Helvetica look-alike) in five text point sizes from 8 to 14 points, Swiss Condensed Bold in three large point sizes, Zapf Calligraphic (a Palatino derivation) in seven sizes from 8 to 30 points, Monospace 821 (a Courier twin), Ribbon 131, and Symbol. These fonts are indelibly burned into the cartridge, but there are four slots in the cartridge, each of which admits a 256K module. Thus, you can add 1Mb of typefaces to suit diverse tastes and needs.

Bitstream includes one module with the cartridge, called the *Deli card*, which contains Letter Gothic, Cloister Black, and Old Dreadful No. 7. Whimsicality appears to be something of a Bitstream trademark. Other modules are called Skyscraper, Soho, Dutch, and Charter, ranging in price from $99 to $129.

For $150, Bitstream will program a module with any typefaces desired from the Bitstream type catalog; the only catch is a minimum order of five modules with identical contents. There is also a personalized programming service that will burn logos, letterheads, and clip art into a module. This is definitely not as flexible a system as the FontBank, but the consistency and quality of Bitstream is unquestionably high. Font City's only other drawback is in unresolved font name conflicts with some Adobe typefaces.

Scalable font cartridges

Since the introduction of the LaserJet Series III printers, a new market for scalable HP format fonts has been created. Hewlett-Packard, Pacific Data, UDP, and Computer Peripherals all have produced cartridges that supplement the internal fonts of newer printers.

Hewlett-Packard's collection of scalable is excellent, both in selection and in execution. HP has three scalable typeface cartridges: WordPerfect, Distinctive Document I/Compelling Publications I, and Brilliant Presentations I/Compelling Publications II, each of which is priced at $349.

The WordPerfect collection consists of Albertus, CG Century Schoolbook, Dom Casual, Futura Book II, ITC Galliard Roman, Microstyle Bold, CG Palacio, Park Avenue, Univers Medium Condensed, and ITC Zapf Chancery Medium Italic.

The Distinctive Documents/Compelling Publications cartridge contains Antique Olive, CG Century Schoolbook, CG Palacio, ITC Souvenir Light, Stymie Medium, Univers Medium Condensed, and ITC Zapf Dingbats.

The Brilliant Presentations/Compelling Publications cartridge is occupied by ITC Benguiat Book, CG Bodoni Book, ITC Bookman Light, Cooper Black, Garamond Antigua, CG Omega, Revue Light, and Shannon Book.

Each HP cartridge is made to be used with HP's LaserJets III and IIIP. To create screen fonts for Windows applications, HP has devised the Intellifont-for-Windows 3.0 program. Working with the printer's own Intellifont technology, this program automatically generates screen fonts by reading the contents of the cartridge and building fonts while an application is running. Some software publishers have incorporated HP AutoFont Support into their products (WordStar 5.5/6.0, WordPerfect 5.0/5.1, and Microsoft Word 5.5 among others), so that the applications themselves will install the cartridge fonts into their screen and printer drivers, foregoing the need for the user to install them manually. For all other uses, HP and Compugraphic (the CG in many of the typefaces used in the cartridges, and originator of the Intellifont scaling technology) have combined to issue Type Director 2.0, a stand-alone font generation and installation program (discussed in the chapter on software).

UDP's TurboScalable Font Cartridge contains 37 typefaces, each of which can be printed in any quarter-point fractional size between 6 and 999.75. There are 14 UDP equivalent type families, most of which are supplied in roman, italic bold, and bold italic. This selection obviously bears a strong resemblance to the type complement found in PostScript printers, and it does bring an HP LaserJet III closer to equaling the power of a PostScript printer. Twenty-three nationalized or special-purpose symbol sets are provided, and drivers are supplied for Windows 3.0, WordPerfect 5.1, Word 5.0/5.5, Xywrite, and WordStar 5.5/6.0.

Pacific Data modestly calls its scalable font cartridge the Complete Font Library Cartridge, containing 51 outline typefaces. This cartridge also adheres to the Intellifont scaling factors of quarter-point fractions up to 999.75 points. The Complete Font Library has the additional distinction of using licensed typefaces, so that designs and names are guaranteed to be compatible with the CG, ITC, or other originals. While this might not be literally a complete font library, it does fill out the printer's font selection in a manner that will meet most if not all desktop printing contingencies.

In truth, the number of typefaces regularly used by all but the wildest typomaniacal personal laser printer owner can be reduced to three or four, and this cartridge can, by that criterion, be legitimately termed complete.

The Complete Font Library Cartridge also exceeds the LaserJet's maximum external ROM addressing capabilities. LaserJets can access up to, but not in excess of, 2Mb of cartridge ROM. This can be distributed across both cartridge slots or all in one slot. Early HP cartridges contained 512K. Pacific Data's 25 in One! cartridge managed to fit all of HP's cartridges into 2Mb. The Complete Font Library Cartridges use memory bank switching (Pacific Data calls it *windowing*), to allow the printer to access more than its permissible limit. Although there are greater than 2Mb in the cartridge, at any one time the printer can "see" only that 2Mb portion that the cartridge presents. When a font not in the currently addressed area is needed, the cartridge switches access to another 2Mb section in which the font does reside, and some fonts previously available are locked out.

Computer Peripherals, Inc. has taken a unique road to scalable-type cartridges by way of TrueType, the Apple-Microsoft-LaserMaster bezier-based outline system. The JetType IIP cartridge is for the LaserJet IIP alone, but because it is the best-selling LaserJet and has been succeeded by the IIP Plus, there are plenty of potential buyers.

The cartridge contains 13 licensed Monotype and proprietary CPI fonts, each of which can be scaled to nearly any size. The cartridge is tailored especially to fit the Windows 3.1 environment, which imports TrueType technology. New Times (the Monotype typeface used by the Times of London), Arial (a cloned relative of Helvetica), and Garamond are the three type families found in the cartridge and form a solid core of conscientious typography. The cartridge's contents are rounded out by Swing Bold (a scriptlike face), Symbol (a Greek and mathematical technical set), and Lotica (a speadsheet font). JetType also includes drivers for WordPerfect 5.1, Lotus 1-2-3, dBase IV/III, and Windows 3.1 and Windows applications.

More than type

Cartridge ROM upgrades reach into more areas than typography alone: you can add Level 5 of Hewlett-Packard PCL, PostScript, and printer emulations to some printers.

Hewlett-Packard PCL

For the Hewlett-Packard LaserJet IIP, HP has produced a PCL 5 upgrade cartridge, putting the printer nearly level with the IIIP in its power. Unlike the Computer Peripherals JetType IIP cartridges, the HP cartridge contains a full implementation of the latest PCL version that includes scalable fonts, typographic effects, plotter language support, and graphic compression. All that it lacks to make it the complete IIIP-in-a-cartridge is the Resolution Enhancement Technology (RET) of the Series III family.

Unfortunately, RET modulation of the laser beam, however desirable, is not a feature easily grafted onto a printer through external ROM. Equally unfortunate, the IIP has only one cartridge slot, forcing the user to choose between this cartridge and the JetType IIP.

The PCL 5 cartridge breaks through the bitmapped barriers of font technology, the greatest shortcoming of the HP laser printer family. Scaling is not just a hot fashion but a real advance, making possible almost unlimited numbers of font sizes from a very compact type set. Users no longer have to have bitmaps for every font size they need, and no longer have to purchase a 72-point size that they will use only in rare instances. Instead they have sizes up to 720 points always on call, all for the $299 price of the cartridge.

If that were not enough, the addition of the HPGL/2 plotter support gives the user great control over how scalable fonts look. Font outlines can be internally translated into graphic vectors you can stretch, rotate, fill, with patterns or grays, and manipulate in ways that were once impossible in an HP laser printer outside of the III family.

HP has obviously been trying to annex to PCL many traits of PostScript, which is clearly superior in nearly every important aspect of page description, without actually including PostScript as a standard item. While the advancements demonstrated in PCL Level 5 have given new power to HP printers, it does not diminish the broad appeal and wide acceptance of PostScript. Hewlett-Packard has tacitly acknowledged this by licensing Adobe PostScript for a cartridge.

Adobe PostScript

For many users, PostScript is the ultimate upgrade. PostScript is a single-purpose computer programming language. PostScript's sole purpose is to produce printed matter from a mathematically defined set of page descriptors that govern every element of the page, from the visible text characters and the photographs or drawings illustrating the text to the invisible margins and the line and character spacings. And, as with any programming language, anyone can learn to write a PostScript program. Adobe encourages people to write PostScript programs. The catch is that, like other interpreted programming languages, an interpreter (actually a second computer program) is needed to run the program and to produce the actual output. That is where Adobe comes in with its PostScript interpreter and rasterizers.

The rasterizer takes the calculated output from the interpreter and renders it into scan lines suitable to the resolution of the device on which the output is to be displayed. Adobe sells (i.e., licenses) its language interpreter and rasterizer for use in any number of devices from printers to computer display systems.

PostScript emulators

Naturally an unprotected monopoly attracts competition. In the case of Post-Script, once a program was written in the language (the language is given away free, remember, and the program written in it is the property of the author), the program needs the interpreter/rasterizer to be of any use. If you know what the language commands are, you can manually plot out the result or, in effect, interpret the page. And, if you can plot out the result yourself, you can theoretically write an interpreter. That is exactly what some enterprising people did.

Pacific Data's Pacific Page

Pacific Data was the first to enter the PostScript cartridge market with Pacific Page, based on the Phoenix Page PostScript emulation interpreter. The first cartridge was for the LaserJet Series II. It worked (depending upon the expectations of the user) either well or not well, but it worked. It required a minimum of 2.5Mb of memory, which caused some distress because the addition of memory effectively added to the price of the cartridge. Some reviewers were dismayed that it co-opted control of the printer, rendering it impossible to use the printer on a network. Also, the printing process for most PostScript files slowed to seeming interminability with the Pacific Page.

The Pacific Page P•E and XL were received with warmer enthusiasm. The P•E was the basic cartridge unit with a revised emulation capable of running with a minimum memory of 1Mb, and the XL was the cartridge combined with an accelerator /2Mb memory board. Pacific Data claimed that the XL was two to eight times faster than a standard PostScript cartridge. In this case, the standard was the Adobe cartridge.

The speed enhancement was derived from the accelerator board, which used an Intel i960 CPU, a reduced instruction set computer (RISC), to relieve the printer's CPU of PostScript interpretation. The lack of networking was also resolved, and Pacific Data introduced networking products, one of which was specifically for the Macintosh. The version for the Macintosh and the IIP, however, was not considered a worthwhile alternative to a PostScript printer in a review by MacWorld, which advised readers to avoid it. This judgment was based partly on the fact that the IIP, built on the Canon LX or P-110 engine was itself a four-pages-per-minute-(ppm) printer, and not the equal of printers constructed from the SX or other engines capable of eight pages per minute.

While Pacific Data ironed out the creases in its PostScript emulation, UDP, Computer Peripherals, and Adobe sent their own PostScript and PostScript-compatible cartridges to the marketplace.

Adobe cartridges

Adobe's cartridge was for the Hewlett-Packard LaserJet II exclusively. It had many of the same limitations as Pacific Page's cartridge, but it received better notices, perhaps on account of its noble parentage. It required 1.5Mb of RAM to print a full letter-size page, and 2.5Mb to print to a legal-size page. There was no support for networking. Only the serial and parallel ports were recognized, and a computer sending data through an optional interface would cause the printer to "hang." Adobe Font Foundry was supplied on disk to generate screen fonts for Windows and Ventura Publisher. A software control panel was also supplied that switched the printer between PCL and PostScript.

CPI's JetPage cartridge

The CPI JetPage cartridge is an emulation product. Its 35 typefaces are equivalents to true PostScript printers such as the Apple LaserWriters Plus, NT, and NTX. Bookman, Avant Garde, Zapf Chancery, and Zapf Dingbats are licensed from ITC, while Helvetica, Helvetica Narrow, Times Roman, Palamino, Century Schoolbook, and Courier are celebrity lookalikes for the originals. The cartridge supports optional I/O input, requires 1.5Mb of RAM, and comes in versions for the LaserJet II and the LaserJet IIP, IID, and III. It can be switched from Post-Script to PCL and back either from the computer or the printer.

UDP's TurboScript cartridge

The UDP TurboScript cartridge (Fig. 11-6) looks very much like another face in the crowd of PostScript-capable cartridge interpreters. There are no licensed Adobe typefaces in its LaserWriter equivalents, but there are more of them. To stand out from the crowd, UDP has added 12 fonts to the 35 routinely gathered in any PostScript-speaking convention. Garamond, Helvetica Black, and Korinna were added to the genealogy, making the cartridge not Laser-Writer but IBM LaserPrinter 4019 compatible. It accepts input from optional I/O boards so that some networks are possible, but its highest data speed seems to fall considerably short of that required by AppleTalk or other similar networks. The interpreter is Custom Applications' Freedom of Press and is one of the most reliable PostScript clones. The software version of FOP even beats a dedicated PostScript printer in speed tests to a laser printer or an ink jet printer. (See the chapter on software for a discussion of FOP.) TurboScript uses no coprocessors and requires 1.5Mb of memory in the printer. The cartridge for the LaserJet II is called TurboScript II, while that for the IIP and III is called TurboScript III.

TurboScript II must reside in the left cartridge slot of the Laser JetII and TurboScript III can be inserted in either slot in the Series III. The cartridge comes with a lively 34-page manual and a software utility on disk.

Ports can be individually selected (parallel only, serial only, or optional I/O only) or the printer can be instructed to receive data from all ports on a first-come-first-serve priority. Two or three computers can be attached simultane-

11-6 UDP's TurboScript offers highly compatible PostScript emulation for LaserJets. (Equipment courtesy UDP Data Products)

ously to the printer. The maximum allowable serial baud rate is 19,200 a practical limit for optional I/O as well. Parallel data transmission is definitely faster, although it precludes the possibility of setting up an interactive link with the printer for PostScript programming, a situation which serial communication can provide.

In order to use the extra fonts in the cartridge, you must select a driver for the IBM 4216 Personal PagePrinter II-030 or II-31. Selection of the LaserWriter or other standard PostScript printer divider will limit the font selection to the normal typefaces.

The utility disk is 5¼-inch IBM format and carries two small DOS batch programs that switch the TurboScript cartridge between PostScript and PCL operation. Not all programs are compatible with spoolers and buffers, which will strip some printer commands from the data stream. In this case, you must reset the printer at the front panel.

The cartridge itself performs admirably. It can print very complex PostScript effects for both text and graphics without error, which indicates that it echoes all of PostScript's commands and functions. Any page that will print on a Laser-Writer Plus or NT (and some that won't, as in Fig. 11-7) will print on the LaserJet with TurboScript. Even illustrations created in Cricket Draw, a drawing program for the Macintosh that generates its own PostScript, not to mention its own derived PostScript functions, printed without fault. Graduated fills, mirroring, binding text to an arbitrary path, rotating text, and other PostScript tricks can be handled by TurboScript.

11-7 Cricket Draw stencil effect uses PostScript clipping functions and graduated fills.

Waterfall

The TurboScript cartridge third-party typefaces, although conforming to Adobe PostScript specifications, appear different than the Adobe type itself. The Nimbus Q fonts are copies of the Adobe typefaces, not duplicates. The lowercase letters of the TurboScript Times Roman equivalent, for instance, are slightly smaller than the lowercase characters of the true Adobe Times Roman. There are also subtle differences in the serifs of all the letters. The "look" of a page of TurboScript Times is, on the whole, not as pleasing as that of the same page printed in Adobe Times. Taken separately and alone, Nimbus Q Times is perfectly acceptable, but, in a side by side comparison, Adobe Times is the better-looking typeface.

Canon LPB-4

For the Canon LPB-4, the printer upon which the HP IIP, IIP Plus, IIIP and so many other small four-ppm printers are based, Canon has marketed the PS-2 PostScript card, the only commercial PostScript upgrade for Canon printers. Similar in concept to the Pacific Page P•E, it uses both the cartridge slot and an internal RAM/co-processor card. The co-processor is a floating point arithmetic chip that handles the long math computations required by PostScript transformations. The chip sits on the memory card, which adds 1Mb to the printer's 512K. The cartridge contains 39 PostScript-compatible fonts. The list price is $695.

PostScript vs. the emulators

The type of printer you choose will ultimately depend on how you will use it. Tests are a good judge of the suitability of a product only in the context of your purposes. If most of your work is text, or text with some graphics, a controller-based printer with a fixed amount of memory is probably the better choice. If, however, your work is mostly graphics, a cartridge-based printer with ample memory and memory expansion could be the better buy. There are other determining factors, such as cost, compatibility, and speed.

Speed

Speed is one thing that PostScript has sacrificed for quality, and printers equipped with PostScript emulation cartridges have lagged behind real PostScript printers in most printing tests. The differences cannot always be attributed to the emulation itself, however. Unless the printer is on an AppleTalk or faster network, PostScript printing can be hobbled by the speed at which the data are sent to the printer. A printer with the minimum required memory will also tend to run at a slower speed than one with 2.5Mb or more of RAM. Some examples are given below.

The PostScript file of some garlic cloves (Fig. 11-8) was printed on a Laser-Writer Plus and on a LaserJet II with TurboScript. The LaserWriter was on AppleTalk, the nominal speed of which is 230.2 kilobaud (230,200 baud), and the LaserJet was serially connected to the computer and receiving data at 19,200 baud. AppleTalk can transmit files to the LaserWriter in the background from a print spooler, called Print Monitor, that is part of the LaserWriter support designed into Macintosh software by Apple. The background operation can be disabled.

Normally, an Apple PostScript dictionary, Laser Prep, is downloaded to the printer the first time a file is sent to the LaserWriter after it has been turned on. Thereafter, Laser Prep is resident in the printer until it is turned off or reset. It is usually downloaded only at the beginning of a session. This downloading adds some time to the printing of the first file. Subsequent files of equal length print faster.

11-8 Complex vector drawing used to test various PostScript options.

The garlic.ps file was sent to the LaserWriter both with the downloaded Laser Prep and without, both in the background and by direct interaction of the printer and the sending program. In the background with Laser Prep, the Laser-Writer Plus took 1 minute, 52 seconds to print. In the background without Laser Prep, the time was shortened to 1 minute, 25 seconds. In the interactive mode, without Laser Prep, the page was printed in 1 minute, 4 seconds, a very respectable time for a fairly old machine.

The LaserJet II and TurboScript were timed at 8 minutes and 25 seconds for the same file, 3 minutes and 57 seconds of which were consumed by transmission of the file. Actual interpretation and printing of the file can, therefore, be timed at 4 minutes and 28 seconds, reasonable, although still 400 percent slower than the LaserWriter Plus.

This result when comparing PostScript cartridge emulations to native Post-Script printers can be deceptive. There are actually some cases in which the cartridge emulation will beat the native PostScript. Figures 11-7 and 11-9 are examples.

Each of the characters in Fig. 11-9 is a Cricket Draw object, an outline filled with a fountain or gradient fill. To each fountain, a halftone screen was applied. The halftone in the upright characters is different from that in the mirrored characters. The mirrored characters have also been slightly distorted to create a wave effect. All things taken together, this figure calls for some very complicated PostScript calculations to produce a printed page. PostScript is a memory-consuming, stack-oriented language. The LaserWriter Plus has 1½Mb of RAM soldered to the logic board, more RAM than is standard in most laser printers, but an amount that cannot be enlarged. The LaserWriter Plus chewed on this draw-

11-9 Another complex Cricket Draw drawing combining several PostScript effects.

ing for about 2½ hours before turning out the page. The LaserJet II used in this test had 2.5Mb of RAM and the TurboScript cartridge installed. It finished the computations and printed the page in about 1½ hours, an hour less than the genuine PostScript printer. The comparative performances of the two printers in Fig. 11-7 is even more dramatic.

Figure 11-7 is composed of the same elements as the upright word in Fig. 11-9, but the fountain is created in a separate object placed behind the characters. The fountain is then revealed selectively by a clipping command in Cricket Draw that acts as a stencil, permitting the fill to show through the characters but not through the empty space around them. The LaserWriter worked for a few minutes and then gave up, returning a stackunderflow error. The TurboScript cartridge and the LaserJet II worked on the problem for about the same duration and quite unexpectedly printed the illustration. It is therefore evident that the amount of memory can affect the outcome of tests between a cartridge emulation and a controller-resident form of PostScript.

Compatibility

Will the printer be on a network, and if so, what type? The addition of an optional interface adds further to the cost of the printer, while many native PostScript printers already include the network interface. Will the cartridge selected support the network? AppleTalk, for instance, which permits either Apple or IBM computers to be connected, is built into the LaserWriters. If it must be added to a printer, then the Pacific Data Products cartridge with PacificTalk is the likely choice. I do not mean to convey a definitive answer, because there are too many circumstantial variables. I mean to suggest that you weigh the type of tasks you do and the environment in which the printer will be used. If you already own a printer, a cartridge may be the only solution.

PostScript beyond the cartridge slot

There is not always an alternative to a cartridge form of PostScript, but for almost any printer based on a Canon engine, it is possible to add PostScript, by replacing the controller/logic board with that of an Apple LaserWriter. This is a project that cannot be covered adequately in a small space, but I can give you the barest outline of the procedure. Fuller directions can be found in my TAB-Windcrest volume, *Build Your Own PostScript Laser Printer and Save a Bundle*.

The Canon CX engine

The Canon CX engine was the first engine to be converted to an Apple Laser-Writer. The concept is simple: Canon laser engines are used in millions of laser printers built by dozens of companies, including Apple. The only basic difference between a printer built by Hewlett-Packard and Apple from the same engine can be found in their respective logic boards, the only proprietary portion of each machine. If all the common parts of the printers are interchangeable, it is logical that the proprietary parts, the logic boards, are also interchangeable. They are.

It takes relatively little dexterity and knowledge to transfer the PostScript-speaking logic/interface brain from an Apple LaserWriter One or Plus into the body of a generic Canon printer. Logic boards can be purchased from many sources, and the engines can be found in new, used, and reconditioned form from even more sources. Besides Apple boards, there is also the PS-Jet+ from Laser Connection, a division of QMS, which can be added to a LaserJet, LaserJet Plus, or LaserJet 500. It is a genuine PostScript board as well and has more memory than the LaserWriter board.

The secret to adding a logic board to a Canon engine is in the video and serial I/O interfaces built into the LaserWriter logic board. The Canon CX engine receives its printing instructions through the video interface which is connected to the DC controller, the site of all of the printer's lower-level functions such as laser scanning, motor control, high voltage regulation, and paper motion.

The video I/O gives the logic board access to all of those functions. The printer, in fact, is a semi-autonomous mechanism, with the logic board having only a supervisory role. The interface to the outside world, that is to say, to a computer is part of the logic board, so that the laser engine can be adapted to practically any type of interfacing with the right logic board.

The LaserWriter One/Plus logic interface board is large (Fig. 10-1), as is the CX laser engine (Fig.11-10). The video I/O and the Serial I/O are located in the lower, right-hand corner of the board, the power connector is located in the left rear corner, and the ROM chips are in the center. There are mounting holes in each of the board's four corners, which mate with standoffs in the laser engine's lid. To make the board and engine work together, construct a video I/O cable that connects from the logic board to the DC Controller at connector J-202. This is the only link between the two boards. The LaserWriter board must receive +5

11-10   Canon CX laser engine.

volts at the two pins of the power connector nearest the large coil. The two outside pins are to ground.

If the engine had a logic board before the coversion, then the required power should be available through that board's power supply connection. If the engine was the type used in the NEC laser fax station, then you must add an external power source.

A serial interface cable must be constructed to link the serial I/O port on the board to the outside port, most often a DB-9 subminiature connector. The port can be configured for either AppleTalk, RS-422, or dual purpose, depending upon which lines are run from the serial I/O. If desired, two ports can be constructed, one a DB-9 for AppleTalk and the other DB-25 for an RS-232/422 serial interface.

The easiest form of port to wire is that for AppleTalk, requiring four lines. A dual-purpose interface is the most useful; however, it is a bit more complicated to make since it requires the addition of a switch (Fig. 11-11) to toggle between RS-422 and AppleTalk modes. The external port connector is installed in the left end of the engine. To finish the printer, you must install three status LEDs which draw their power and signals from the connector J-201 on the DC controller board.

The Canon SX engine

The Canon SX engine and interface board are smaller than their predecessors (Fig. 11-12). Logic boards for the SX are mounted in the bottom of the printer. There are no external interfaces to construct because the interface connectors are built into the logic boards themselves (Fig. 11-13).

The HP LaserJets have parallel and serial connectors, with a slot for the insertion of an optional I/O board for AppleTalk, Ethernet, or multiple serial ports. The Apple LaserWriters II are ported variously. The II SC is not meant for a network and therefore has two SCSI ports and an Apple Desktop Bus port for connection to a single computer (Fig. 11-13). The IINT relies on the same ports as the LaserWriter Plus, AppleTalk and RS-232/422. The LaserWriter II NTX and IIfx have the same two ports for computer and network as the NT, but an external disk drive SCSI port has been added to their logic boards. The IIg has an Ethernet connection as well.

The problem of transferring a LaserWriter II logic board into a stock SX engine such as the LaserJet II is that the connector (Fig.11-14) on the logic boards has no counterpart in the LaserJet. The LaserWriters receive power through five pins and send and receive data through others (Table 11-1).

The easiest way to mate a LaserWriter II logic board to a LaserJet II is to replace the LaserJet's DC controller board with one from a LaserWriter II, thereby providing the matching connector for the logic board. The DC controller adds to the expense of the job, however, by about $375. It is less expensive to construct a cable to lead from the DC controller and the power supply to the LaserWriter logic board. The only difficulty is that a source for the female connector is extremely hard to locate.

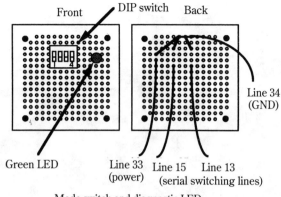

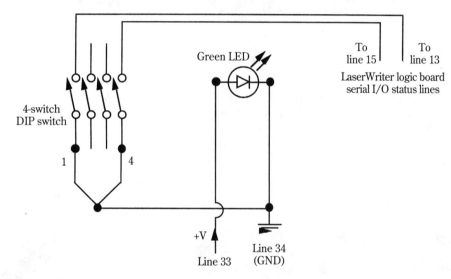

11-11 Diagrams of switch used to select LaserWriter interface mode.

Simpler, although not as flexible, are the JetScript controllers from QMS-Laser Connection. This conversion requires that the LaserJet be teamed with an IBM PC or compatible. An input/output interface is inserted into the LaserJet, and a Post-Script controller with 3Mb of RAM is installed in the computer's open expansion slots. This is a monogamous relationship; the printer cannot be shared.

The JetScript is, in effect a PostScript cartridge for the computer. The interface transmits at a moderately high baud rate, and the output is undeniably genuine, but the system places restrictions upon the printer that may not be acceptable in an office with shared resources.

Why bother with a conversion at all if one can add a cartridge? The best reason is that the printer that has an integral PostScript controller generally per-

11-12 Logic boards for Canon SX engines are typically small, although this LaserWriter II SC board is very small.

forms better in the round than the printer that has been upgraded with a cartridge. This performance advantage is especially great for the printers of the LaserWriter II NTX class, i.e. those with 68020 and later generation CPUs and the potential for RAM expansion. Therefore, at the entry level, you should consider building a LaserWriter One or Plus from a CX engine.

If you already have an SX engine, then build an NTX. The NT does not offer any real improvement over the LaserWriter Plus, and the trouble to convert an SX

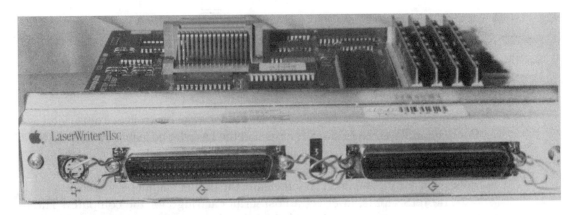

11-13 Interface connectors of SX engines are built into the logic boards.

11-14 Apple's oddball logic board connector.

Table 11-1. LaserWriter II connector J-1 pin functions.

Pin	Function	Pin	Function
A1	Not connected	B1	Not connected
A2	$\overline{\text{CCLK}}$, command strobe	B2	Not connected
A3	$\overline{\text{VDO}}$, video data	B3	$\overline{\text{CMND}}$, command
A4	$\overline{\text{VSYNC}}$, vert. sync. pulse	B4	$\overline{\text{CPRDY}}$, PCA pwr. ready
A5	$\overline{\text{CBSY}}$, command busy	B5	$\overline{\text{PRNT}}$, begin printing
A6	$\overline{\text{STATS}}$, dc contllr. status	B6	Not connected
A7	$\overline{\text{VSREQ}}$, vert. sync. request	B7	SBSY, dc cont. send busy
A8	$\overline{\text{PPRDY}}$, prntr pwr ready	B8	$\overline{\text{RDY}}$, printer ready
A9	+5 volts dc	B9	$\overline{\text{BD}}$, beam detect
A10	LED 1	B10	LED 3
A11	LED 2	B11	LED 4
A12	Ground	B12	Not connected
A13	Ground	B13	+5 volts dc
A14	Ground	B14	+5 volts dc
A15	Ground	B15	+5 volts dc
A16	Ground	B16	+5 volts dc

Table data supplied by Don Thompson.

engine into a LaserWriter is better expended if the end product is an NTX. If an NT equivalent is all that you desire or can afford, and if you require networking, the Pacific Data cartridge and PacificTalk interface are worth your time to evaluate. If you do not require networking, the UDP TurboScript cartridge is the best bet.

PostScript beyond the 300 dpi horizon

The high standard for resolution at the time that PostScript was brought to the desktop by Apple was 300 dots per inch (dpi). This has become the *de facto* standard for laser printing, but it is no longer the high-end standard. It was a good standard, and, to paraphrase H.H. Munro, as good standards go, it went. Now we have printers that can improve on those 90,000 dots per square inch fourfold, and there are still others beyond the horizon.

11-15 Xänte Accel-a-Writer high-resolution logic board replacement for LaserJet.

High-resolution controllers

Higher-resolution laser printer controllers are available from companies such as LaserMaster and Xänte. From a company that was founded in 1989, the Xänte Accel-a-Writer upgrades (Fig. 11-15) have been remarkably successful in gaining acceptance.

The Accel-a-Writers are direct replacements for the controller/interface boards of the Apple LaserWriter, LaserWriter II, HP LaserJet II, and Personal LaserWriter printers. The Accel-a-Writer IV is typical of the group. Using an advanced Micro Devices 29,000 RISC CPU, it comes with 6Mb of RAM installed. Memory can be expanded to 16Mb. It uses the Phoenix Raster Image Processor for PostScript interpretation, and the normal 35 fonts are printer resident.

As with the LaserWriter NTX, a SCSI interface is part of the extended font access structure, so that a hard drive can be attached for hundreds of megabytes of font storage. External interfaces include AppleTalk, Serial, and Centronics parallel, all of which are active simultaneously, allowing IBM and Macintosh PCs to be connected through different ports and yet to have full use of the printer. Most important, Accel-a-Writer drives the LaserJet Series II at 600 × 600 dots per inch. Processing speed is said to be improved by as much as 12 times over the LaserWriter Plus. In actual printing circumstances, the increase in speed is likely to be closer to 4–5 times better.

The boards have a series of DIP switches that control the resolution and printing speed. The more memory installed, the faster the printer can work, since the Accel-a-Writer can work on the rasterization of one page in memory while printing another page. With the board set to a resolution of 300 × 300 dpi, printing naturally proceeds at higher speeds than when set for 600 × 600 dpi. Unlike most PostScript printers that have a fixed partition for downloaded fonts (512K on the LaserWriter II NTX), the font-caching memory of the Accel-a-Writers is dynamically allocated.

Fonts are built as needed in a PostScript printer from the outlines stored in ROM. Each type style or each point size used in a document must be created as a character set and stored as an image in the printer's font memory. After a font has been used for a job, it is purged from memory to make room for the fonts used by the next job.

Downloaded fonts—font outlines sent to the printer from the computer—complicate the situation, because the raster form of the fonts must be calculated and stored, and the outlines themselves must have a place in memory as well. Outlines are also purged as the download area is filled. If the same font is used in two documents, it may have to be downloaded a second time if the original download was wiped out for successive outlines. The Accel-a-Writers can keep more outlines in memory, thus reducing download time.

In practice, Accel-a-Writers do indeed produce excellent output. The comparison under magnification of a character printed at 300 dpi and one printed at 600 dpi shows the difference (Fig. 11-16). Even more striking is the quality imparted to scanned photographs that have been printed at 600 dpi. Scanned images look indistinguishable from newspaper halftones (Fig. 11-17), even though true halftoning uses dots of varying sizes while the Accel-a-Writer merely uses more dots to simulate halftones.

The price of such a high-resolution upgrade is high, running to $1,600 for a minimum configuration of 6Mb, but a 600 dpi printer can practically eliminate the need for a service bureau or print shop. In many cases, you can avoid the printing press altogether, with the finished work coming directly from the Accel-a-Writer-driven laser printer. For those who need such high-resolution printing, the boards are inexpensive when compared to the $4,000 price attached to high-resolution printers.

ABCDE
abcde

11-16 Highly magnified output of Accel-a-Writer board shows no degradation of characters.

11-17 Half-tone simulation of Accel-a-Writer 600 dpi resolution is exceptional.

What the manufacturers don't want you to know

The upgrade I am about to describe falls into the believe-it-or-not category, that area between light and shadow that Rod Serling called "The Twilight Zone." Consider, if you will, the possibility that the 300 dpi laser printer you are already using is inherently capable of 400×400 dpi performance and could be made to do so for less than the price of a carton of paper. Consider yet again, that some printers could print at true 600 dpi resolutions for the same expenditure. Is this yet another sighting of Elvis?

This information was given to me by Chuck Rogers of Computer Peripherals Unlimited in Haverhill, Massachusetts. I purchased a Canon CX laser engine from that company, then a liquidator of overstock and leased equipment, a couple of years ago. It formed the basis of my LaserWriter conversion later written of in Computer Shopper and *Build Your Own PostScript Laser Printer and Save a Bundle*.

The printer engine was part of a NEC-package Group 4 facsimile station for Federal Express, the remainder being a 400 dpi scanner, fax modem, and a CPU to control the whole agglomeration. Because it was designed for use in Group 4 facsimile printing, the laser engine had to print at 415 dpi, the Group 4 standard. The engine itself was really identical to the engine used in the Hewlett-Packard LaserJet Series One, LaserJet 500, and the Apple LaserWriters One and Plus, except for the higher resolution.

In the business of selling equipment, Computer Peripherals Unlimited found—strange as it sounds—that there was not much of a market for a 400 dpi laser engine. The fact that all laser printers using that engine were 300 dpi machines seemed to make prospective buyers wary. Apparently, most people were more concerned about direct compatibility than about higher resolution. So, in order to make the engines more attractive, a way was sought to degrade the laser engines to 300 dpi output.

Because CX engines were identical in all respects except resolution, Chuck Rogers decided that it must be something very simple that controlled the number of dots per inch on the printed page. After all, the NEC laser engine had no high-level interface/controller board whatsoever, receiving raw raster data over the video I/O from the CPU that ran the fax. If a simple dumb laser engine could print at 400 dpi, than it should also print at 300 dpi—and so it could.

Chuck Rogers found that there were two determinants for printer resolution: one, the rotational speed of the scanning mirror, and two, the pulsing of the laser beam that produces the dots. The former determines the number of horizontal lines that are scanned in a given period of time, and the latter determines the number of discreet dots that are placed in each line.

The scanning mechanism of the laser printer consists mainly of a series of focusing lenses and a rotating hexagonal mirror. Each face of the hexagonal mirror causes the laser beam to traverse the length of the drum as the mirror rotates. If the mirror can be made to rotate faster (with everything else such as paper traveling speed remaining constant) more lines will be scanned down the length of the paper in any given period of time. Therefore, by increasing the speed of the mirror's drive motor, the vertical resolution of the printer can be increased. The only limiting factor is the motor itself, which, beyond a certain speed, will suffer accelerated wear. For the ordinary 300 dpi printer, 400 lines per inch would incur minimal additional stress on the motor.

Thus, it is possible to have a printer with a horizontal resolution of 300 dpi across the line and 400 lines per inch down the page. This would cause a foreshortening of the normal 300×300 output by .75 on the vertical axis.

The horizontal resolution is governed by the duration of the laser beam pulse, which is regulated by the DC controller. The shorter the pulse, the more pulses can be fired in any given time. In the time spent by the scanning of the beam from one side of the drum to the other, the 300 dpi pulse would lay down 2400 dots in an eight-inch line. If the pulse could be shortened so that 400 dpi were possible, then the dot count for an eight-inch line would rise to 3200, an in-

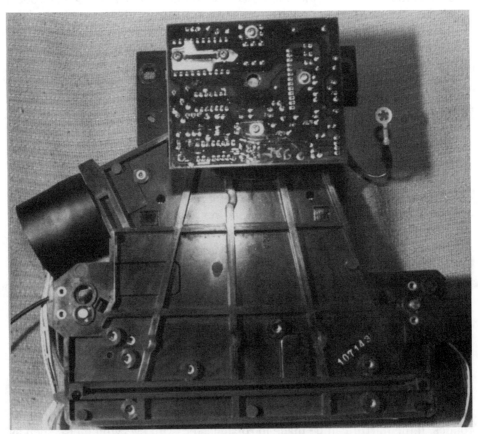

11-18 Laser-scanning mirror motor PCB is mounted on bottom of laser-scanning unit.

crease of one third. This would change the horizontal aspect to .75, since the usual 2400 dots would be printed as the beginning of a 3200 dot line (24/32 = .75).

So by decreasing the pulse duration and increasing the mirror's rotational velocity, the printer could be made to print at a uniform 400 dpi by 400 lines per inch, thereby preserving the 1:1 aspect ratio of the 300 dpi printer. The printed output would be reduced in size from the original to .75 on each axis.

Chuck Rogers, working in reverse, wished to decrease both the lines per inch and the dots per inch of his 400 dpi engines. To do so meant that he must slow the scanning mirror and lengthen the pulse of the laser. Using retro-engineering, the process by which apparatus are dissasembled and their components studied to ascertain their functions, he was able to discover that the speed of the mirror's motor, mounted on the bottom of the black triangular scanning assembly, was set by a tachometer, a device to measure revolutions of a motor. The tachometer was a phase-locked loop (PLL) design, and the actual speed was set by comparison to a reference frequency generated by a crystal (Fig. 11-18).

Crystals vibrate regularly when excited by electricity or other stimuli, and each crystal has its own peculiar harmonic, or natural resonance. A crystal can be used for timing purposes by counting the vibrations in any span of time. Since

11-19 300 dpi DC controller board from CX engine. Filter regulating horizontal dpi is at top, below and between two connectors toward right.

their frequency is constant, they make excellent references, as in quartz clocks. All that was needed to change the rotational speed of the motor was to change the frequency used by the tachometer as a reference: the higher the frequency, the faster the motor would revolve the mirror, and, conversely, the lower the frequency, the slower the mirror would be spun by the motor. Substituting a crystal of a lower value produced the desired reduction from 400 to 300 lines per inch.

The dots per inch are regulated in a similar manner. There is a crystal (actually a ceramic filter) on the DC controller (Fig. 11-19) that furnishes a reference frequency for the laser pulse modulation. When the frequency is raised the pulse rate is increased, and more dots are put on the drum. As with the motor, a decrease in frequency slows the pulse rate, causing the laser to pulse less frequently and to produce fewer dots. Another substitution of crystals brought about the expected and desired reduction of dots per inch to 300. (To reverse this process, as we would like, let us suppose the crystal has a frequency of 104 kHz for 300 dpi. To raise the dpi to 400, you would multiply 104 by 4/3, and the answer, 138.666667, would be the frequency (400 dpi/300 dpi) of the new crystal.) Thus Computer Peripherals Unlimited could very quickly and cheaply make a saleable 300 dpi laser engine from an unsaleable 400 dpi engine.

Theoretically, the optics used in the Canon laser engines are capable of resolving as many as 2500 dpi. The only limiting factor is the mechanical one of making components that can withstand the rigors involved at those resolutions and remain within their tolerances. The motor bearings, for instance, wear more quickly at higher rates of speed. Chuck stripped down a motor from the 400 dpi NEC engines, compared it to one from a standard model 300 dpi HP type of printer, and found that they were dissimilarly wound. He theorized that the motor used in the NEC engines was rated for 600 dpi use, since that was the only functioning high-resolution alternative at that time. He reasoned further that the motor simply had been slowed down by Canon for use at 400 dpi, in much the same manner as he had done to reach 300 dpi. It was therefore reasonable to assume that you could run the motor safely at twice the revolutions per second to drive the mirror for 600 lines per inch. Of course, a concomitant increase in the beam pulse rate would bring the dots back into a 1:1 aspect ratio.

It is quite reasonable to assume, then, that the standard motor might be driven to produce 400 lines per inch without an appreciable attrition of the motor's life expectancy, since the increase in revolutions is well within tolerances for such high speed motors. Adding another 33 percent to the dot pulse rate would place next to no stress at all on the laser, rated for 2500 dpi. Therefore, should you wish to do so, you can increase your printer's resolution from 90,000 dots per square inch to 160,000 dot per square inch at very little expense. And for those of you who possess the NEC engines, it is likely that you can achieve 360,000 dots per square inch output from your printers. Theoretically, if you wished to do so, you could replace the motor for one rated for higher revolutions, bringing the printer to 1200 dpi.

The above is particularly relevant to Canon engines of all types not only the CX. But not surprisingly, you can apply the same techniques with equal success to other brands of laser engines that use the same scheme of tachometer-governed motor speed and crystal-regulated laser pulsing. Believe it or not.

Naturally, some questions arise. The first is, how do companies that market high-resolution controller boards get away with selling them for the prices they charge, when the same effect can be realized for $10 or $20? Well, it is easier to convince someone to pull the logic board and make a quick substitution than it is to persuade that same person to tear down the printer to make component-level modifications.

There is also the problem of matching the input to the output. All current standard printer controllers and computer software assume a 300 dpi machine is connected to the controller board, and the output is calculated at 300 dpi. Thus, when printed at higher resolution, the page is scaled down. So different ROM instructions are needed for the printer to make an 8×10 page at 600 dpi than at 300 dpi. But this could also be done very cheaply. For the most part, output can be scaled from software, so that a 600 dpi document would merely have to be printed at 200 percent in order to fill the page. In other words, convenience is what you are paying for when you buy one of the higher resolution boards.

The second question is, why hasn't this knowledge been disseminated in the past? It is amazing that it has not been widely and loudly proclaimed. The reason for the silence is inexplicable.

Part 4

Other Hardware

Chapter 12

Daisy wheel and thermal printers

There are two types of printers that have not yet been mentioned: daisy wheel and thermal transfer. The reasons for this are quite simple. Daisy wheel printers are obsolete, and thermal printers are divisible into two types—the very expensive and the very cheap—neither of which lend themselves to the kind of upgrade to which this book is dedicated.

Daisy wheel: they ought to be called Sinclairs

Daisy wheel printers were once state of the art in letter-quality printing, but then, dinosaurs were once state of the art in organic matter. Today, all that a dinosaur can be used for is a museum exhibit.

Daisy wheel printers perfectly reproduced the look of a hand-typed page without the erasures and the whited-out patches. Their print wheels could be changed to change the character typefaces, and they could handle carbons and multipart forms. They can still do all of those things, but nobody wants them. You can buy excellent machines that have languished for years in warehouses, still in their manufacturer's shipping cartons, for less than $75. What is the problem with daisy wheel printers? Obviously, it isn't price.

The worst flaw of the daisy wheel printer is its painfully plodding pace. Daisy wheel printers are faster than the fastest typists, but printers are measured against electronic competitors, not human ones. The very slowest dot matrix printer is easily three or four times as fast in its near letter quality (NLQ) mode as the normally snail-like daisy wheel printer, and you have to look really hard to find a dot matrix printer that slow. One hundred characters per second in NLQ is common from dot matrix printers. The near letter quality printout of a 24-pin printer, and even of many 9-pin printers, is as readable and presentable as the formed characters from a daisy wheel.

Not many people read their correspondence with a magnifier, and without magnification, dot matrix NLQ is impeccable. So, speed is the major lack of daisy wheel printers, and the advantage they once enjoyed for clarity and cleanness of character formation has eroded to the point of insignificance.

The second flaw in the daisy wheel printer is its inability to deal with graphics. Modern computing is graphic-intensive, and daisy wheel printers have only the crude X and O graphic capability of the old text-only terminals, on which clever and apparently underemployed persons once typed out pictures composed of mixtures of periods, colons, dashes, and brackets. Those days are gone forever: everything is now bitmapped, and only bit-addressable printers have a place in the bit graphic environment. As DOS is pushed farther and farther into the background or substrata of computer operations by graphical user interfaces (GUIs), text-only printers will lose that little viability still remaining to them.

Another problem with daisy wheel printers is their bulk: not only are they dinosaurs, they are brontosaurs. Most are so heavy they must be shipped by ground motor freight. The only reason to use a daisy wheel printer is if you already have one or the makings of one. If you happen to have a daisy wheel electronic typewriter, you might be able to convert the typewriter into a printer by the addition of a module to act as interface between the computer and the printer. This is an old project and has been performed thousands of times in the last dozen years. IBM Actionwriter typewriters can, for about $10, be converted. The necessary interface is sold by Mendolson Electronics for $9.95.

The Smith-Corona electronic typewriters (Fig. 12-1) can also be converted into computer printers. In the rear (Figs. 12-2 and 12-3) there is a connector into which you plug a cable from an external box (Fig. 12-4). The box, about the same size and appearance as an external disk drive or modem, is called the Messenger Module, a combination parallel/serial interface (Fig. 12-5). You connect the cable permanently attached to the Module to the typewriter and attach the Module to your computer through the appropriate cable to either a serial or parallel port (Fig. 12-6).

The Module receives data from the computer and translates it for the typewriter, which responds as if the data had been entered from the keyboard. You can configure the serial interface for all of the normal serial parameters, including baud rates up to 19,200. The serial settings are controlled by two DIP switches on the printed circuit board (Fig. 12-7). You must open the case to gain access to the switches, which are behind the front panel.

The only setting likely to give trouble is the one that translates the ASCII carriage return (CR) and line feed (LF) characters. The various combinations are fairly confusing, and it takes some experimentation to obtain the proper one. The combination that will work depends both upon the type of computer used and the

12-1　Smith-Corona electronic typewriter with daisy wheel print head.

12-2　Rear of Smith-Corona typewriter. Interface connector is at left.

software that generated the text to be printed. You need to know whether, when your computer sends a CR, it means only a CR (return to beginning of line) or it means a CR and LF (return to beginning of line and feed paper up one line). If the printer double spaces when it should single space, then the CR/LF should be turned off, and separate CR and LF commands instituted from the DIP switches. If the printer overwrites the same line, then the computer wants a CR/LF sequence executed for every CR sent, and the switches have to be set accordingly.

The typewriter, once correctly configured, will emulate a dedicated daisy wheel printer. As a bonus, the typewriter can be toggled on and off line, allowing the user to make manual text entries on the same page as the text sent from the computer. This is about the only justification for using a daisy wheel printer, that

12-3 Enlargement of DB-9 interface connector.

12-4 Smith-Corona Messenger Module adapts typewriter to computer printer usage.

it can double as a typewriter, replacing two machines with one. The speed, of course, is slothlike, in the 10–12 characters per second range, depending upon which Smith-Corona model typewriter you use. The internal buffer of the module is only 322 characters and cannot be expanded, so don't expect to punch the Enter key and get control of your computer again any time soon.

12-5 Parallel (left) and serial (right) interface connectors of Messenger Module.

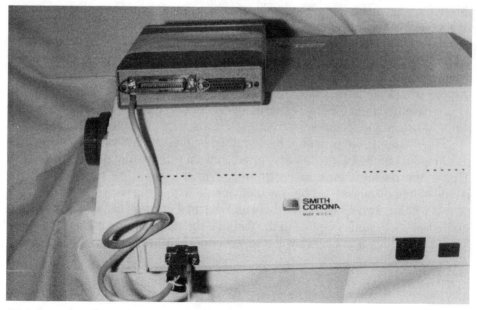

12-6 Permanently attached cable plugs into typewriter.

12-7 Communications parameters are set by DIP switches inside module.

Thermal transfer: Just a note

Thermal transfer printers use a print head with no moving parts. There are heating elements embedded in the print head's face that melt either the coating of a special paper or a wax-coated ribbon to make the dots from which the printed matter, be it text or graphics, is composed. The fax machine is a typical thermal printer.

The thermal printer is virtually silent. It can be fast. It can print stunning colors. My problem with thermal printers is that they tend to divide themselves into one of two categories, neither of which is especially amenable to the premise of this book. Thermal printers tend to be at either end of the price/value spectrum. At the very low end, represented by the Okimate 20 or the IBM PC jr printer (made by Canon and liquidated a few years ago for about $15–$20 apiece), they are not capable or worthy of upgrading. At the high end of the spectrum, they are incredibly expensive and very proprietary creations, machines which their owners would and could only upgrade through their factory representatives. There have been relatively few thermal printers that have fallen into the middle range of prices and features where the great majority of printers are.

The Citizen PN48 printer, a beautifully designed and excellently made little machine, is unique of its type and price, and there is nothing in it to upgrade. This is the reason I have given thermal printers only a passing wave of the hand—not in dismissal, but by way of invitation to join the parade.

As a balm, owners of daisy wheel and thermal printers capable of being upgraded can take some comfort in the fact that the upgrade procedures that work for dot matrix impact printers will also work for their printers.

Chapter 13

Printer sharing You got to have connections

Next to internal RAM and ROM upgrades, the most productive additions to a printer can be the external devices that multiply a printer's usefulness by making it serve more than one computer. The use of some sort of interface multiplexing, that is the multiplying of inputs to a single interface, can solve many problems where a printer must be shared. Sharing devices can also be used when one computer is connected to more than one printer through a single interface.

Switch boxes

The simplest sharing device is a switch box. These come in various configurations of input and output ports, but the usual arrangement in the basic boxes is either serial-in/serial-out or parallel-in/parallel-out. Their function is to switch between computers sending data to a peripheral or between peripherals receiving data from a computer.

Manual

Manual switch boxes similar to the one in Fig. 13-1 are the most basic peripheral-sharing apparatus. This box has a rotary switch in the front that allows the user to select between output destinations. In the rear are the input connector (Fig. 13-2, top) a standard female Centronics 36 parallel interface port, the same as that found on most printers, and two output connectors, also female Centronics (Fig. 13-2, bottom), labelled A and B, thus giving the name *A-B box* to this sort of switch.

13-1 Typical A-B rotary manual switch box.

13-2 Rear of switch boxes shows all connectors to be female.

After you have turned off all the devices to be interconnected, including the computer or computers, you place the box within reach (what use is it out of reach?), and plug the cable from the computer into the top receptacle. You then get a funny look on your face, because the output connectors are also female Centronics 36, rather than DB-25, and a normal printer cable will not work between the box and the printers to be connected. You must have male-to-male Centronics connector cables for the printers. Cables of this description are usually not ready to hand, so be certain to purchase the correctly terminated cables when purchasing the switch box.

Once you have connected all the cables and turned on all the devices again, the switch becomes operable. It requires no power. It will direct the data stream from the computer to the peripheral indicated by the switch position. You might, for example, wish to connect a high-speed 9-pin printer to one output for churning out draft quality pages or invoices on continuous form paper, and a 24-pin printer to the second port for single-sheet letterhead printing. With a twist of the switch, you can direct the forms to the 9-pin printer and the business correspondence to the 24-pin printer.

A typical setup with an A-B box is two dot matrix printers hooked up to a single computer. If you have a serial switch box, you may use one output for a printer and the other for a modem. However, for devices that are actively communicating with the computer, such as a modem, it might be better to use an automatic switch box that is specifically bidirectional. Some switch boxes are unidirectional. Note that nowhere have I mentioned laser printers. This is not an oversight, and a look inside the switch is required to explain this reservation.

Inside, the simple structure of the switch is revealed, along with the reason why such switches are not recommended for use with laser printers. Almost all manual switch boxes use a switch termed *make-before-break*. This is shorthand electronic jargon for the electrical condition that exists within the switch itself during switching. The knob rotates the electrical contacts from the input connector between the contacts for each of the output connectors, and, as it rotates, it makes contact with the next connector before it breaks contact with the previous connector, thereby setting up a brief shorting condition between the computer and the peripherals.

Although this shorting has not been conclusively demonstrated to be dangerous, Hewlett-Packard, a company with excellent customer relations, has declared that mechanical rotary switch boxes void the warranty on its laser printers. A voltage spike across an interface can be disastrous, and the condition produced by the switch boxes is conducive to electrical anomalies. For a savings of about $15, it is not worth the risk.

Automatic

Automatic switch boxes are inherently more convenient than mechanical ones, and they are regarded as perfectly safe for laser printers. They need only be connected to the peripherals and the computers and then left alone. The cheapest automatic switches (Fig. 13-3) require no external power and can mediate between two incoming signals on a first-come-first-serve basis. Its operation is transparent to the user. In a normal situation, delays are unlikely because a printer is idle more often than it is busy.

In peripheral sharing, there must arise some occasions on which the printer is busy when a second user wishes to use it, and then the second user must wait. Moreover, different programs printing to the same printer will frequently establish

13-3 Simple automatic serial switch box and two RJ-11 serial port adaptors.

incompatible page and type parameters, and fail to reset the printer to its previous state when a printing job is completed. Some programs issue form feeds, while others set lines-per-page limits and rely on the printer to feed the page when the line count exceeds the limit. Some programs, such as spreadsheets, print in landscape mode, while word processors normally print in the portrait mode. When conflicting parameters are left in the printer, unexpected and unwanted results result. For instance, if the software fails to force a form feed for the last page of a printing job, the next job will begin printing on that last page of the previous job, and formatting for all subsequent pages will be offset by that amount.

Automatic switches with some intelligence can take care of problems arising from conflicting software parameters. They can be instructed to intercept or pass on various control codes, and to routinely issue certain orders to the printer. Of course, unless properly instructed, this kind of supervision of the printer can cause conflicts. And the switch can do nothing about the waiting that is imposed when the printer is busy.

Dresselhaus Computer Products, makers of the Dots-Perfect upgrade for the Epson printer family, manufactures smart printer-sharing devices, the Smart-Print Printer Sharing System. These devices look like the AC power strip into which your computer and peripherals are plugged. There are parallel and serial versions, designed to share one printer among two, four, or six computers. The inputs are all DB-25 female, and the output is always a DB-25, also female, whether in the parallel or the serial models. Serial models can be used with telephone wire and RJ-11 modular adapters rather than the ordinary serial cables. Parallel cable lengths can reach to 50 feet, and serial cables can be as long as 1,000 feet.

The printer sharing is conducted through a combination of hardware and software. Alone, the hardware offers automatic switching on the first-come-first-served basis of dumb automatic switches, and any computer with the proper interface can use the switch. With the software, written for IBM-compatible computers only, the switch can instruct the computer to buffer the data to the computer's hard drive while the printer is busy, thereby freeing the computer as though printing had actually taken place. When the printer becomes free, the switch can then retrieve the spooled file and direct it to the printer in the background.

The software includes a pop-up menu to control the printer settings, giving the user an alternative to running down the hall or across the room to set up the printer from its control panel for the next job. The advantage of the SmartPrint system of buffering is that the switch uses resources already installed, namely the computer's hard drive, saving the cost of external RAM within the buffer. If there are forty megabytes of free space on the drive, the software and switch can use as much as is needed for spooling. Of course, a small or nearly full hard drive could present less space for spooling than might a RAM buffer.

Buffers, converters, and low-level LANs

Buffers are sold for individual and for multiple users. Individual user buffers are the answer to the question, What can be done when no internal RAM buffer can be added? The external buffer may contain as little as 64K of RAM or as much as 16Mb. If your printer has no buffer or a very small one, even the 64K buffer will make a noticeable improvement in your daily printing, freeing the computer in seconds for most jobs. In fact, if your jobs are text only, 64K might be all the buffer you need. The larger jobs (those with graphics or many fonts), require the larger buffer. It is not likely that a single user would ever need 16Mb of buffer; 1Mb could probably take care of most jobs, and 4Mb would certainly do so.

Buffering for groups is usually found in combination products. Many automatic switches come with some amount of RAM buffer, usually expandable, and some offer data conversion in addition, translating serial to parallel or parallel to serial, either unidirectionally or bidirectionally.

Converters

A simple single-user bidirectional converter is shown in Fig. 13-4. It has a parallel male Centronics 36 connector on one end and a 25-pin DB female serial connector on the other. There is a DIP switch array (Fig. 13-5) which sets the translation parameters. The array shown allows baud rates up to 19,200, as read from the table (switches 1 to 3 in Table 13-1), and enables either hardware or software handshaking (switch 4). The method of translation, serial to parallel or parallel to serial, is set by switch 8. Parallel data transmission speed is stated by the manufacturer to be 19,200 bytes per second. There is a reset switch, a power indicator LED, and an input for the 9-volt power supply.

Inside (Figs. 13-6 and 13-7), the converter is a sandwich of two small PC boards with a common connection through a multipin plug and socket. There are two IC positions that can be filled with 256K × 4-bit DRAMs, thereby creating a 256K buffer for incoming data (Fig. 13-8). You can purchase the converter either

13-4 Automatic bidirectional parallel/serial data converter, left, and 36-pin Centronics gender changer, right.

13-5 In the ATEN data converter, data translation and serial communication parameters are set by DIP switch.

with the chips installed or without; the difference in price is about $70. (The chips themselves cost about $10, so the other $60 is what you would pay for not picking up a soldering iron.)

The buffer is a significant feature for two reasons. The obvious benefit is that you have two products in one small, unobtrusive box, and the 256K buffer is capable of storing the output from several jobs without overflow. The second benefit is that the data transmission rate through the parallel port is increased to 3.5K per second, or nearly double the unbuffered rate, further reducing the waiting time for the printer.

Table 13-1. ATEN Data Converter baud rate settings.

Baud rate	Switch 1	Switch 2	Switch 3
19,200	●	●	●
9600	●	●	○
4800	●	○	●
2400	●	○	○
1200	○	●	●
600	○	●	○
300	○	○	●
150	○	○	○

Legend   ● On
         ○ Off

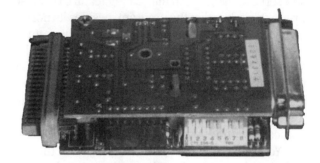

13-6 The inside of data converter shows two simple boards sandwiched tgether.

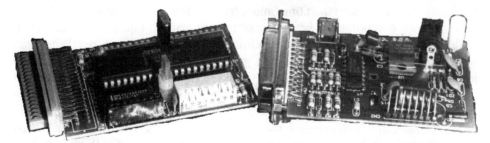

13-7 Open face sandwich of boards shows serial section on right and parallel section on left.

Carrying the principle of the small, single-user converter/buffer to its logical extreme are intelligent boxes like those manufactured by Dresselhaus and Buffalo Products. These are stand-alone data managers, some with very sophisticated functions. Both are good representatives of their types.

Data managers

The Dresselhaus Multi Printer Switch is a crossover version of that company's SmartPrint. There are dual input ports, one parallel and one serial, and there are one serial and four parallel outputs. Data translation is automatic, parallel to serial

13-8 Empty chip locations can be filled with 256K × 8-bit SRAMs for 512K buffer.

and serial to parallel. An interesting feature of the software provided with the Multi Printer Switch is that the program, besides its normal spooling capability, can be set up to direct output from specific applications software packages to specific printers.

If you always want your letters printed on a daisy wheel printer, then you can set up the program always to send the word processor's files to the daisy wheel's port. If that printer is busy, then the file will be spooled to the hard drive for later printing. In the same way, your spreadsheets can always be sent to the 132-column printer, and your checks can always be printed on the laser printer, automatically, without user intervention.

You can cascade, or link in series, both the SmartPrint and the Multi Printer Switches, in any combination, to increase the number of printers and computers on line. To connect more than one SmartPrint switch to one printer, thereby permitting more computers to have access to that printer, one of the SmartPrint switches must be modified to act as a hub, into which satellite SmartPrints can be plugged. The modification involves moving a shunt from one end of a shorting block to the other and clipping a resistor on the PC board of the SmartSwitch that will become the hub. Satellite switches are then plugged into the inputs of the hub, and the strobe used by the hub switch to detect activity on its inputs will cause the satellites to strobe their own inputs. Connecting a Multi Printer Switch to SmartPrint switches is easier, requiring only that the output of the SmartPrint Switch be plugged into the appropriate serial or parallel input of the Multi Printer Switch. This approximates a low-level or no-slot LAN (Local Area Network).

Data managers, such as those, sold by Buffalo Products, have numerous configurations of input/output ports and memory capacities (Figs. 13-9, 13-10, 13-11). There is complete flexibility in the assignment of ports, whether to peripherals or to computers, and data translation is bidirectional and simultaneous. Data managers use the concept of *channels* to make this flexibility possible.

A user can assign a channel to a peripheral or to another computer, and then the computers and peripherals can communicate one to one. More than one computer can use the same channel to a printer simultaneously; the data manager will allocate the printer's time automatically, storing jobs in its inter-

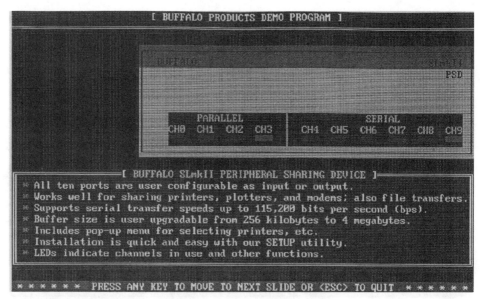

13-9 Descriptive screen showing characteristics of Buffalo SL Mark II switch box and buffer. (Software courtesy Buffalo Products)

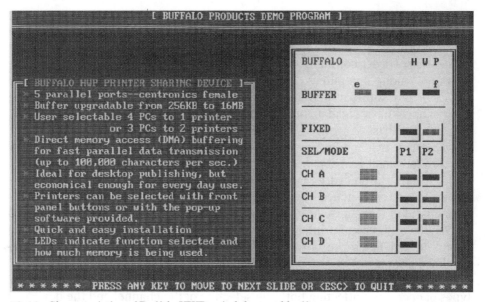

13-10 Characteristics of Buffalo HWP switch box and buffer. (Software courtesy Buffalo Products)

nal buffer until they are sent out to the printer. The buffer can be expanded from 256K to 16Mb on most models. (The Buffalo boxes use special memory modules obtainable only from Buffalo Products, while other brands of data managers use regular DRAMs.

[BUFFALO HXM PERIPHERAL SHARING DEVICE]
* 4 ports—2 serial, 2 parallel
* Buffer upgradable from 256KB to 16MB
* Ratio of PCs to peripherals:
  user selectable as 3/1, 2/2, or 1/3.
* Direct memory access (DMA) buffering
  for fast parallel data transmission
  (up to 100,000 characters per sec.)
* Supports serial data transfers up to
  115,200 bits per second (bps).
* Ideal for sharing serial printers,
  plotters, or modems.
* Peripherals can be selected with
  front panel buttons or with the
  pop-up software provided.
* Quick and easy installation
* LEDs indicate function selected and
  how much memory is being used.

BUFFALO   H X M
BUFFER   e   f
FIXED
COMPUTER   P1|P2|P3|P4
CPU-A
CPU-B
CPU-C
CPU-D
FIX/FRE
COPY

* * * * * PRESS ANY KEY TO MOVE TO NEXT SLIDE OR <ESC> TO QUIT * * * * *

13-11 Buffalo HXM parallel and serial switch box, converter, and buffer. (Software courtesy Buffalo Products)

The user can control priority for usage of a peripheral, if necessary, and a channel can be reserved so that data are not queued but receive immediate processing. Direct communication and file transfers can also occur over the channels among computers. Serial transmissions proceed at any speed up to 115,200 baud, and parallel connections permit speeds up to 100,000 cps, although normal parallel data processing occurs at speeds closer to 2,000–16,000 cps on 386 CPUs.

The data manager's functions can be controlled from its front panel, or through terminate-and-stay-resident (TSR) software pop-up menus (Figs. 13-12, 13-13, 13-14). The software responds to either mouse or keyboard input, and displays the currently active channel and its peripheral as well as the channel's transmission parameters. As you can see in Fig. 13-12, the root menu allows you to compile a library of printer macros that can be sent from the menu. This is useful for redefining the printer's characteristics prior to a printing job or returning a printer to its previous condition after a job has been completed.

Channel control as illustrated in Fig. 13-13 allows you to perform several types of operations affecting both the selection of the channel and the device on that channel. If you want to print, you have the option of specifying the printer to which the output will be sent or allowing the data manager to use the next available printer (Fig. 13-14).

Because the boxes are bidirectional and compatible with all manner of peripherals, you can use them equally well for modems, printers, computers, plotters, and other serial or parallel devices. A small office can share a modem or fax

180   *Printer sharing: You got to have connections*

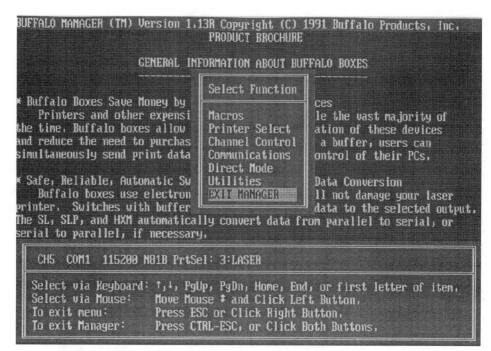

13-12 Buffalo's pop-up TSR menu system allows most functions to be implemented from software. (Software courtesy Buffalo Products)

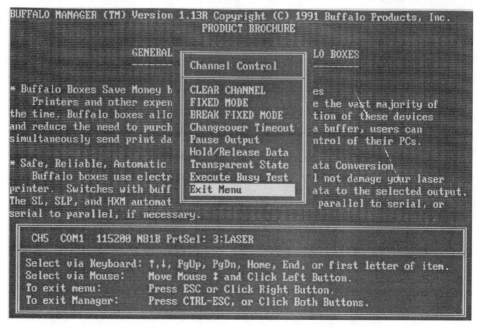

13-13 Channel selection and parameters in pop-up menu form. (Software courtesy Buffalo Products)

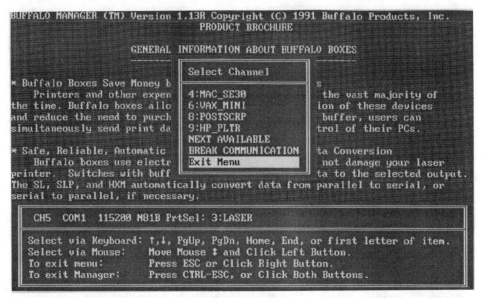

```
BUFFALO MANAGER (TM) Version 1.13R Copyright (C) 1991 Buffalo Products, Inc.
                         PRODUCT BROCHURE

              GENERAL INFORMATION ABOUT BUFFALO BOXES

                        ┌──────────────────────┐
* Buffalo Boxes Save Money b│ Select Channel      │s
    Printers and other expen│                     │ the vast majority of
the time. Buffalo boxes allo│ 4:MAC_SE30          │ ion of these devices
and reduce the need to purch│ 6:VAX_MINI          │ buffer, users can
simultaneously send print da│ 8:POSTSCRP          │ trol of their PCs.
                            │ 9:HP_PLTR           │
                            │ NEXT AVAILABLE      │
* Safe, Reliable, Automatic │ BREAK COMMUNICATION │ ta Conversion
    Buffalo boxes use electr│ Exit Menu           │ not damage your laser
printer.  Switches with buff└──────────────────────┘ ta to the selected output.
The SL, SLP, and HXM automatically convert data from parallel to serial, or
serial to parallel, if necessary.

  ┌─────────────────────────────────────────────────────────────────┐
  │  CH5   COM1   115200  N81B  PrtSel:  3:LASER                      │
  └─────────────────────────────────────────────────────────────────┘
  Select via Keyboard: ↑,↓, PgUp, PgDn, Home, End, or first letter of item.
  Select via Mouse:    Move Mouse ↕ and Click Left Button.
  To exit menu:        Press ESC or Click Right Button.
  To exit Manager:     Press CTRL-ESC, or Click Both Buttons.
```

13-14 Channels can be identified by the device attached to simplify routing. (Software courtesy Buffalo Products)

modem and a laser printer, and execute file transfers between computers through a box. With ten ports on each of the larger boxes, cascading similar to that used by the Dresselhaus switches, the ability to use any type of output device and any computer, and the versatile software, this product line also verges on a LAN.

Other products that qualify as no-slot LANs are those made by and similar to the special purpose printer network devices sold by ASP Computer Products. The most basic form of their printer-sharing network is the SNAP series of connectors. Each computer is furnished with a transmitter module that plugs into the parallel port, and the shared printer is given a receiver module. Both modules have RJ-11 compatible plug sockets that accept telephone wire. The network can add computers at any time, up to a total of sixteen, by simply plugging in another transmitter.

JetWay

The JetWay printer-sharing device is a thin box, about as large as a medium-sized paperback book (Fig. 13-15). It is a standalone switch and buffer that works with any printer having a parallel port and any computer having a serial port. The box itself has either four (JW421) or eight (JW821) input ports, all RJ-11, and one output, a DB-25 parallel port, the same as on an IBM or compatible computer. The cabling to the box is made from four-conductor telephone wire, with the four wires connected straight through. Normal telephone wire has the four lines reversed end to end. Serial port adapters are plugged into the computers, and the four-conductor cable is plugged into the adapters. The cables terminate at the JetWay, where inputs are numbered 1–8.

13-15 ASP's JetWay printer-sharing and data buffer device. (Equipment courtesy ASP Computer Products)

The JetWay is software-driven. Each of the eight ports is configured from a setup program (Figs. 13-16, 13-17, 13-18, and 13-19) or from DOS ECHO commands. The baud rate can be as high as 115,200. Each computer must set its own output serial port (Fig. 13-17), the baud rate (Fig. 13-18), and the logical printer device which DOS normally uses for printing (Fig. 13-19). That is, if the printer is connected normally through the default LPT1 logical port, then you must inform the software so that DOS can reroute the output to the selected serial port. The software then sets the JetWay to the baud rate desired, and requests the user's permission to modify the computer's AUTOEXEC.BAT file, so that the printer port assignment and serial port settings can be made automatically at startup. Each of the JetWay input ports is thus independent of every other, and a user cannot accidentally reconfigure another port (with one exception—see below). From this point, printing becomes transparent through the serial port to the JetWay.

Users can send "job control commands" to the JetWay through the DOS ECHO command. These commands provide a means to alter the JetWay's performance for individual printing jobs. The port parameters (baud rate, timeout, handshaking) can all be set. These changes affect only the JetWay, and the computer must then be reconfigured to match the new settings. There are beginning job and end of job commands that append a character string to the beginning or ending page of a particular job. The JetWay can also be instructed to print up to ten copies of a document. Each of these commands is user- or job-specific, and cannot affect other users on other ports, but there is one command, called "Initialize All Ports," that can and will reset the communications parameters of all of the JetWay's ports to the factory settings and flush all jobs currently in memory. This is clearly not something you want to do without consulting the other users in advance.

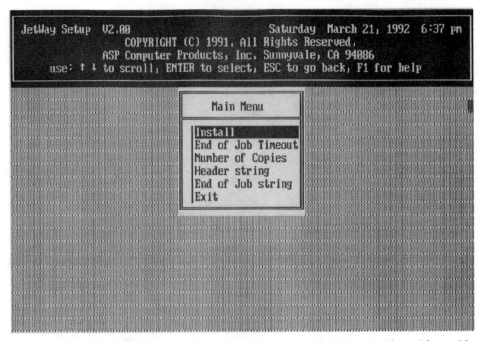

13-16 Setup of the JetWay for each computer is done through software, either with or without mouse. (Software courtesy ASP Computer Products)

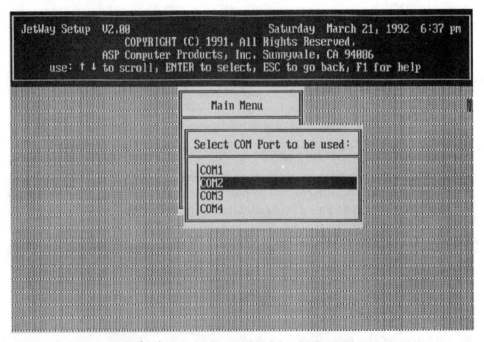

13-17 Computer port selection. (Software courtesy ASP Computer Products)

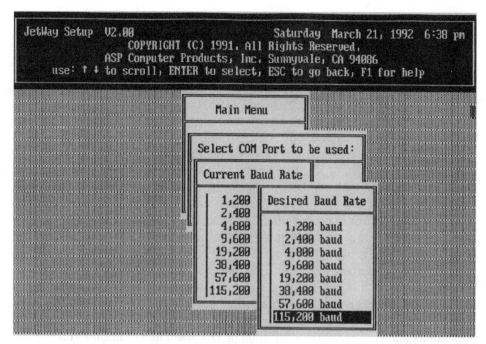

13-18 Baud rate for selected port and for JetWay port. (Software courtesy ASP Computer Products)

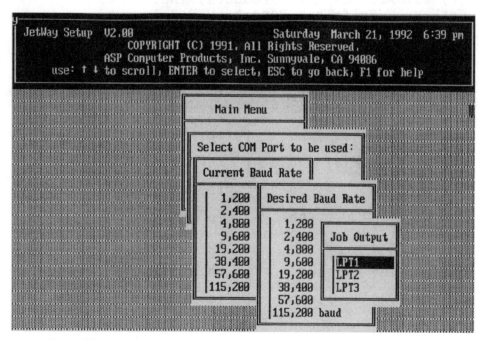

13-19 Logical BIOS printing device is indicated for redirection. (Software courtesy ASP Computer Products)

The JetWay is particularly valuable when printing to a laser printer into which a PostScript cartridge has been installed. Some PostScript emulation cartridges balk at input from AppleTalk or other high-speed optional interfaces, but because the JetWay is connected to the printer's parallel port, it can provide multiple users a substitute form of moderately fast networking that will not cause the cartridge to hang up.

The JetWay is also a buffer. The default shipped with the box is 256K, but the buffer can be expanded with 4-bit DRAMs to 4Mb. The buffer is used to queue printing jobs when multiple users are online and the printer is busy. You determine the amount of RAM you need to install by the two common factors of average job size and number of users: the more and larger the files to be queued, the larger the buffer. You can print out the JetWay's memory complement and the settings of each of the ports with a self-test built into the switch's ROM (Fig. 13-20). The self-test button is on the top edge of the unit, recessed in the cabinet and activated by a push from a ballpoint pen tip or an unbent paperclip. It is also a good way to ensure that the LaserJet has been prepared to accept input from the parallel port. If the self-test fails to print, the LaserJet is probably set to receive data from another port, and you must use the front panel menu to change the input port. There are three LEDs on the JetWay to indicate its status. There are no buttons or DIP switches to bother you.

```
(C)1991 ASP Computer Products, Inc.
JetWay     Self-Test Report. VER 2.10


Memory Test Passed.
Available Memory:    256K-Byte
```

PORT	BAUD RATE	TIMEOUT	ROBUST XON
SERIAL 1	115,200	10 SECONDS	OFF
SERIAL 2	57,600	10 SECONDS	OFF
SERIAL 3	9,600	10 SECONDS	OFF
SERIAL 4	9,600	10 SECONDS	OFF
SERIAL 5	9,600	10 SECONDS	OFF
SERIAL 6	9,600	10 SECONDS	OFF
SERIAL 7	9,600	10 SECONDS	OFF
SERIAL 8	9,600	10 SECONDS	OFF

13-20 JetWay self-test shows memory installed and parameters for each JetWay serial port.
(Software courtesy ASP Computer Products)

The JetWay itself can be mounted on the LaserJet, on a wall, or on some other convenient surface. The only restriction is imposed by the length of the cord on the external power supply. The cable from the JetWay to the printer should not be longer than 25 feet. The serial cables from the computers to the printer should be 50 feet or shorter. ASP sells RJ-11 adapters and cable sets.

ServerJet

ASP also makes the ServerJet (Fig. 13-21), an optional interface with buffer designed specifically for the Hewlett-Packard LaserJet family (II, IID, III, and IIID, the SX engines). The interface board is slipped into the optional I/O slot of the LaserJet (Figs. 13-22 and 13-23), which is concealed beneath a small hatch next to the standard interfaces. The ServerJet comes in five models (see Table 13-2), but all use the ASP implementation of RJ-11 and straight-through-wired telephone cable. Some models are furnished with an extra parallel input/output port, through which an additional computer (input) or second printer (output) can be connected. If there is a second printer, the port has only a pass-through function, and jobs are sent directly to the auxiliary printer, bypassing the LaserJet. Thus, a dot matrix printer can be added to the network for printing that requires carbons, color, or draft proofing.

13-21 ASP's ServerJet, an optional I/O card for the LaserJet SX engines. (Equipment courtesy ASP Computer Products)

The ServerJet is software-driven, like the JetWay, and uses the same method of setup. The printer output is redirected and options not available on the JetWay are added to the setup software (Figs. 13-24 and 13-25). There is also a pop-up TSR that enables you to switch jobs from within applications between the two at-

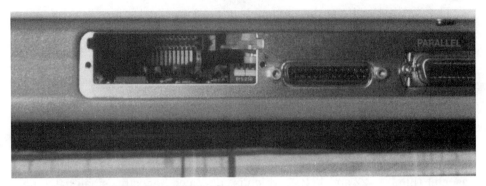

13-22 Optional I/O slot on rear of LaserJet.

13-23 ServerJet installed with RJ-11 terminated cable. (Equipment courtesy ASP Computer Products)

Table 13-2. ASP ServerJet models.

Model	Serial inputs	Parallel I/O port
ST400	4	N
ST500	4	Y
ST600	6	N
ST700	6	Y
ST1200	12	N

tached printers. The ServerJet answers to the same "job control commands" as does the JetWay, including the Initialize All Ports command. There are also commands to configure and to select the parallel port.

Like the JetWay, the ServerJet is also a buffer. The standard incoming data buffer is 256K and can be as large as 4Mb, taking some of the strain away from

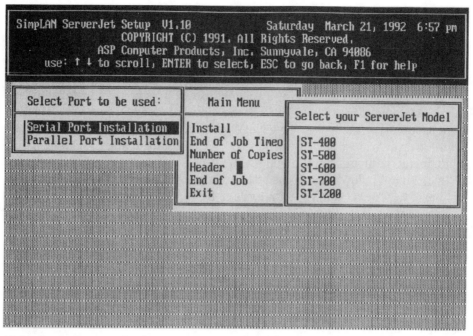

13-24 ServerJet setup is same as for JetWay, except some models have additional parallel port for input/output. (Software courtesy ASP Computer Products)

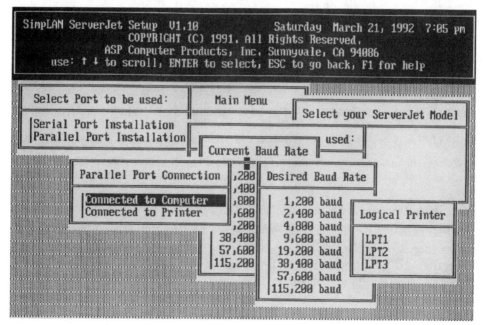

13-25 Parallel port can be connected to a second printer for output or to a computer for input. (Software courtesy ASP Computer Products)

the internal RAM of the LaserJet and freeing the computers much sooner than would be the case if the printer's own RAM were the sole repository for incoming data. The ServerJet may not be compatible with some emulation cartridges used in the LaserJets, in which case the JetWay is a good alternative, lacking only the second printer port option.

The ServerJet can also print a self-test to verify its correct installation and current settings (Fig. 13-26). The self-test button is located in a very inconvenient spot on the side of the ServerJet's port housing. Again, like the JetWay, a failure to print is most likely due to the user's failure to set the LaserJet configuration menu for input from the optional I/O.

Note that Windows users must use the Printer Setup from the Windows Control Panel to redirect output to the printer for both the JetWay and ServerJets. The proper port is designated LPT1.OS2, which is the DOS logical serial output specified in the ASP configuration software.

```
(C)1991 ASP Computer Products, Inc.
SimpLAN ServerJet Self-Test Report. VER 2.20


Memory Test Passed.
Available Memory:   256K-Byte
```

PORT	BAUD RATE	TIMEOUT	ROBUST XON	I/O
SERIAL 1	115,200	10 SECONDS	OFF	INPUT
SERIAL 2	19,200	10 SECONDS	OFF	INPUT
SERIAL 3	9,600	10 SECONDS	OFF	INPUT
SERIAL 4	9,600	10 SECONDS	OFF	INPUT
PARALLEL	N/A	10 SECONDS	N/A	OUTPUT

13-26 ServerJet self-test shows status of ports. (Software courtesy ASP Computer Products)

Macintosh users

For Macintosh users, ASP supplies MacPrint from Insight Development Corporation (Fig. 13-27). MacPrint consists of a serial cable, Chooser software drivers for various HP printers, including the LaserJets and DeskJets, and font support files for many of the font cartridges used in HP printers. With the drivers and a ServerJet from JetWay, Mac owners can print directly to a LaserJet or DeskJet as they would to a Macintosh serial printer (Fig. 13-28). The font files are installed in the System (System 6.04 or higher and System 7.0 compatible) with LJ prefixes, distinguishing them from PostScript, TrueType, and other Mac exclusive

13-27 MacPrint system of software drivers and cable for printing to HP LaserJet and DeskJet printers. (Software courtesy ASP Computer Products and Insight Development)

13-28 MacPrint opening screen allows selection from variety of HP printers. (Software courtesy ASP Computer Products and Insight Development)

fonts (Fig. 13-29). Access to font cartridges is thereby made simple, ensuring the best 300 dpi printing from the LaserJet and preserving the Macintosh's WYSI-WYG display (Fig. 13-30).

An alternative to the MacPrint printer drivers is sold by Orange Micro in their Grappler series of Macintosh interface products. The Grappler 9-Pin and Grappler LX are interface conversion cables that connect the serial port of the Macintosh to the parallel port of a 9-pin dot matrix (Grappler 9) or 24-pin dot matrix or laser printer (Grappler LX).

The Apple ImageWriter (9-pin) and ImageWriter LQ (24-pin and laser) Chooser software is included, and is modified to support the printer connected to the Grappler interface. The Grappler LS (Fig. 13-31) is sold for printers with a serial port, or for users of ASP or Pacific Data interface/sharing devices. It provides only the software and a serial cable.

Devices very much like the ASP ServerJet for the Hewlett-Packard LaserJets can also be purchased from Pacific Data and from LaserPlex through Chenesko

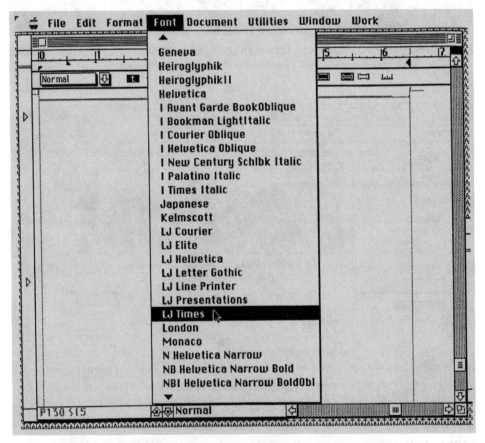

13-29 MacPrint installs LaserJet fonts with LJ prefix to set them apart from regular Macintosh fonts. (Software courtesy ASP Computer Products and Insight Development)

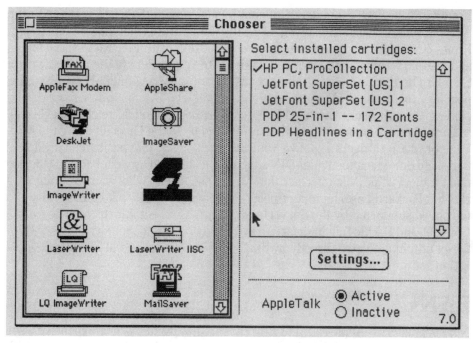

13-30 MacPrint Chooser drivers support numerous font cartridges. (Software courtesy ASP Computer Products and Insight Development)

13-31 Grappler LS supports serially connected HP LaserJets and DeskJets in ImageWriter LQ emulation only.

Products. The Pacific Connect Optional I/O is used in the same printers as the ASP ServerJet, and in the Wang LDP8III-DSK and the Siemens Nixdorf High Print 7800 and PT10. It comes in one configuration, with four RJ-11 serial inputs and a 36-pin Centronics connector, making it the equivalent of the ASP ServerJet ST 500. The Pacific Connect also acts as a print buffer, with 256K standard, expandable to 1.5Mb, 2.5Mb less than the ServerJets. In most other respects, including the top baud rate of 115,200, they appear identical to the ServerJets. Macintoshes are supported, and can print directly to the LaserJet using the MacPage or MacJet drivers supplied with the interface. Cable packages for all four ports and one Macintosh mini-DIN adapter are supplied as well. Pacific Data also makes the PacificTalk interface for Macintosh users who want to connect a Hewlett-Packard LaserJet to an AppleTalk network. AppleTalk runs at twice the top speed supported by the ServerJet or Pacific Connect interfaces. The Pacific Connect and PacificTalk interfaces are the only ones that support Chooser Post-Script printing initiated directly by the Print menu command of Macintosh application software.

LANs

Networks such as AppleTalk and Ethernet are not particularly inexpensive ways to share computer peripherals. AppleTalk hardware is built into all Macintosh personal computers, LaserWriter printers (except the Personal LaserWriter SC and LaserWriter II SC), and the ImageWriter LQ, and you need only purchase and install the cables to make the network functional. AppleTalk boards can be added to IBM and compatible personal computers that allow connection to a LocalTalk network. The IBM PC can then share the LaserWriter or ImageWriter LQ. The boards are about $135 each, and a number of IBM PCs can run the cost up quickly, but it is the easiest and fastest way to put a LaserWriter at the disposal of a PC. The additional cost of the cables can be kept down by using PhoneNet or AppleTalk-compatible connectors from third-party sources.

Ethernet is the most common PC network hardware, and the new Apple LaserWriter IIg has a built-in Ethernet port, so there is no extra cost in acquiring the LaserWriter on network. To install an Ethernet or similar network simply to share a printer is not cost-effective.

Cabling

One of the most vexatious items in computing is the cable. It is never the right one for the job. Just when you thought that you had every possible cable you would ever need, you buy a switch box and find out how naive you are. Switches, converters, buffers, and all their permutations can use some very improbable cables, and the documentation will make them sound perfectly ordinary.

Boxes with parallel connectors might have any one of four connectors in common use, requiring that you purchase a new cable for every computer and peripheral attached. Remember especially that there are two ends to every cable: You might be able to plug into the computer or into the peripheral, but you might not be able to plug into the box. The four types of parallel connectors in general use are the female DB-25, as used in the IBM-PC and other computers, the female Centronics 36, as used in most printers, the male DB-25 as used on the computer end of a normal parallel cable, and the male Centronics 36 as used on the printer end of a normal parallel cable. If you are lucky, switch boxes might accept input from a normal DB-25 male to Centronics 36 male cable, but the outputs are then likely to require a male Centronics 36 to male Centronics 36 in order to connect to the printer or printers. You might also find, as in the ASP ServerJet, that to connect the parallel port of a switch as an input from a computer, you will need a cable with DB-25 connectors on both ends and with straight-through wiring. In a pinch, you can link two normal parallel printer cables together with a female Centronics 36 to female Centronics 36 gender changer to make a DB-25 to DB-25 cable. To connect a Dresselhaus parallel SmartSwitch to a Multi Printer Switch, you would need a cable with a DB-25 male connector at one end and a DB-25 female connector at the other and straight-through wiring.

Serial cabling is where the real fun begins, since there are so many serial connectors and so many wiring schemes behind those connectors. To keep it as simple as possible, let us assume that the basic cable will have DB-25 connectors on either end, and that adapters or additional cables will be added as necessary to make the basic cable work with computers equipped with DB-9 and mini-DIN 8 connectors. The rule is simple and invariable: If using an adapter or adapter cable, always use the straight-through or modem cable to connect to the main DB-25 cable.

The real problem with cabling to switches and buffers and the like is that there are two antiquated serial denominations for the devices attached to a serial cable: data communications equipment (DCE), and data terminal equipment (DTE). The former encompasses modems and the latter printers. Their primary difference lay in the assignment of the transmit and receive lines: Modems used line 2 to transmit and line 3 to receive, while printers used the reverse. In the ancient world (say 1975), serial ports on computers would be hard wired for either DTE or DCE devices, and the same cable would work on either port, since the ports themselves contained the differentiations. Then serial ports became generalized (and therefore cheaper), and it became necessary to configure the cable for the device. Nobody suggested that all peripherals be redesigned as well, since there was too large an installed base. Thereafter, modem cables and printer cables appeared; the modem cables were wired straight through and the printer cables had lines 2 and 3 crossed end to end.

This discussion leads us to switch boxes, which may or may not need something that you consider unreasonable. The ATEN converter with the serial port at one end and the parallel port at the other requires that the serial port be considered a DCE device; i.e., a modem cable is needed. You would assume that the device, meant for a printer, would use the printer cable, but it does not. The

Dresselhaus SmartSwitch requires straight-through cabling, not only from the computer to the switch but from the switch to the printer as well. Yet, when you want to daisy chain or cascade the switch, then the cable must be of the DTE or printer variety, with lines 2 and 3 crossed. And don't forget that all of the Dresselhaus SmartSwitch connectors are female DB-25, but that the connectors of the Multi Printer Switch are both male and female (Parallel: male In and female Out. Serial: female In and male Out.)

To connect a computer with the products that use RJ-11 connectors you need an adapter for whatever connector your computer uses at the serial port. Then you must be certain whether you need straight-through wiring (as is necessary with the ASP interfaces and sharing boxes) or normal telephone wire, which reverses all four conductors end to end.

If you want to make an adapter for the ASP products, you should be aware that a DB-25 to RJ-11 adapter has six lines on the RJ-11 end. The first and sixth lines are not connected. Line 2 of the DB-25 goes to line 4 of the RJ-11; DB-25 line 3 goes to RJ-11 line 2; DB-25 lines 5 and 6 are connected together on line 3 of the RJ-11; and DB-25 line 7 goes to RJ-11 line 5. A DB-9 to RJ-11 is adapted as follows: DB-9 line 2 goes to RJ-11 line 2; DB-9 line 3 goes to RJ-11 line 4; DB-9 line 5 goes to RJ-11 line 5; and DB-9 lines 6 and 8 connect together at RJ-11 line 3.

A Macintosh will need a printer cable to the RJ-11 adapter—so much for rules!

Chapter 14

Paper handling

Paper handling might not seem to be a matter to be included in a book about printer upgrades, but how much time do you want to spend feeding paper into your printer? As little as possible, right? Even though paper parking has made it possible to feed single sheets without removing the continuous form paper, why feed just one sheet at a time? And how often does that paper cassette empty out and stop a printing job while the laser printer waits for want of paper?

Bottom-feeding mechanism

For the dot matrix printer with a bottom-feeding mechanism, say the Citizen GSX140 Plus or 200 GX, the best method to feed long runs of paper is through the bottom. The paper is less likely to slip into misalignment when fed from the bottom, reducing the attention that the user must give the printer. The best printers are the ones that run unattended.

The only problem with bottom-feeding paper is that the paper has to be under the printer. Since the paper cannot feed if the printer is sitting on the paper stack, the obvious solution is a printer stand. Citizen makes stands for its printers (Fig. 14-1) consisting of three pieces of molded plastic that snap together to form an elevated platform for the printer. The stand is color-coordinated with the printers, if your interior designer must be consulted. While printer stands can be purchased from most accessories dealers for as little as $6–$10, this stand has one feature that is unique: a wide slot in each of the side pieces that permits the printer to be placed in a vertical position (Fig. 14-2) to facilitate the feeding of the paper through the bottom slot. This is the kind of feature that the printer manufacturer can include in accessories for its own printers that would not be feasible for the maker of generic printer accessories.

14-1 Citizen narrow carriage printer stand is formed of three snap-together pieces. (Equipment courtesy Citizen America)

14-2 Citizen printer stands allow printer to be placed in vertical position for feeding of paper through bottom slot. (Equipment courtesy Citizen America)

Automatic sheet feeder

For letterhead printing, most manufacturers make cut sheet feeders or automatic sheet feeders for their printers. They attach in various manners, but the Citizen units are typical.

The cut sheet feeder shown in (Fig. 14-3) is designed for 50 sheets of paper. It comes assembled, except for the wire paper guides that slide into the holes in the top of the back of the paper bin. Flip up the clear portion of the printer cover and fit the feeder unit down over the center of the printer, aligning the corners

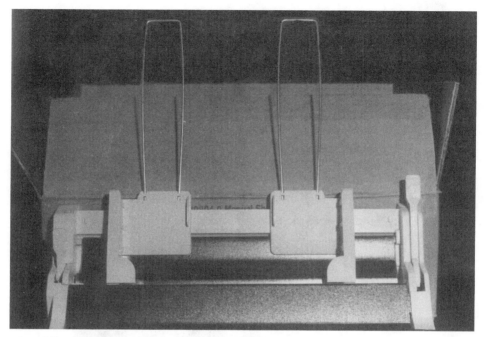

14-3 Manual sheet feeder ensures correct and rapid insertion of cut sheets. (Equipment courtesy Citizen America)

with the triangles in the top of the case (Fig. 14-4). Then snap down the unit securely into place. Load the paper by pulling forward the lever on the left-hand side and stacking the paper between the moveable side pieces. Push back the left-hand lever into an upright position and use the right-hand lever to feed the paper into the printer. This ensures that the paper feeds straight and that the top of form is correctly placed.

The automatic sheet feeder in Fig. 14-5 is designed to feed up to 100 cut sheets into the printer in a continuous stream, as though the printer were using edge-perforated forms. The automatic feeder requires only slightly more assembly than the manual sheet feeder, once again to add wire guides. The automatic sheet feeder fits into the same position as the manual feeder, and it must be selected as the paper source in order for the printer to operate properly.

The 140 Plus can use a macro to set the printer for auto sheet feed and to disengage the feeder. You can leave in place both the manual and auto sheet feeders while the printer is using continuous form paper. You can therefore leave letterhead in the printer for formal letters, while perforated paper is used for more informal documents, and you can switch between paper sources without significant effort.

The Okidata Microline printers have a slightly different manner of notifying the printer that a sheet feeder has been installed. Printers that accept feeders have a port (Fig. 14-6) into which you can plug a cable attached to the feeder. This provides a logical connection between the printer and feeder.

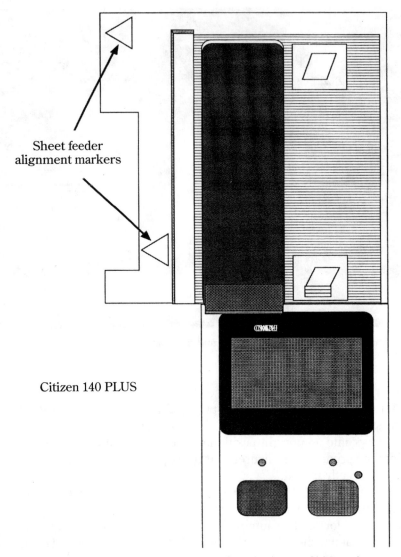

Sheet feeder
alignment markers

Citizen 140 PLUS

14-4 Location of mounting markers for sheet feeders on Citizen printers.

Cassettes

Paper handling in laser printers is usually described in one word: inadequate. Most laser printers have paper cassettes with a maximum capacity of 250 or fewer sheets. Some printers have optional second cassettes. However, most people using printers for large printing runs eventually feel the urgent need to purchase a paper bin, a device that either attaches to or substitutes for the paper cassette and can feed 1,000 or more sheets at one loading. Bins are manufactured by numerous third-party companies, including UDP, AGT, and Elite. They

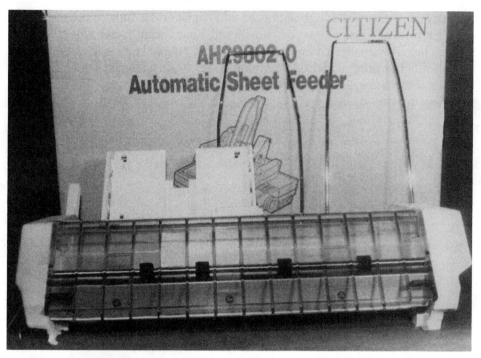

14-5 Automatic sheet feeder will insert up to 100 cut sheets continuously through printer.
(Equipment courtesy Citizen America)

14-6 Circular DIN port for connection of sheet feeder signal cable on Okidata Microline 192 is located to left and below hatch in this case.

are very convenient, although some can add considerable bulk to the larger SX-style engines, and space must be considered a significant factor when you purchase a bin. The smaller LX engines often accept optional oversize cassettes that fit beneath the printer and add nothing to its basic footprint. But, then, the smaller printers are also only 50% as fast as their larger siblings. There are compromises in every design.

Part 5

Software: when hardware won't do

Chapter 15

Software: The substitute for hardware

Software is the other half of a computer. If everything were hardware, "What a wonderful world it would be," say the hardware designers. And the software designers placidly observe that everything isn't hardware. The dictum is that hardware is always faster than software, but the word *always,* like the word *never,* is an adverb as much observed in the breach as in the compliance. Sometimes hardware leaves a breach that software must fill. For almost every hardware solution to a problem, there is an alternative solution in software. Many times the software is preferable, if only for the elegance of its execution.

Spooling buffers

RAM is getting cheaper, and printer buffers are getting cheaper, too. But what if you cannot afford a printer buffer or cannot justify the expense? What if your printer will not accept more RAM, and you can't, for whatever reason, add an external buffer? The solution is to use what you have.

Spooling is the action of taking the output that would normally go directly to the printer and redirecting it to a temporary holding area in the memory of the computer. The area may be in RAM or on some fixed memory such as the hard drive or floppy media. The principal advantage of spooling is that it places the actual printing process in the background of normal operations, and is the most frequently used and useful form of multitasking, not to mention the first usually implemented on any computer platform. The second advantage is that it is the most-effective solution to time-intensive printing jobs, for it uses the resources already in place. (See the section on Dresselhaus SmartSwitches in the previous chapter.) The principal disadvantage of spooling is that it steals or usurps resources that would otherwise be used in the foreground task, thereby decreasing performance and degrading the system overall. The degree of this degradation increases as the allocation of resources to the background task increases, due to the size of the printing job or to the speed at which the job proceeds to its completion. The larger the job or the faster that you want it processed, the greater the loss of foreground efficiency.

One of the most familiar of all spoolers is the Print Manager supplied with Windows 3.0. To the program that prints through the Print Manager, the Manager appears to be a printer, mimicking the responses of a printer to the program's printing routines. To the printer, the Manager appears to be the original source of the printing instructions and file data. It is this mediation that makes the Manager both a useful and sometimes overbearing servant. The more jobs you send to the Manager, the more slowly the foreground tasks are carried forward.

Mouse cursor motion suffers discontinuity or "jumpiness." Screen updating is taxed. Mathematical calculations take longer, and word processors cannot keep up with even moderately speedy keyboard entry. Part of this is due to the cobbled relationship of Windows to DOS, because Windows events are CPU-dependent rather than ROM-directed.

Graphical interfaces impose more demands on the entire computer than DOS. Faster, more powerful CPUs help make such slowdowns more tolerable or less intrusive. Graphics accelerators also improve system responses. More memory is definitely helpful, as are faster and larger hard drives. Better code writing would undoubtedly bring better results.

On the Macintosh, spooling is largely the province of LaserWriters (Fig. 15-1). Background printing is handled by Print Monitor, a small spooler that uses the hard drive and small allotments of RAM to relieve the foreground application of the printing task. Its operation is much less querulous than is that of its counterpart in Windows. The Macintosh is not blessed with an outstanding multitasking environment, but it has inherent many of the necessities for successful background printing.

The Macintosh operating system, unlike Windows or DOS, is largely ROM-resident. The routines that define, manipulate, and manage the priority of the graphical interface elements and tasks are proprietary ROM code. The software portion of the system can concern itself with the actual channeling of data from the user to the computer and from the computer to the peripherals, rather than with the low-level tasks of defining what a window is, where it is located, what its contents are, and how those contents are being changed. The operation of a background task is therefore more truly in the background than it is in Windows.

There are some commercial spoolers for the Macintosh, most notably Super-Spool for ImageWriter printing and SuperLaserSpool, which works with laser printers (other than the LaserWriters) and the DeskWriter. Also, Orange Micro's Grappler support software includes a spooler for background printing with any attached printers (Fig.15-2). The spooler permits documents to be moved about in

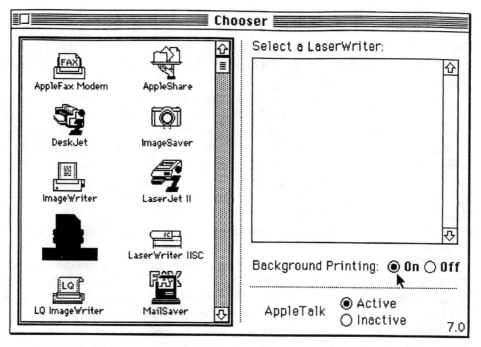

15-1 Mac's Chooser DA allows LaserWriter printing to occur almost transparently in background with spooling to disk.

15-2 Orange Micro's Grappler spooling software has options not available with Apple's Print Monitor.

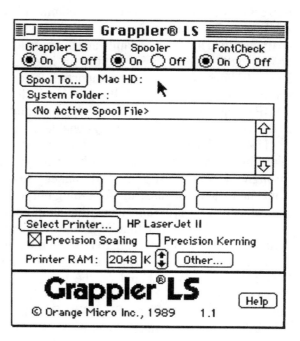

the queue, to be deleted, and for printing to be suspended or cancelled. DeskJets and LaserJets are supported, but font cartridges are not. The intention is to make the HP printer emulate the ImageWriter LQ, so Macintosh fonts are used. Unfortunately, the spooler itself does not recede into the woodwork (or wallpaper) as it is going about its business.

Compared to LaserWriter spooling through Print Monitor, it is a nuisance. Foreground tasks are too frequently interrupted by the Watch cursor as the spooling intrudes, absorbing processor time and attention and forcing visible and distracting pauses in screen activity. Still, for those who use HP printers, who require fidelity to the Mac's WYSIWYG promise, and who desire background printing, this combination package of spooler and printer driver might be the only choice.

The DOS world has relatively more choices than does the Windows world, largely because of the greater age of the environment. But a glimpse at one spooler is sufficient to show what you can gain and what you sacrifice by the use of spooling software.

DMP is a shareware spooler with about as many options as you could imagine or want. It can spool output to RAM, to disk, or to both, using whatever your computer system has to offer. It can strip printer commands or pass them on; it can print to disk; it can hold up printing until commanded to resume. It can run the printer at full speed at the expense of system speed, or it can reduce printer throughput to optimize foreground tasks. DMP can be set up to work with virtually any printer, whether serial or parallel, with text or with graphics, and it costs all of $18.

DMP is a command line–actuated program, with options and option parameters set by switches embedded in the command line entry. The simple command DMP, when issued from the correct PATH, will start the spooler with its default characteristics in effect. Defaults are the parallel printer port LPT, printer speed of 75% (on a scale of 0–99), use the 6K internal buffer, issue form feeds, page length 66 lines, and others less important for casual use. There are also default settings for the serial port, if the printing is directed to one of the COM ports (DMP recognizes COM1 and COM2): 2400 baud, 8 bits, no parity (N), 1 stop bit. XON/XOFF handshaking is always enabled.

DMP works at the system level to intercept the BIOS call to the printer. It takes the incoming data and spools it to a file and then drives the printer directly through the designated port. DMP makes use of the system interrupts to read from and write to the disk, and for timing purposes. By reading interrupts, it can coexist with other programs using the computer at the same time.

It is important to note that DMP itself redirects the printer output, so it is imperative that you do not attempt to redirect the printer functions using the MODE or other DOS commands. This means that the ASP setup program used with the ServerJet and JetWay should not be permitted to modify the computer's AUTOEXEC.BAT file, or the ASP_DATA.BAT file should be manually altered to remove the redirection. The ASP_DATA.BAT file calls the ASPMODE.EXE and ASPBAUD.EXE programs and passes to each the parameters needed. The ASP-

MODE program sets the logical printer and the COM port. ASPBAUD sets the baud rate for the COM port specified. The contents of the typical ASP_DATA.BAT file looks something like this:

ASPMODE 1 2
ASPBAUD 2 15

meaning that the logical printer is LPT1:, located on COM2:, and COM2: is set to 115,200 baud. To make DMP compatible with the JetWay or ServerJet, run ASP's setup software first, but do not permit it to add the CALL to your computer's AU-TOEXEC.BAT file, and do not select a baud rate higher than 19,200. After exiting the ASP software, run DMP with the command DMP/COM2 R19200, which will set DMP to the serial port at its highest baud rate. The ServerJet or JetWay and DMP will then work together.

In Windows 3.0, you might have to change the port in the Printers Control Panel, so that a print file is created rather than attempting to print to the serial port designated for DMP. The file can then be printed using DMP. Also, those running Windows on a 1Mb machine might find that DMP must be run from Window's DOS command line or from a DOS window, since DMP will take some DOS memory needed to start Windows. An insufficient memory condition occurs if DMP is run from DOS before Windows has been installed.

It is generally true that all programs running in a graphical environment, whether Windows, GEM, or a runtime version of such an environment (say, TimeWorks Publish It!), will not print properly if the spooler is also running. Much more reliable printing will result from printing to disk first, and then using DMP's PF (print file) utility afterward to send the file through DMP to the printer. Indeed, any program that drives the printer with its own subroutines rather than relying upon the BIOS calls and, DOS must print to a file in order for DMP to be of use. Many of the more expensive word processors circumvent the DOS and BIOS printing routines, largely on the principle that there will be no interference with printer control codes and no system overhead to attenuate printing. This is sometimes necessary rather than optional, due to the waywardness of some programs in their formatting and special features codes.

DMP's commands can be strung together; e.g., DMP/COM2 R19200/DC:/G+, which sets the output port to COM2:, the baud rate to 19,200, the spooling buffer to drive C:, and turns off translation of line feed and other control characters because a graphic file is to be printed. Once you define a suitable set of printing parameters for your needs, you can save the set as a configuration file with the DMP/WCF (write configuration file) command. The next time DMP is run, the spooler will look for the configuration file and automatically adopt the mode defined by its contents. DMP can also accept parameters which have been passed to it from DOS commands like SET.

More than one file can be specified at a time by linking them on the command line. DOS wildcards are acceptable in filenames and paths. Once the queue has been started, DMP begins spooling the first document. This occurs in the foreground, but when the spooling is complete, printing occurs in the background, and the computer is free to execute a foreground task. This is where the real time savings are garnered. Small files are no test of the spooler, since it is an intermediary and can actually add to the printing time. Long files or multiple files accrue the greatest benefit from spooling.

Spooling can be interrupted by a switch /S–, and killed with another, /SK. Spooling can be resumed with the /S+ switch. If more than one printer is connected, say one to a serial port and the other to a parallel port, printing can be alternated between the ports with the /COM and /LPT switches once you have defined the parameters for each.

If a program cannot print to a file, DMP can take the data meant for the printer and print it to a file for you, using the /PF switch (not to be confused with the separate utility PF, which spools and prints already existing disk files). Again, this is best done with programs in nongraphical environments and which do not drive the printer themselves. You can append disk files to an existing file with the /AF switch, or overwrite an existing file with the /OF switch.

DMP can use any type of RAM as its spool site. Expanded memory, extended memory, and the high-memory area are all supported, as are RAM disks. The manual that is compressed with DMP contains extensive instructions on how to use memory managers to allocate RAM for spooling. In order of their preference by DMP, spooling is directed to these areas: internal buffer (6–40K), high memory, expanded memory, extended memory, and disk. Any disk can be used, whether fixed or removable, but if you remove a disk while spooling is proceeding from that disk, you can expect to cause a fatal system error. In addition, disk input/output to floppies is much slower than to either hard drives or RAM.

When you load the spooler, the startup configuration is sent to the screen in confirmation (Fig. 15-3). The spooler displays the current control character handling and the capacities of the various buffers enabled. If no buffers are specified, the internal buffer is used, and a warning is posted that no other buffers have been allocated. At any time during its operation, the spooler can report on

```
C:\ZIP>dmp/dc:/com2 r19200/g+
 Installing DMP Printer driver / spooler. Version 2.03
 Copyright (c) 1989,1990 T. McGuire.
 ***** Unregistered copy of program *****
All character conversions off.
Output to serial port COM 2        19200bps, 8N1 Busy signal: CTS

Spool buffer summary:   bytes used / available
     Internal                0       6144
     Disk drive C:           0    3158016
Total bytes spooled:         0

C:\ZIP>
```

15-3 Installation of DMP Spooler is simple, although many options for spooling exist.

its status in replay to the DMP command typed in DOS (Fig. 15-4). The amount of buffer space in use reflects the size of the spooled file remaining to be printed. If the printer is connected to the parallel port, a speed quotient is reported that is composed of the speed actually in use and the speed as set. If the speed is at its maximum, you can opt to increase the limit.

```
C:\ZIP>dmp
 DMP Printer driver / spooler. Version 2.03
All character conversions off.
Output to serial port COM 2       19200bps, 8N1 Busy signal: CTS

Spool buffer summary:    bytes used / available
     Internal               2823        3321
     Disk drive C:        104448     2367488
Total bytes spooled:      107271

C:\ZIP>
```

15-4 A status report for DMP can be ordered at any DOS prompt.

The conclusion is that the spooler will do a good job of getting you back to work, but there will still be some initial waiting, and the more of your computer's resources that you turn over to the spooler, the less you will have for more important programs. If you cannot add a RAM buffer, the best way to spend your money is on RAM for your computer. It is the cheapest and most useful expansion you can make, for the RAM can be used both for spooling and in normal operations. The conflicts that can arise between the spooler and some software are usually solved simply by using the main application to print to disk—a method that will ultimately save time, since the disk can receive the data faster than a printer can. Conflicts between the spooler and some external hardware, such as intelligent switches, can be harder to resolve, although most of the spooler's basic functions can be turned off or changed to remove their effects. If the external device contains a buffer, you probably don't need the spooler, or one was provided with the device.

Soft fonts

Ever since the Macintosh and its bitmapped typefaces transformed computer printing, fonts have been spreading like a virus from computer to computer. Any text printed on an ImageWriter from MacWrite looked one hundred percent better and more interesting than anything printed on any other dot matrix printer from the best DOS word processors. The LaserWriter added high resolution and font scaling to the mixture, and there was an explosion of fonts and font vendors.

The problem for DOS users, though they would never have admitted it, was that fonts are a much more difficult item to manage in DOS programs than they are on a Macintosh. If you don't have one, you can't have the other.

What are all of the other people with their millions of dot matrix or ink jet printers to do?

Some of the most important changes in printer font technology have been made not in the printers themselves, but in the computers that drive them. It was not the ImageWriter, a simple 9-pin dot matrix printer from C.Itoh, that made the printout look so attractive: it was the Macintosh and its graphical environment that created the page from first to last. When Adobe Type Manager (Fig. 15-5) further enhanced the Macintosh's print quality by using outline fonts on screen and on paper from the same computer-based font, then the graphical environment became the de facto standard for high-quality printing and the Macintosh was the *ne plus ultra* of graphical environment computers. Windows has changed that to a great degree.

15-5 Adobe Type Manager set up control panel for Macintosh.

Windows, whatever its many faults, has been the agent of change in DOS computers and in DOS-based printing. Windows 3.0 has brought consistency to printing, giving a single typeface foundation to all its dependents. Gone are all the idiosyncratic methods of type selection and type printing that had sprung up in the lawless DOS world. Every word processor used a different method to display output on the screen in a way that suggested how it would look when printed. One had to imagine, for instance, that reverse video was really boldface, italic, 12 point New Century Schoolbook. Now you know what it looks like. All the leading word processors have migrated to Windows. Adobe Type Manager is now in its second DOS version. Windows is without exception the best thing that has happened to printers since the Macintosh.

Even outside Windows there are oases of clean type and typographic variety.

Dot matrix

Every printer that is not a formed character printer is a dot matrix printer, but in this section I am speaking only of the impact dot matrix genus, the broad and deep base of all printers.

Low-resolution Surprisingly, even without benefit of Windows, you can get typographical products for a very few dollars that will make even 9-pin printers look better in print. There are many fonts that you can download to the printer that will add interest to the page. Fonts can be found on bulletin boards and in catalogs of shareware or public domain software. Typefaces not found in even the best dot matrix printers can be sent to the printer's download buffer for use in jobs where you need something different from the old and rather conventional Letter Gothic or Prestige Elite.

If you are of a mind to do so, you can even create your own downloaded typefaces. There is usually a chapter in the printer's manual that describes the matrix used by the printer to create its fonts, and how that matrix can be used by the printer owner to define a new character set. Basically, the discussion is as follows.

A printer character's height is determined by the spacing of the nine pins which make up the print head: the pins are stacked vertically in the print head and form a column. In any one column, eight of the pins can be fired, either the eight counted from the top or the eight counted from the bottom. Six columns form the width of each character, but since the horizontal spacing is not determined by pin placement in the print head, there are dot positions located between each of the columns, making eleven points in all along the width. This is the matrix of the dot matrix. The horizontal dots are conceived to be in rows. Any point in the matrix can be referred to, therefore, as a cell formed by the intersection of a row and column, or as a point formed by the lines defining the cells (Fig. 15-6).

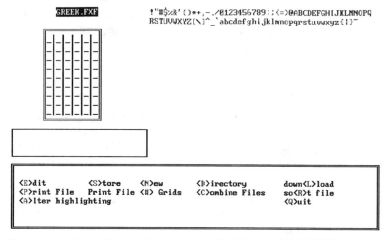

15-6 Cell matrix of a font editor for 9-pin printers, in this case FXMATRIX.

You can copy a character set from the printer's ROM into the printer's download buffer, and can then alter the contents of the buffer to make a new character set from the existing one. Individual characters are called from the buffer by their ASCII position in the character set: ASCII character number sixty five (hexadecimal 41) is the uppercase letter A. Once you call a character, you can change its shape or erase and replace it in any way that the matrix permits.

About the only restriction placed on the design of a character is that adjacent columns cannot have adjacent horizontal dots; i.e., horizontal dots must skip columns. Aside from that, you are free to manipulate the character set in any way. Foreign language character sets are especially good subjects for downloading, since Greek and Cyrillic alphabets are not often found as ROM-resident type in dot matrix printers.

Naturally, you do not want to have to go to the trouble of redrawing the entire alphabet everytime that you want to use a different character set. The design of the character set is usually stored in a disk file (created in BASIC or some other high-level language) that can be recalled easily and sent to the printer using the correct escape sequences. Better than BASIC are the numerous font-editing programs that you can find in shareware or public domain software catalogs, on bulletin boards, or on large networks such as CompuServe or Genie.

One font editor for Epson FX and Epson-compatible printers is called FX-MATRIX, a shareware program written by J. David Sapir of Jimmy Paris Software (Paris is an anagram of Sapir). The program can create files entirely from user-supplied input, or it can load existing files (some of which are supplied with the software) for the user to modify. Once you have created the font, you can save it to a file. You can download character sets from within the program or with a separate program. You can then switch the printer from the ROM-resident fonts to the RAM-resident one and back with escape sequences.

The font editor displays the matrix and the default ASCII character set (Fig. 15-6). You can select a position within the set by cursor, and move the character from that position to the editing matrix (Fig. 15-7). You move the cursor by the arrow keys, and can turn the cells or interstitial dots on or off at will, within the constraints affecting adjacent horizontal dots. You can select these and other operations from a menu at the bottom of the screen; items from the menu are chosen from the keyboard. You can move the character in the editing matrix in all four directions to change the baseline or shift the spacing. You can mirror it or merge it with another character from the ASCII set. You can choose from three logical tests to determine if highlighted cells from the two characters cancel each other or remain highlighted. If desired, you can send the entire cell matrix for any character or for a range of characters to the Epson printer for a permanent record (Fig. 15-8). Also, you can print out the whole ASCII character set as a hard-copy reference (Fig. 15-9).

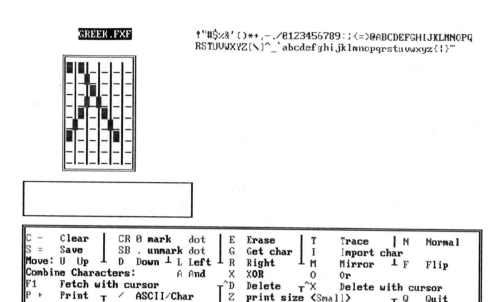

```
GREEK.FXF          !"#$%&'()*+,-./0123456789:;<=>@ABCDEFGHIJKLMNOPQ
                   RSTUVWXYZ[\]^_`abcdefghijklmnopqrstuvwxyz{|}~
```

```
C  -    Clear     │ CR 0 mark   dot  │ E  Erase      │ T   Trace     │ N   Normal
S  =    Save      │ SB . unmark dot  │ G  Get char   │ I   Import char
Move: U  Up   ⊥ D  Down ⊥ L Left ⊥ R  Right    ⊥ M   Mirror   ⊥ F   Flip
Combine Characters:        A  And  │ X  XOR        │ O   Or
F1      Fetch with cursor         ┬^D  Delete   ┬^X   Delete with cursor
P  +    Print  ┬  / ASCII/Char    │ Z  print size <Small>      ┬ Q   Quit
```

15-7 Layout of a character on matrix. Note the use of lines and cells.

Using the editor, the patient and creative user can amass a library of typefaces for use in any document. Font downloading takes only seconds, and the
printed results from a carefully constructed typeface are excellent. And, although the editing takes place in a draft display mode, the characters can be
printed in either draft or NLQ print modes.

High resolution Twenty-four pin printers have the same options and
sources for their typefaces as do the 9-pin printers. Ordinarily, the 24-pin printer
will have a larger selection of internal fonts than will a 9-pin sibling, but the
improved quality of printing from the denser dot matrix only encourages you to
seek out new fonts. You can find fonts in ready-to-use form in public domain and
shareware catalogs, and on bulletin boards or other electronic services.

There are also font editors for the 24-pin printers. Jimmy Paris Software has
LQMATRIX, an upscale version of FXMATRIX, for the 24-pin Epson and NEC
printers. Naturally, designing characters for a 24-pin printer involves more work,
since the matrix contains more cells.

For both 9-pin and 24-pin Epson printers, you can obtain the highest-quality
soft fonts with Type Director from Hewlett-Packard, described below.

Laser and ink jet

The real font frenzy has been and continues to be in the laser printer and ink jet
printer markets. There are innumerable fonts of fixed size, from 4 points to 72
points, in all styles. The commercial selection alone is enormous and grows

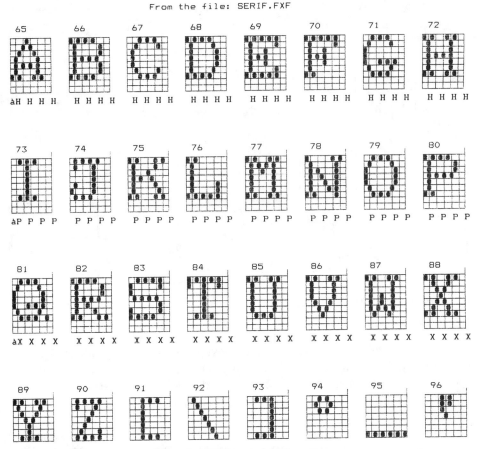

From the file: SERIF.FXF

15-8 A sample printout of cell matrices for lowercase characters.

larger every month, and the scalable fonts for Hewlett-Packard Series III printers have added territory in which that growth can continue with new vigor. Some of the more important products are listed here.

Type Director You would expect Hewlett-Packard to be a primary source of downloaded fonts for its laser printers. All of the LaserJets except the original can use the downloaded typefaces, and the DeskJets all have download font areas when memory cartridges have been installed (see the section on DeskJet memory expansion). The very best of the HP's downloaded fonts are the scalable typefaces that can be used with either the Series II or the Series III printer families.

When used with the Series III printers, these fonts are automatically scaled to the required size by the printers' built in Intellifont scaling technology. Most of the fonts, like the Intellifont technology itself, are Agfa-Compugraphic creations, and represent in electronic form the high quality and lineage of traditional CG typefaces.

216 *Software: The substitute for hardware*

Contents of SERIF.FXF

à 33-!: à!	à 34-": à"	à 35-#: à#	à 36-$: à$	à 37-%: à%
à 38-&: à&	à 39-': à'	à 40-(: à(	à 41-): à)	à 42-*: à*
à 43-+: à+	à 44-,: à,	à 45--: à⁻	à 46-.: à.	à 47-/: à/
à 48-0: à0	à 49-1: à1	à 50-2: à2	à 51-3: à3	à 52-4: à4
à 53-5: à5	à 54-6: à6	à 55-7: à7	à 56-8: à8	à 57-9: à9
à 58-:: à:	à 59-;: à;	à 60-<: à<	à 61-=: à=	à 62->: à>
à 63-?: à?	à 64-@: à@	à 65-A: àA	à 66-B: àB	à 67-C: àC
à 68-D: àD	à 69-E: àE	à 70-F: àF	à 71-G: àG	à 72-H: àH
à 73-I: àI	à 74-J: àJ	à 75-K: àK	à 76-L: àL	à 77-M: àM
à 78-N: àN	à 79-O: àO	à 80-P: àP	à 81-Q: àQ	à 82-R: àR
à 83-S: àS	à 84-T: àT	à 85-U: àU	à 86-V: àV	à 87-W: àW
à 88-X: àX	à 89-Y: àY	à 90-Z: àZ	à 91-[: à[	à 92-\: à\
à 93-]: à]	à 94-^: à°	à 95-_: à_	à 96-`: à`	à 97-a: àa
à 98-b: àb	à 99-c: àc	à100-d: àd	à101-e: àe	à102-f: àf
à103-g: àg	à104-h: àh	à105-i: ài	à106-j: àj	à107-k: àk
à108-l: àl	à109-m: àm	à110-n: àn	à111-o: ào	à112-p: àp
à113-q: àq	à114-r: àr	à115-s: às	à116-t: àt	à117-u: àu
à118-v: àv	à119-w: àw	à120-x: àx	à121-y: ày	à122-z: àz
à123-{: à{	à124-¦: à¦	à125-}: à}	à126-~: à~	

15-9 Sample printout of entire character set from FXMATRIX.

Screen fonts for your programs can be generated automatically on the fly if the software has AutoFont support written into its code, or, for Windows applications, if you have obtained a copy of Intellifont for Windows. Intellifont for Windows is given away by HP and can be ordered over the telephone (303-353-7650) or downloaded from the HP Peripherals Forum libraries on CompuServe (Library 4, "LaserJet", IFW1.ZIP).

When used in printers other than the Series III LaserJet, HP's scalable fonts must be individually created in fixed sizes for the printer and for the screen display using Type Director, a font utility from Agfa-Compugraphic and Hewlett-Packard. This process requires some advance planning. You must know which typefaces, styles, and sizes you will be likely to need, and the programs with which you intend to use the fonts. You must also estimate the amount of disk space required to store the font files and the application support files that Type Director produces. You can create new fonts for new applications whenever you desire, but it saves time and confusion to work up all the necessary files at one sitting.

The typefaces are sold in disk collections. Type Director can be purchased alone or with a basic group of 12 typefaces called the Premier Collection (Fig. 15-10). Fonts can be scaled from 4 to 200 points on printers outside the III Se-

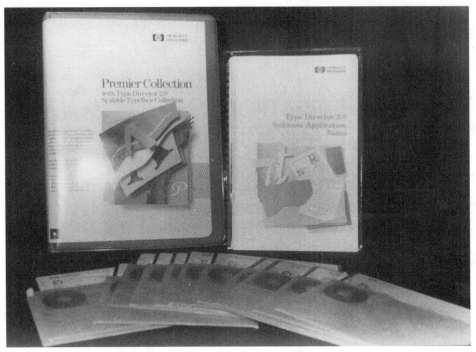

15-10 Hewlett-Packard's Type Director and Premier Font Collection. (Software courtesy Hewlett-Packard)

ries. Type Director requires 640K of RAM and a hard drive, and it supports mouse entry or keyboard selection through the arrow keys. The main menus (Fig. 15-11) provide for establishment of the program and system environment in which the fonts will be used, the display type and resolution, the printer type, and the programs supported (Fig. 15-12). The most popular software is listed for selection, while other programs not specifically named are lumped together as a generic unlisted application.

Best of all, this program creates typefaces for use with Epson 9-pin and 24-pin printers and compatibles, bringing font scaling to the great majority of printers, many of which were left in the typographic equivalent of a ghetto by the new technology.

Users load type files from disk and then place the type families in a directory in Type Director (Fig. 15-13). After loading all the typefaces necessary for the session, you move to the Make Fonts menu. Here the typefaces are listed, and you select those to be turned into screen and printer font files. Typefaces are listed as styles, and you are prompted to enter the sizes to make (Fig. 15-14). When the point sizes for all the selected typeface styles have been entered, Type Director creates necessary font files. Depending on the number of fonts (a font being a typeface in a specific style and point size) to be generated, this can take five or more minutes. As fonts are created, they are automatically placed into the

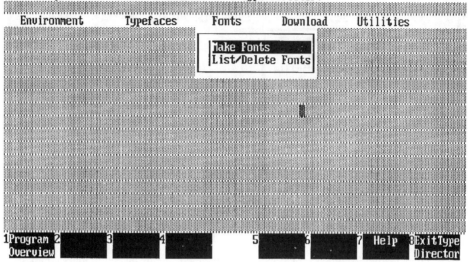

15-11 Type Director's menu driven environment. (Software courtesy Hewlett-Packard)

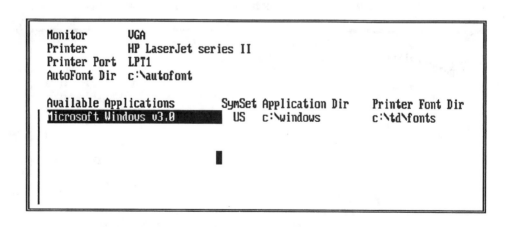

15-12 Type Director's hardware and software setup is in Environment menu. (Software courtesy Hewlett-Packard)

MAKE FONTS

Highlight a desired typeface, then press ENTER to save your selection.

Typefaces		Device	Ori	SymSet
	T SETUP [TDFONTS]			
	ndows v3.0			
	izes	Device	Ori	SymSet
CG Century Schoolbook		[P&S]	[P]	[US]
CG Century Schoolbook Bold		[P&S]	[P]	[US]
CG Century Schoolbook Bold Ital		[P&S]	[P]	[US]
CG Century Schoolbook Italic		[P&S]	[P]	[US]
Cooper Black		[P&S]	[P]	[US]
ITC Zapf Chancery Medium Italic		[P&S]	[P]	[US]
Revue Light		[P&S]	[P]	[US]
Revue Shadow		[P&S]	[P]	[US]
Uncial		[P&S]	[P]	[US]
University Roman		[P&S]	[P]	[US]

ESTIMATED SPACE REQUIRED 492K   SPACE AVAILABLE 1094K

1 Make Fonts	2 Get Setup	3 Save Setup	4 Delete Setup	5 Clear Screen	6	7 Help	8 Exit Menu

15-13 Fonts loaded from disks for selected Environment are displayed in fonts menu. (Software courtesy Hewlett-Packard)

MAKE FONTS

To select a typeface from the list, press ENTER.
    After all characteristics are specified, press F1 to make fonts.

MAKE FONT SETUP [TDFONTS]
Active Application: Microsoft Windows v3.0

Typeface	Point Sizes	Device	Ori	SymSet
↑CG CentSchl BdIt	10 12	[P&S]	[P]	[US]
CG CentSchl It	10 12	[P&S]	[P]	[US]
Cooper Black	14 24	[P&S]	[P]	[US]
ITCZapfChncyMdIt	14 24	[P&S]	[P]	[US]
Revue Light	12 14	[P&S]	[P]	[US]
Revue Shadow	12 14	[P&S]	[P]	[US]
Uncial	10 12	[P&S]	[P]	[US]
University Roman	10 12	[P&S]	[P]	[US]
ITCZapfChncyMdIt	36	[P&S]	[P]	[US]
↓				

ESTIMATED SPACE REQUIRED 492K   SPACE AVAILABLE 1094K

1 Make Fonts	2 Get Setup	3 Save Setup	4 Delete Setup	5 Clear Screen	6	7 Help	8 Exit Menu

15-14 Fonts are chosen from type families, and user specifies sizes to be created. (Software courtesy Hewlett-Packard)

proper directories so that they can be used immediately in the application that you specified. You can remove fonts from the application as desired.

If space is scarce—as it can be on a small hard drive or with very large type—you can order a reduced character set, choosing only those characters that will actually be used and omitting the more exotic ones that are seldom, if ever, used. You can also make a custom font menu for the target application using the Application Utility, which creates software support files for your program based on the fonts you designate for inclusion (although font menus are usually created automatically from the Type Director files).

The program can download up to 32 fonts to the printer, assigning each a distinctive font ID. Downloading might or might not be a good idea, depending on how the target application handles fonts and font ID numbers. Type Director does everything that needs to be done, and does it well. It is easy to use, and there are help files for almost every menu item or procedure. It brings pseudoscalable fonts to printers that do not have the Intellifont scaling hardware.

There are no real drawbacks except those attending soft fonts *per se:* creating and installing them consume time and disk space, and downloading a large number of fonts can be tedious. The fonts themselves are as good as can be found anywhere, even in PostScript, and are better than many found in type cartridges. For Epson and Epson-compatible impact dot matrix printers and for programs not running in Windows, Type Director is the best product available to enlarge and enliven typography.

Adobe Type Manager Adobe Type Manager from Adobe Systems arguably is the most useful printer utility ever written. It is a form of Display PostScript for type scaling only, using PostScript outline fonts for both display and printing. Adobe Type Manager is small, works entirely in the background, and produces the best printed type that can be had from your printer if you use Windows or a Macintosh computer.

ATM is basically the PostScript rasterization program, rewritten and transferred from the printer's ROM to the computer's RAM. The PostScript outline fonts that had previously been either in the printer or downloaded to the printer, are now kept in the computer. When a font is called for which there is no bitmapped version, ATM builds a bitmap from the appropriate outline font file. First, it scales the outline to the correct size. Second, it compares the outline to the resolution of the output device, whether printer or CRT, and fills in the outline with raster or scan lines of dots. Thus, the optimal appearance of the type is maintained across all platforms, whatever their configuration and resolution.

The advantages of such a system are plain: Typographic consistency from desktop to print shop is assured; the Adobe PostScript fonts are made available to almost everybody; and WYSIWYG computing is moved one step closer to reaching its one-for-one ideal state. The disadvantages are a little less plain: It takes time to build a typeface from scratch (a factor which, for display type building, cannot be hidden); it takes computing power (a factor which owners of older machines will be the first to notice); and it works only in a narrow, although widening Window.

Some of its necessary defects have been obviated by careful and clever programming. The speed of ATM has been improved so much over that of the original PostScript rasterizer, that Adobe has incorporated ATM into latter versions of the PostScript interpreter itself. Other faults can only be removed as more people move their computing to Windows and Windows itself is improved.

TrueType Speaking of improvements to Windows, the most desired is the inclusion of TrueType, the much travelled PostScript clone. Microsoft has added TrueType support to Windows 3.1, and has managed thereby to improve the pitifully slow printing from Windows using Windows typefaces.

TrueImage, the parent of TrueType, was begun as a PostScript alternative-plus product, compatible but different and cheaper. Microsoft and Apple acquired TrueImage and TrueType in order to wriggle free from the grasp of Adobe. Support for TrueImage and TrueType was to become the cornerstone of display and printing technology for both companies, but it has since been curtailed as the impracticality of supplanting Adobe has been recognized. Apple's System 7.0 for the Macintosh includes TrueType fonts, but they are not of much use, largely because so much has been invested in PostScript by so many already. TrueType in Windows, however, stands a better chance of success, since the alternatives have had relatively less of a headstart than they had in the Macintosh. Time and performance will tell. TrueType has been adopted in cartridge form by some companies, and it has been incorporated into some printers. The developmental problems in TrueType, such as dropouts (the tendency for portions of a character to disappear as the point size is reduced) and its general problem of acceptance, can be traced to the root problem: While PostScript is fully mature and in the vigor of its ascendancy, TrueImage is in its infancy after a premature birth. It is too early to tell what will come of it.

Roll your own fonts If you have an HP printer or compatible, you can choose to make your own soft fonts. There are many fonts already in the public domain and shareware catalogs, but if you cannot find what you want, you can build your own with a font editor.

One soft font editor, Quick Font!, is available through bulletin boards, national services, and from the publisher, Jamestown Software. It is a slick, fully functional, mouse-driven editor, capable of loading and modifying existing fonts or of creating new fonts from the baseline up.

The opening screen (Fig. 15-15) shows the Open File Dialogue box, from which you can select a typeface to edit. You can create a new file by clicking the mouse outside of the box, cancelling the dialogue. Movement up and down the levels of subdirectories is accomplished by clicking on the name of the parent or subdirectory. The default file form recognized has the .SFP extension (Fig. 15-16) used by Hewlett-Packard for its soft fonts, which means that Quick Font! can be used to alter HP fonts. You can change the extension mask to load other font file types consistent with the HP file structure, but designation of an invalid

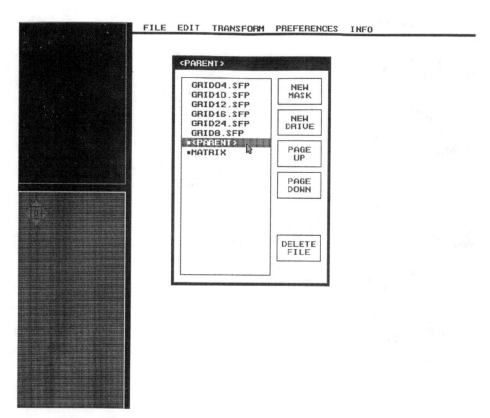

15-15   Quick Font editing program for HP compatible soft fonts.

file type will cause Quick Font! to crash back into DOS when it attempts to open the invalid file.

Once you load a file, the first ASCII alphabetic character (number 65 or uppercase A), is displayed in the editing grid (Fig. 15-17). It becomes rapidly apparent that editing a soft font that is to be downloaded to a laser printer is a lot of work. To make things easier, Quick Font! includes some basic drawing tools for Bezier curves, arcs, ellipses, circles, and boxes (Fig. 15-18). It also provides pattern filling and transformations, allowing characters to be made into slanted pseudo-italic formations, outlined text, shadowed text, or white on black text. Lines can be either black on white or white on black, according to which mouse button is clicked to terminate the line. You can magnify an area, or copy, cut, erase or paste an area. You can copy entire characters between font files, since the clipboard content is maintained. Characters or parts thereof can be flipped horizontally or vertically when pasted, and there is a choice of patterns to apply.

You can move through the character set from the keyboard simply by typing the letter to be edited or by selecting the Get New Character command from the Edit menu. If changes have been made to the character already in the matrix,

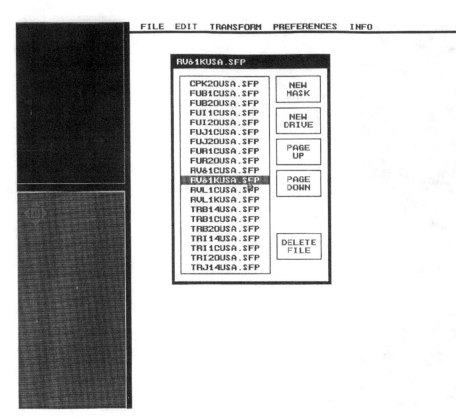

RV&1KUSA.SFP

CPK2OUSA.SFP
FUB1CUSA.SFP
FUB2OUSA.SFP
FUI1CUSA.SFP
FUI2OUSA.SFP
FUJ1CUSA.SFP
FUJ2OUSA.SFP
FUR1CUSA.SFP
FUR2OUSA.SFP
RV&1CUSA.SFP
RV&1KUSA.SFP
RVL1CUSA.SWP
RVL1KUSA.SFP
TRB14USA.SFP
TRB1CUSA.SFP
TRB2OUSA.SFP
TRI14USA.SFP
TRI1CUSA.SFP
TRI2OUSA.SFP
TRJ14USA.SFP

NEW
MASK

NEW
DRIVE

PAGE
UP

PAGE
DOWN

DELETE
FILE

15-16 Any font with .SFP suffix can be edited.

you have the option of saving or abandoning the changes before the next character is displayed.

Statistics for the font currently open are displayed at the lower left of the screen. The characteristics of the whole font can be altered by changing the file header, making a monospace font from a proportionally spaced one, for instance.

The Quick Font! editor does not produce screen or display fonts, only download font files, and is, therefore, more useful for DOS programs than for graphically based programs. Its mouse interface could use some improvement to bring it into line with other mouse-driven programs. Menu items are not highlighted when a menu is first pulled down. You must release the mouse button and then click again on the pulled-down menu in order to select an item. Better to be able, in one operation, to pull down the menu by depressing the mouse button, highlight menu items as the mouse moves through the menu with the button down, and select an item by releasing the mouse button.

Despite its limitations and minor faults, for the purpose of font creation, Quick Font! is quite useful. The program requires 512K RAM, DOS 3.x or higher, and works with Hercules, EGA, or VGA display cards. Version 1.5B of

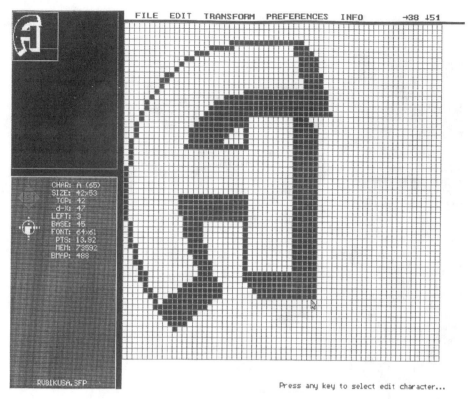

CHAR: A (65)
SIZE: 42x53
TOP: 42
d-x: 47
LEFT: 3
BASE: 45
FONT: 64x61
PTS: 13.92
MEM: 73592
BMAP: 488

RU81KUSA.SFP

Press any key to select edit character...

15-17   Large matrix of soft fonts is evident.

Quick Font! is in the Hewlett-Packard System Forum Library 2, DOS utilities, as QFONT1.ZIP on CompuServe.

Page description languages

The larger alternative to font files is the environment in which fonts exist, the Page Description Language (PDL). There are two major PDLs in use, Hewlett-Packard PCL, currently at Level 5, and Adobe PostScript.

PostScript has by far the greater utility and the wider acceptance of the two, being the standard PDL used in commercial typesetting equipment. PostScript is device-independent and can render the same effects on any device at the best resolution of that device. Therefore, the user of the desktop machine is able to move his work from a laser printer for proof printing to a phototypesetting machine for final press run without any conversion. This fact has guaranteed that page makeup programs running on desktop computers can be used successfully as front end devices for Compugraphic or other high-end equipment. PostScript is undeniably better at some things than is PCL. While font scaling has been

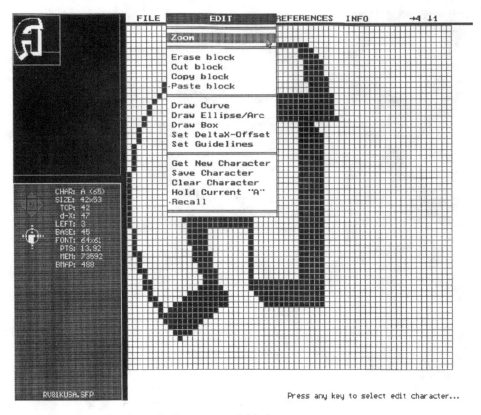

15-18 Numerous drawing primitives are available from menu.

added to PCL, and vector graphics are now possible with the importation of HP plotter commands to PCL, those are capabilities inherent in even the oldest Post-Script printer and handled much more competently by PostScript. PostScript is also better at fountains, binding text to arbitrary paths, clipping, text distortion, and other effects applied to text.

HP PCL is, on the other hand, the clear leader in desktop printing, simply because there are more Hewlett-Packard and PCL-compatible printers in use than any other type of laser printer. PCL is the language of the desktop, since most of the documents created in PCL are confined to the desktop environment, the in-house publications or the day-to-day personal missives of commerce and private communication. PCL is very quick with bitmapped graphics and fonts, and it can generally turn out a page of text much more quickly than a PostScript printer at any given font point size, if that size is available.

The only fly in the ointment, so to speak is that most people do not own laser printers, either of the PostScript or the PCL persuasion. Getting PostScript or PCL output from a common dot matrix impact or ink jet printer has long been desired.

Hewlett-Packard PCL

If you want or need to make PCL-compatible output on a dot matrix printer, there is now a way to do so cheaply.

LaserTwin LaserTwin, a product of Metro Software, is a printer utility that will "fool" the software drivers of your computer's applications into "thinking" that a PCL printer is attached. LaserTwin, in other words, is a PCL emulator. The emulation is LaserJet Series II compatible and is RAM-resident. It supports virtually the entire library of PCL effects: landscape orientation, gray scales, downloaded fonts, and all typographic styles such as bold, italic, underline, outline, and shadow.

LaserTwin works with almost any printer from Alps to Toshiba at its highest resolution, requires as a minimum an IBM PC, PC-XT, AT, PS/2, 386, 486, or their clones, DOS 2.0, hard drive and floppy.

As with all neat things, there are catches. The two most important ones are that it takes a great amount of time to drive a dot matrix printer at its highest graphic resolution (e.g., 316 or more dots per inch), and that it takes a great amount of disk space to store soft fonts which would normally be resident in the printer. At the price, however, if you can live with the catches, LaserTwin cannot be bettered for PCL output on a plain vanilla printer.

Adobe PostScript

PostScript is now available in cartridges and in cartridge emulations for laser printers, but it was available as a software emulation even before the cartridges hit the marketplace.

UltraScript The rock-bottom PostScript software emulation is UltraScript, a commercially distributed program developed by QMS and Adobe Systems, and formerly marketed through the QMS subsidiary Laser Connection. At one time it was ambitiously spread among several computer types, including the Amiga. It then suffered some occultation, due in part to the internal conflict resulting from the production of both PostScript hardware and software by QMS. The original program received complimentary reviews. It has been resurrected by PM Ware under OEM license from QMS. Not all software, good or bad gains its deserved fate, and the migration into a new publishing house should not be held against UltraScript. Many excellent products, from Willy's Jeep to Cricket Draw, have been sheltered under many roofs.

UltraScript requires as a minimum an AT or more powerful CPU, 1Mb of RAM, and 3Mb of free space on the computer's hard drive. It will run with less space given to it, but it will slow considerably. UltraScript PC has 13 fonts, while UltraScript PC Plus has 47 fonts. There are Mac versions called UltraScript and UltraScript Plus for the Macintosh.

The opening screen of UltraScript is shown in Fig. 15-19. The topmost rectangle shows the printer port and the default printer (the HP DeskJet), its resolution, paper size, and some headings that come into use as the program prints. The center rectangle contains the File, Configure, and Quit menus. The File

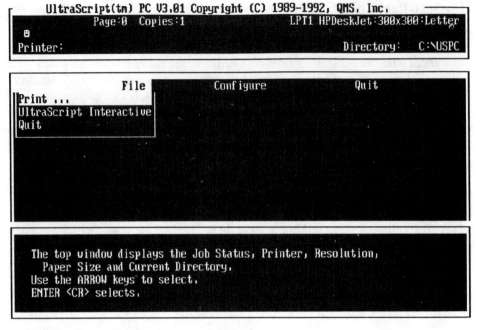

```
┌──── UltraScript(tm) PC V3.01 Copyright (C) 1989-1992, QMS, Inc. ────┐
│          Page:0  Copies:1                    LPT1 HPDeskJet:300x300:Letter │
│  ⊟                                                                         │
│  Printer:                                     Directory:    C:\USPC        │
│                                                                           │

              File              Configure              Quit
 ┌──────────────────────────┐
 │Print ...                 │
 │UltraScript Interactive   │
 │Quit                      │
 └──────────────────────────┘




 ┌──────────────────────────────────────────────────────────────────┐
 │  The top window displays the Job Status, Printer, Resolution,      │
 │    Paper Size and Current Directory.                               │
 │  Use the ARROW keys to select.                                     │
 │  ENTER <CR> selects.                                               │
 └──────────────────────────────────────────────────────────────────┘
```

15-19 UltraScript's opening screen.

menu Print command leads to submenus and dialogue boxes from which files are selected and the printing command is issued (Fig. 15-20). The Configure Menu contains two items, one to select the printer (Fig. 15-21) and the other to select the output destination, whether to a file or a port. UltraScript supports laser, BubbleJet, and impact printers as well as the default DeskJet, and, although more choices would be nice, you are likely to find a compatible printer from the rather short list offered. The box with the bright outline is the active one, and the grey-edged boxes are spawned from the first. The contents of the second and third boxes are updated (rather slowly, it must be said) when the printer choice is changed. You can select the items in those boxes by using the left or right arrow keys to activate their respective boxes, and then using the up and down arrow to change selections. Output is generally directed to a hardware port, so that if you have redirected printer output in DOS, as you would with DMP or for an ASP product, you must select from the logical BIOS devices rather than the hardware alternatives.

Attempting to print a file with a missing font will generate an error (Fig. 15-22). When printing, the middle rectangle is darkened and messages are displayed regarding the printing progress (Fig. 15-23). The percentage of the file rendered to the moment is displayed in the upper left corner of the top rectangle.

US does an adequate job with PostScript interpretation. It seems to have no trouble with purely graphical files. It is, however, very slow on a 286 PC. Figure

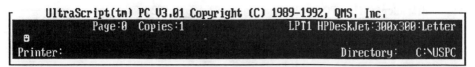

15-20 File selection box of UltraScript.

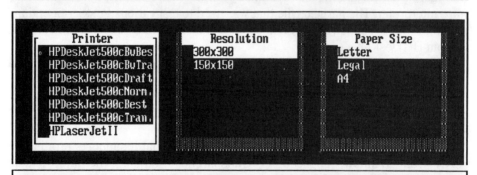

15-21 Printer selection and communications parameters in UltraScript.

```
  UltraScript(tm) PC V3.01 Copyright (C) 1989-1992, QMS, Inc.
 F%:100 D:1   Page:0  Copies:1                LPT1 HPLaserJetII:300x300:Letter

 Printer: OK                                  Directory:   C:\USPC


 ┌─UltraScript Output─────────────────────────────────────────────
 %%[ Printing File SAMPLE1.PS ]%%
 %%[ Starting Server ]%%
 QMS UltraScript PC
 %%[WARNING: Font "Albertan" not found, substituting Courier.]%%
 %%[ Starting Server ]%%

 Press Any Key To Return To Previous Menu




         CTRL-Break will suspend Printing
```

15-22   Center rectangle reports errors on file being printed.

15-24 was rendered from a demonstration file. It was printed on an HP LaserJet II equipped with 2.5Mb RAM. It took seven minutes and forty-five seconds to print. When printed to the TurboScript cartridge in the same printer, the file printed in forty-four seconds. On a LaserWriter Plus, the file printed in forty-five seconds. It was more than three times slower than even another PostScript emulation software interpreter. The garlic.ps file that was used to test various PostScript options took one hour to render, although it took less than five minutes of that time to print it on an HP DeskJet.

This is not to say that UltraScript should be tossed aside. It is capable, and running on a faster computer than that 12MHz 80286 upon which it was tested, it would turn in a speedier performance. It supports a variety of printers, including the Epson LQ-2550 and the HP DeskJet 500C, putting color PostScript output within reach of most people.

The biggest advantage offered by UltraScript is that it supports printing directly from Windows applications, transparently handling the intermediate process of spooling, so that printing proceeds as though the output were going directly to the printer. It requires, however, at least 2Mb of RAM in the computer to run from Windows.

For Macintosh users, UltraScript runs either under System 6.07 or System 7.0. It will also print directly from applications under either System (running in the background of MultiFinder 6.07 or Finder 7.0). UltraScript need not be on the startup disk to work with Mac applications, but it requires a hard drive.

```
┌─ UltraScript(tm) PC V3.01 Copyright (C) 1989-1992, QMS, Inc. ──────────┐
│ Printed:100% Page:2  Copies:1              LPT1 HPLaserJetII:300x300:Letter │
│ ▣                                                                          │
│ Printer: OK                                            Directory:   C:\USPC │
└────────────────────────────────────────────────────────────────────────────┘

┌─UltraScript Output──────────────────────────────────────────────────────┐
│ %%[ Starting Server ]%%                                                   │
│ 47 FSM fonts                                                              │
│ Sorting                                                                   │
│ Printing                                                                  │
│ 0 Type 1 fonts                                                            │
│ Sorting                                                                   │
│ Printing                                                                  │
│                                                                           │
└───────────────────────────────────────────────────────────────────────────┘

┌───────────────────────────────────────────────────────────────────────────┐
│                                                                             │
│                    CTRL-Break will suspend Printing                         │
│                                                                             │
└───────────────────────────────────────────────────────────────────────────┘
```

15-23 Top rectangle contains data on printer activity and printer type.

15-24 Sample output from UltraScript to LaserJet.

Freedom of Press Perhaps the best PostScript emulation interpreter is Freedom of Press (not Freedom of *the* Press), published by Custom Applications, Inc. It is used by UDP in their PostScript cartridge, and it works as well in software form as it does burned into hardware. In some ways, the software interpreter is better than its hardware counterpart.

Freedom of Press comes in two forms, Freedom of Press, with a full set of 35 PostScript-compatible fonts and Freedom of Press Light, with 17 fonts and more limited printer support. Both FOP and FOP Light come in versions for the Macintosh and MS-DOS computers.

As with most programs that have cross-platform versions, there are positive and negative comparisons that can be made between the twins, and preference for one over the other could be attributed to prejudice shaped by an inclination toward one computer rather than another.

FOP for the Macintosh is decidedly easier to use than its MS-DOS sibling. The Macintosh version has two parts. The spooler, called FP Spooler runs under MultiFinder or System 7.0, resides in the background, and emulates a LaserWriter as a printing device. Freedom of Press itself takes the files spooled by FP Spooler, translates them from PostScript into raster data for the selected printer, and sends them to the printer. If both the spooler and FOP are running simultaneously under MultiFinder in System 6.0x, and you print a document from another program, the spooler and FOP automatically and transparently take the print file and send it to the printer, just as though the document were being sent immediately to the printer rather than through two other programs. Under System 7.0, the automatic feature does not work, but printing begins as soon as you switch to FOP from the program that was the source of the print file.

FOP Light for the Macintosh can render PostScript files to more than twenty brands of printers, as well as to PCX file format, the screen, to itself, and to PCL files (Fig. 15-25). Output can even be sent to the Trash for test purposes, the equivalent of printing to a null device in DOS. Most of the common printer brands are represented by at least one model, and some—like Epson and Hewlett-Packard—by a dozen or more (Fig.15-26).

Once you have selected a printer, there are options for each printer which permit flexibility in destination port selection (Fig. 15-27),baud rates (from 300 to 57,600 for serial connections, Fig. 15-28), resolution, and color for those that are capable. Color is usually selected at the sacifice of high resolution (Fig. 15-29).

FOP also has preferences of its own to set, including whether the program should run in the background, whether files should be deleted automatically after printing, and whether PostScript binary data ought to be accepted, an important consideration if bitmapped files are being printed.

File selection and printing can be conducted either manually or automatically. In background operation, files generated by the spooler are sent to a PS Output

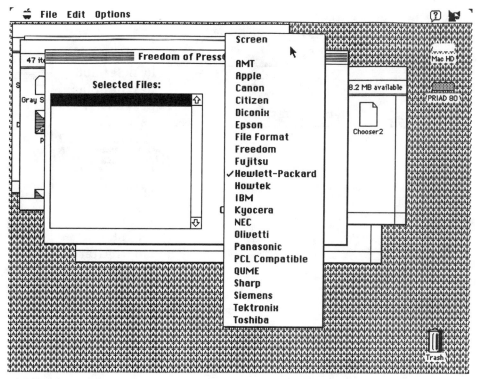

15-25 Printer brands supported by Mac version of Freedom of Press Light. (Freedom of Press Light software courtesy Custom Applications)

folder contained in the Freedom of Press folder within the System Folder. Any files sent to the PS Output Folder are selected for printing by FOP without user intervention, and the printing begins if Auto Print has been checked in the File menu. Manual operation lets you choose files and establish their order of printing.

On the Macintosh, PostScript files are generated in three different ways. Some programs like Cricket Draw or Adobe Illustrator can generate their own PostScript and save the text files to disk. In most programs, PostScript is generated only when a LaserWriter has been selected as the printer and only at the time the Print command is selected from the File menu of the applications. Under Systems prior to System 7.0, you created PostScript files by giving the Print command, clicking on the OK radio button in the LaserWriter print dialogue box, and then holding down the Command-F keys or Command-K keys immediately. This would send a control sequence to the operating system to direct the PostScript output to a Print file rather than to a printer. (When a LaserWriter is the printer, the operating system converts the document to be printed into PostScript and then sends the PostScript

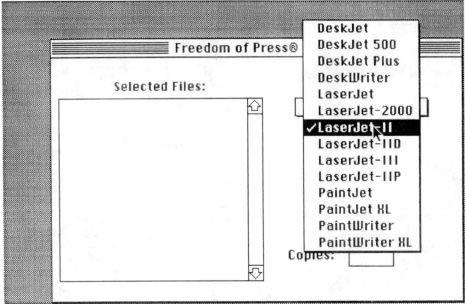

15-26   HP printers supported by Macintosh Freedom of Press Light. (Freedom of Press Light software courtesy Custom Applications)

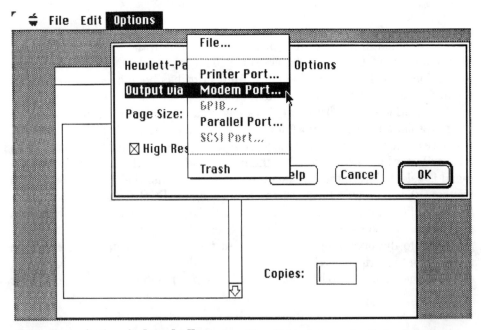

15-27   Port selections for LaserJet II. (Freedom of Press Light software courtesy Custom Applications)

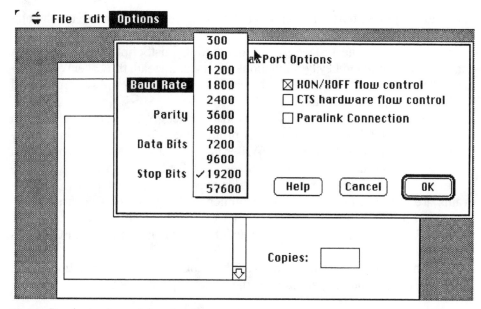

15-28 Baud rates for serial port on Mac. (Freedom of Press Light software courtesy Custom Applications)

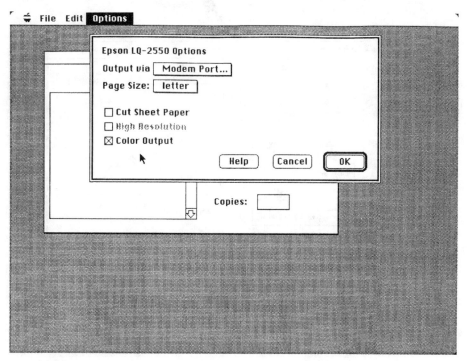

15-29 Color PostScript output is supported for some printers. (Freedom of Press Light software courtesy Custom Applications)

output to the printer port. The command key sequence merely redirects the output to another destination.)

In System 7.0, the procedure for generating PostScript output has been changed. No command key combinations are used. Instead, the LaserWriter dialogue box contains a check box which, when selected, orders the system to send the PostScript output to a file.

The spooler provided for FOP runs in the background and is selected in Chooser as though it were a LaserWriter printer (Fig. 15-30). (Background printing must be turned off for the LaserWriter in Chooser if background operation for FOP WAS set in the FOP preferences. The FP Spooler runs in the background as a MultiFinder application under System 6.0x. In System 7.0 all programs are run in a multitasking environment.) When printing occurs from a program, the PostScript created for the LaserWriter is sent to the LaserWriter named FP Spooler, and the spooler sends it to the PS Output Folder. FOP takes the file from there.

Printing in the foreground, you see the progress of the translation of the PostScript file into bitmapped data for the selected printer as a moving horizon-

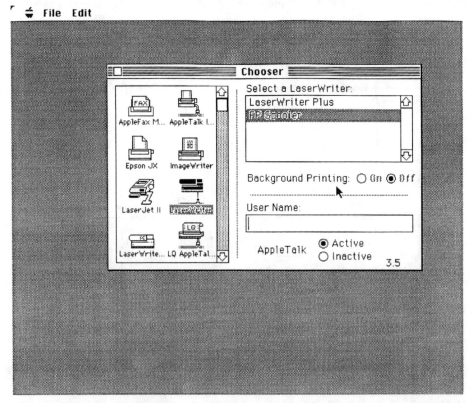

15-30 FP Spooler is selected as a LaserWriter from Mac's Chooser DA. (Freedom of Press Light software courtesy Custom Applications)

tal bar. When the file has been translated, then the actual printing is done, with a small page icon gradually filling with black as the printer completes the tasks.

The mechanics aside, the program performs with not quite absolute fidelity to the LaserWriter. The fonts used by FOP are the same ones used in the UDP cartridge and are not quite as attractive as Adobe fonts. But FOP also can use Adobe Type Manager fonts, so that can be worked around with any fonts not supplied with FOP. In that regard, FOP Light would be a better choice than the full-featured FOP, since the fonts in the Light version are restricted to the Times, Courier, and Helvetica families. Any other PostScript fonts included in a document would come from ATM and would be, therefore, exactly what was expected.

Freedom of Press is very quick when used with a laser printer. The demonstration file from another program which took seven minutes and forty-five seconds to render was rendered by the DOS version of FOP in one minute and fifty-six seconds, same computer and same printer. The garlic.ps file was printed in 22 minutes and 58 seconds, compared to the hour recorded by another PostScript emulation program, again to the LaserJet II. The Macintosh version printed in less than two minutes.

Both the Macintosh and the PC were connected to the LaserJet through an ASP JetWay, which is serially connected to the computers and connects to the parallel port of the LaserJet. The maximum speed permitted by the Mac version of FOP is 57,600 baud, while the MS-DOS version uses the serial port at whatever speed has been set. The maximum speed of the JetWay serial ports is 115,200. Therefore, the 80286 PC communicated with the LaserJet at twice the speed of the Mac, which was running the serial modem port at 57,600 baud. Yet, because the Macintosh used was an SE/30, which has a full 32-bit 68030 CPU running at 16 MHz and floating point arithmetic co-processor, it was able to beat the MS-DOS version of FOP, despite the serial handicap. The Macintosh version requires Macintosh Plus or later machine, System 6.02 or higher, 2Mb of RAM (MultiFinder or System 7.0 partition, or Finder with a 2Mb machine), and 2.5Mb of hard drive space. It can use as much as 8Mb of RAM.

The MS-DOS version of FOP Light (as distinguished from the Macintosh version) is of one piece, but it requires a separate setup program. FOP is installed from a floppy drive to the computer's hard drive. It creates a directory called FREEDOM, with several subdirectories, including one where PostScript files can be placed for automatic printing by FOP.

FOP requires an 80286 or later machine, 4Mb of disk space (program files and working space combined), DOS 2.1 or higher, and 640K of RAM. An optional memory card and floating point co-processor are recommended.

After installation, the program runs the setup software, a separate program called FPCHANGE, which configures FOP for your computer and printer. You are asked to select the drive from which FOP will be working, the model of printer (more than 130 are listed), the port to which the printer is connected, and the paper size. You may run FPCHANGE at any time thereafter if you wish to change any of the parameters, such as the printer. FPCHANGE will ask permission to alter your computer's PATH command line to allow FOP to be run from anywhere in DOS. After that, FOP runs from the configuration file.

To use FOP on the MS-DOS machine, you must first have a PostScript file for FOP to interpret. Generating PostScript files on MS-DOS computers is a program-by-program affair. Each word processor or page makeup program has its own procedure for saving the PostScript file to disk. This is why each program has a manual. FOP is not selective about the source of the PostScript file: you can write your own or import it from another computer.

Assuming that you have managed to save a PostScript file, you run FOP, either by typing FREEDOM, which will cause FOP to load and to print any Postscript files that it finds in the subdirectory PS, or by typing FP-ASK, which causes FOP to load and to inquire the name and location of the file you want to print. This interactive command line is the one that will probably prove most useful. The opening screen is shown in Fig.15-31.

```
                    Freedom of Press
        Copyright 1990 by Custom Applications Inc.
              (Revision 2.5  07-Sep-90)

              Serial # FP1028684
          Licensed to H.W. LaBadie, Jr.


Output Device: HP-LaserJet-II on LPT1

Current Search Path:
Current File Name:
Current File:
Currently INITIALIZING




    ┌Percent of File Interpreted═══════════════════════
    │
    │0─10──20──30──40──50──60──70──80──90──100│
    │
    └Percent of Page Imaged═══════════════════════
```

15-31 MS-DOS version of Freedom of Press Light is text based. (Freedom of Press Light software courtesy Custom Applications)

Once a file has been specified for printing, FOP goes about interpreting it for the printer, one page at a time, with progress shown as a moving bar as in the Macintosh version. After the page has been interpreted, it is sent to the printer, with another bar graph representation of the progress to the moment (Fig. 15-32).

FOP on the MS-DOS side is more complicated to run , because of the vicissitudes of saving PostScript from programs with inconsistent approaches to

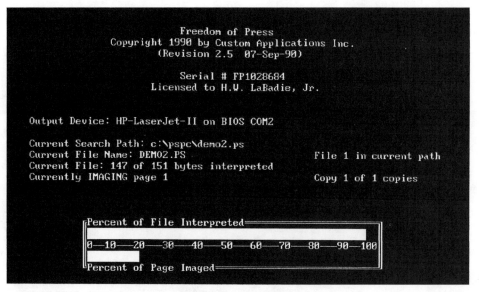

```
                     Freedom of Press
         Copyright 1990 by Custom Applications Inc.
                  (Revision 2.5  07-Sep-90)

                    Serial # FP1028684
               Licensed to H.W. LaBadie, Jr.


  Output Device: HP-LaserJet-II on BIOS COM2

  Current Search Path: c:\pspc\demo2.ps
  Current File Name: DEMO2.PS                File 1 in current path
  Current File: 147 of 151 bytes interpreted
  Currently IMAGING page 1                   Copy 1 of 1 copies



        ┌Percent of File Interpreted═══════════════════════════
        │0─10──20──30──40──50──60──70──80──90──100│
        └Percent of Page Imaged═══════════════
```

15-32 Report of file printing progress is shown as moving bar graph (Freedom of Press Light software courtesy Custom Applications).

printing and file saving, and because changes to its parameters—including the printer—must be made from an independent program. Its performance, however, is excellent.

GoScript, PreScript, T-Script There are other PostScript interpreters. GoScript is from LaserGo, the oldest of the software substitutes for PostScript printers. PreScript is another interpreter, published by Pan Overseas Computers. For the Macintosh, Teletypesetting publishes T-Script. None is quite as polished as FOP.

Appendix A

Sources

RAM chips, SIMMs, and SIPPs

RAM chips can be purchased from many vendors. RAM boards and SIMMs can usually be purchased from the same dealers who sell chips. Prices are extremely volatile, so even the price listed in the most recent magazines will likely be three months out of date. Always call several dealers to ensure that you get the best price. Watch out for those dealers that have minimum order requirements or special handling charges. What you save on the RAM might be more than lost on the extra charges. Most computer magazines have listings for RAM vendors; Computer Shopper lists dozens. Here are some:

Access Computer Components, Inc.
P.O. Box 797602
Dallas, TX 75379
(800) 332-3778

B.G. Micro
P.O. Box 280298
Dallas, TX 75228
(214) 271-5546

H. Co.
17922 Sky Park Cir. #F
Irvine, CA 92714
(800) 726-2477

H & J Electronics International
2400 West Cypress Creek Rd.
Ft. Lauderdale, FL 33309
(800) 275-2447

IC Express
15140 Valley Blvd.
City of Industry, CA 91744
(800) 877-8188

Jameco
1355 Shoreway Rd.
Belmont, CA 94002
(800) 831-4242

JDR Microdevices
2233 Samaritan Dr.
San Jose, CA 95124
(800) 538-5000

Kenosha Computer Center
2133 91st St.
Kenosha, WI 53140
(800) 255-2989

L.A. Trade
20930 South Normandie
Torrance, CA 90502
(800) 433-3726

Leo Electronics, Inc.
P.O. Box 11307
Torrance, CA 90501
(800) 421-9565

Microprocessors Unlimited
24000 South Peoria
Beggs, OK 74421
(918) 267-4961

MicroTech
7304 15th Ave. N.E.
Seattle, WA 98115
(800) 521-9035

Shecom
22755 Savi Ranch Pky., Unit G
Yorba Linda, CA 92687
(800) 366-4433

Storage Devices, Inc.
17300 Saturn Ln., Suite 110
Houston, TX 77058
(800) 835-3023

Universal Memory Products
15451 Redhill, Suite E
Tustin, CA 92680
(800) 678-8648

Panasonic RAM upgrade kits:

Macaw Orchard
P.O. Box 9385
Salt Lake City, UT 84109
(800) 657-2885

Dot matrix ROM upgrades
Epson NLQ ROM

Dots-Perfect for FX/JX, MX, RX:

Dresselhaus Computer Products
8560 Vineyard Ave. Bldg. 405
Rancho Cucamonga, CA 91730
(800) 368-7737

Dots-Perfect will also work in the following printers, manufactured by Epson but packaged under other names:

IBM Graphics Printer, IBM Personal Computer Printer, IBM 5152, Hewlett-Packard 82905 A & B, Texas Instruments PHD 2500, Texas Instruments 99/4, Victor 6020, Wang PC-PM010, NorthStar MX, Sperry 5, Sperry P80RA, Hewlett-Packard 82906A, Wang PC-016-FX.

Installation of Dots-Perfect in Hewlett-Packard models will render them unresponsive to HP codes, converting them to Epson compatibles.

Okidata IBM ROM

Alpha Scientific
P.O. Box 66
Chesterfield, MO 63006
(314) 878-6871

Seikosha 1000 & 2000 Apple ROMs

Seikosha America
Parts Department
(800) 825-5349

Dot matrix interfaces
Epson

RS-232 Interface and Buffer
RS-422 Interface and Buffer
Mega Buffer Centronics Interface and Buffer

Image Technology, Inc.
5994 South St. Paul Way
Littleton, CO 80121

Okidata

Okidata sells service manuals, parts, and accessories to end users through a network of dealers and regional parts distributors. To find the dealer or distributor nearest you, call or write to:

Okidata, an Oki America Company
532 Fellowship Rd.
Mount Laurel, NJ 08054
(800) OKI-DATA, (609) 235-2600

Panasonic

Panasonic sells accessories such as optional interfaces through its Retail Accessories & Supplies Center.

Panasonic Retail Accessories & Supplies Center
2130 Townline Rd.
Peoria, IL 61615-1560
(800) 346-4768

Panasonic service and repair manuals can be purchased from:

Matsushita Services Co.
Division of Matsushita Electric Corp. of America
Service Literature Distribution Center
P.O. Box 848
Arlington Heights, IL 60006

Matsushita is the parent company of Panasonic, Technics, Quasar, etc. Service manuals can be purchased for individual products or for an an entire line of products. You can subscribe to yearly purchase plans that will cover all products issued in a product line during the twelve months from July to June of the year following. The yearly plan includes all subsequent technical supplements for service revisions.

For other printer companies, see the listing at the end of this appendix.

Color options

Color kits, ribbons, etc. for Citizen and Seikosha printers are available from:

Citizen America Corp.
2450 Broadway Suite 600
P.O. Box 4003
Santa Monica, CA 90404-3060
(213) 453-0614

Seikosha-Epson America
10 Industrial Ave.
Mahwah, NJ 07430
(800) 338-2609, 1-201-327-7227

or from authorized dealers such as:

Lyco Computer
P.O. Box 5088
Jersey Shore, PA 17740
(800) 233-8760

Printers Plus
1400 Duke St.
Alexandria, VA 22314
(800) 321-5781

MidWest Micro-Peripherals
6910 U.S. Rte. 36 East
Fletcher, OH 45362
(800) 972-8822

Ink jet printer options
Canon Bubble Jets
Sheetfeeders, font cards for Bubble Jets:

Canon USA, Inc.
Printer Division
1 Canon Plaza
Lake Success, NY 11042
(800) 848-4123, 1-516-488-6700

Hewlett-Packard DeskJet cartridges
Hewlett-Packard Co.
Customer Information Center
(800) 752-0900

Headquarters for DeskJet Printer Division:

Hewlett-Packard Co.
Vancouver Division
P.O.Box 8906
Vancouver, WA 98668-9977

HP Direct
P.O. Box 44548
San Francisco, CA 94144-4548
(408) 553-7888, (800) 538-8787

There are Hewlett-Packard authorized dealers and regional sales offices located through the United States and in most countries around the world. Consult your local directory or directory assistance to find the HP representative nearest to you.

Other dealers:

Business Computer Systems
2216 Commerce Pky.
Virginia Beach, VA

Computer Business Mart
10215 Buena Vista #A
Santee, CA 92071
(800) 441-1491

Computer Discount Warehouse
2840 Maria
Northbrook, IL 60062
(800) 726-4239

First Source International
36 Argonaut, Suite 140
Aliso Viejo, CA 92656
(800) 535-5892

Pacific Data Products
25 in One! Cartridge for the HP DeskJet
9125 Rehco Rd.
San Diego, CA 92121
(619) 552-0880

UDP Computer Products
2908 Oregon Ct. Suite I-2
Torrance, CA 90503
(800) 888-4413

Computer Peripherals, Inc.
DeskSet!
667 Rancho Canejo Blvd.
Newbury Park, CA 91320
(800) 854-7600

Logic boards, paper motors, etc. for Hewlett-Packard DeskJets

Hewlett-Packard Corporate Parts Center
333 Logue Ave.
Mountain View, CA 94043
(415) 968-9200

Page printer options and accessories

The major companies producing third party accessories and options for laser and other page printers are:

Pacific Data Products
9125 Rehco Rd.
San Diego, CA 92121
(619) 552-0880

Font cartridges, PostScript emulation cartridges, programmable font cartridges, memory expansion boards, printer network hardware, plotters.

UDP Data Products
2908 Oregon Ct. Suite I-2
Torrance, CA 90503
(800) 888-4413

Font cartridges, PostScript emulation cartridges, memory expansion boards, paper cassettes.

Computer Peripherals Inc.
667 Rancho Canejo Blvd.
Newbury Park, CA 91320
(800) 854-7600

Font cartridges, PostScript emulation cartridges, memory expansion boards, printer network hardware.

Adobe Systems
1585 Charleston Rd.
P.O. Box 7900
Mountain View, CA 94039-7900
(800) 833-6687

Adobe PostScript cartridge for Hewlett-Packard LaserJet Series II.

Bitstream
215 1st St.
Cambridge, MA 02142
(800) 522-3668

FontCity selectively programmed font cartridge.

Makers of high-resolution controller boards

D P Tek
9920 East Harry
Witchita, KS 67207
(316) 687-3000

LaserMaster
6900 Shady Oak Rd.
Eden Prairie, MN 55344
(619) 944-9696

Xänte Corporation
2559 Emogene St.
Mobile, AL 36616-0526
(205) 476-8189

Source of Custom Crystals for laser engine high-resolution modification:

U.S. Crystal
Fort Worth, TX
(817) 921-3013

You will need to know several things before ordering crystals to boost the dpi and lpi of your laser printer. First, determine the frequency of the crystals by multiplying the frequency of the crystals already in the printer by $X/300$, where X is the number of dpi or lpi that you wish to achieve. In most cases, be satisfied with 400 dpi, since it will place acceptable amounts of stress on the scanning motor. The frequency will be in Megahertz (MHz). Second, determine the tolerance, sometimes found on the crystal, sometimes obtainable from service literature, perhaps obtainable from the technical help line of the printer manufacturer. If you cannot determine the tolerance, let it be 1%, which has a good chance of being right. Third, you will need to know if the crystal is series or parallel capacitated. If it is series, which is the case in all CX engines and probably the case in others, then you are home free. If it is parallel, then you must find out the value from the usual sources.

With that information, you can order crystals. But be prepared to order 20 or more of each and to have them sent to your company (make one up if necessary).

The manufacturer of your printer also makes proprietary accessories for the printer, and may be the only source for some types of options, such as RAM cards, paper cassettes, network interfaces, or PostScript options. Proprietary options will always be higher priced than a third party option, if it exists.

Other hardware

LaserWriter II 32-pin logic board connectors

AT&T Fastech Printed Circuit Board Connector Systems
Insulation displacement connector (IDC) 963T-32, comcode number
105732515.

Cables, switch boxes,buffers, data converters, printer sharing

Altex Electronics, Inc.
11342 IH-35 North
San Antonio, TX 78233
(800) 531-5369, (512) 637-3200

Cables, cable components, gender changers, manual and automatic switch
boxes, data converters, printer-sharing hardware.

ASP Computer Products, Inc.
160 San Gabriel Dr.
Sunnyvale, CA 94086
(800) 445-6190, (408) 746-2965

Makers of SNAP, JetWay, and ServerJet printer-sharing/network
products.

Buffalo Products, Inc.
2805 19th St. SE
Salem, OR 97302-1520
(800) 345-2356

Makers of automatic multiple input/output switching buffers and data
converters.

Cables To Go
(800) 225-8646

Cables, gender changers, switches.

Central Computer Products
300 Central Ave.
Fillmore, CA 93015-1921
(800) 456-4123

Buffers, data converters.

C-Gate International
2960 Gordon Ave.
Santa Clara, CA 95051
(408) 730-0673

Cables, switch boxes.

Computer Friends, Inc.
14250 NW Science Park Dr.
Portland, OR 97229
(800) 547-3303

Parallel Link printer-sharing devices.

Dalco Electronics
223 Pioneer Blvd.
Springboro, OH 45066
(800) 445-5342

Cables, cable components, gender changers, manual and automatic switch boxes, data converters, printer-sharing hardware.

Dresselhaus Computer Products
8560 Vineyard Ave. Bldg. 405
Rancho Cucamonga, CA 91730
(800) 368-7737

Automatic printer switches and printer-sharing devices.

National Computer Accessories
769 North 16th St., Suite 200
Sacramento, CA 95814-0527
(916) 441-1568

Cables, switches, buffers, data converters, printer stands.

PowerPlus
4932 Sharp St.
Dallas, TX 75247
(800) 878-5530

Cables, gender changers, manual and automatic switch boxes, buffers, data converters, printer stands.

Technologic Systems
421 South Main St.
Marysville, OH 43040
(513) 644-2230

Buffers.

Vendors of printer options

Chenesko Products, Inc.
2221 Fifth Ave., Suite 4
Ronkonkoma, NY 11779
(516)467-3205

LaserPlex printer-sharing interfaces for HP LaserJets, toner cartridges, and toner refilling materials.

Laser Press and Graphics (LPG)
4888 Stamp Rd.
Marlow Heights, MD 20748
(800) 628-4517

Laser printer options and accessories, bin feeders, PostScript and font cartridges, printer-sharing devices and interfaces, soft fonts, RAM cards, high-resolution controllers, etc.

Printer Connection
8394 Terminal Rd.
Newington, VA 22122
(800) 622-7060

Laser printer accessories and upgrades.

Printers Plus
P.O. Box 3069
Chesterfield, MO 63006
(800) 562-2727

Options and accessories for most printers.

Printer Works
3481 Arden Rd.
Hayward, CA 94545
(510) 887-6116

Laser Printer upgrades, high-resolution controllers, PostScript controllers, paper cassettes, etc.

Publishing Perfection
W 88 N 16444 Main St.
P.O. Box 307
Menomonee Falls, WI 53051
(800) 782-5974

Laser printer options and upgrades, high-resolution controllers, PostScript options, font cartridges, soft fonts, etc.

Mendolson Electronics Co., Inc.
340 East First St.
Dayton, OH 45402
(800) 422-3525
IBM Actionwriter typewriter computer printer interface.

Soft fonts

The number of companies making downloaded fonts is very large and growing. Agfa-Compugraphic, Adobe, International Typeface Company (ITC), Linotype-Hell, Monotype, and other houses famous for their conventional type have converted their libraries of designs to electronic form, and the same typefaces that were once used only in printing presses are now seen in computer displays. Most of these faces are licensed to vendors who create collections for various computer platforms. Although the fonts downloaded to the printers will be the same, the screen fonts for an IBM and a Mac will be in different formats.

In addition to licensed fonts, some companies sell "equivalent" typefaces; that is, copies of faces with well-known names. Instead of a licensed form of Monotype Times Roman, the vendor will draw its own type, modelled after the Times Roman, and call it TMS RMN or some such pseudonymous confection. Type names are copyright protected, but type designs are not. In many instances, the copies are of a quality equal to the originals, and in many instances they are not. Ask to see a printout from any type product before purchasing. Do not judge by name alone.

Adobe Systems, Inc.
(800) 833-6687, (415) 961-4400

Agfa-Compugraphic
(800) 633-1900, (800) 227-2780

Bitstream
(800) 522-3668, (616) 497-6222

Casady & Greene, Inc.
(800) 359-4920, (408) 624-8716

Linguist's SoftWare
Macintosh Foreign Language PostScript Fonts
(206) 775-1130

Linotype-Hell
(800) 633-1900

Font vendors:

For Hewlett-Packard Intellifont-for-Windows and Type Director 2.0, see listings above and below.

Image Club Graphics, Inc.
1902 11th St. SE, Suite 5
Calgary, Alberta, Canada T2G 3G2
(800) 661-9410

Precision Type
47 Mall Dr.
Commack, New York
(800) 248-3668

Other software

MS-DOS

DMP Spooler

DMP Software
1223 Wilshire Blvd., Suite 199
Santa Monica, CA 90403

$18 registration/purchase fee.

FX Matrix Epson 9-Pin Printer Font Editor
LQ Matrix Epson 24-Pin Printer Font Editor

Jimmy Paris Software
906 Old Farm Rd.
Charlottesville, VA 22903
(804) 295-5496

$18 registration/purchase fee

Quick Font! 1.5 (laser printer and ink jet printer soft font editor)

Jamestown Software
2508 Valley Forge Dr.
Madison, WI 53719
(608) 271-2090

$80 registration/purchase fee

Downld.COM Soft font downloader

R.J. Holmgren
(212) 749-7882
BBS: (516) 536-8723

Public domain/shareware publishers

Public Brand Software
P.O. Box 51315
Indianapolis, IN 46251
(800) 426-3475

The Software Labs
3767 Overland Ave., #112-115
Los Angeles, CA 90034
(800) 359-9998

Commercial software

Freedom Of Press
Freedom Of Press Light
Freedom Of Press Professional

PostScript compatible emulation software for MS-DOS and Macintosh computer systems.

Custom Applications, Inc.
900 Technology Park Dr., Bldg. 8
Billerica, MA 01821
(800) 873-4367, (508) 667-8585

GoScript!

PostScript software emulation.

LaserGo, Inc.
9235 Trade Place
San Diego, CA 92126
(619) 530-2400

LaserTwin

Hewlett-Packard PCL software compatible emulator for IBM and compatible MS-DOS computers. Supports most dot matrix, ink jet, and laser printers.

Metro Software, Inc.
1870 W. Prince Rd., Suite 70
Tuscon, AZ 85705

UltraScript PC and UltraScript for Macintosh.

PostScript emulation software for IBM MS-DOS and compatibles and Macintosh.

PM Ware
346 State Pl.
Escondido, CA 92029
(800) 845-4843

Macintosh

Bitmapped fonts can be created and edited in Apple's Resource Editor, available from most Macintosh public domain software publishers. Other printing utilities are also available in shareware or public domain software.

Public domain/shareware publishers

Budgetbytes
P.O. Box 2248
Topeka, KS 66601
(913) 271-6022

Educorp
742 Genevieve, Suite D
Solana Beach, CA 92075
(619) 259-0255

Commercial software

MacPrint

Chooser-selected printer drivers for Hewlett-Packard LaserJet and DeskJet printers. Support for LaserJet font cartridges.

Insight Development Corp.
2200 Powell St., Suite 500
Emeryville, CA 94608-9976
(510) 652-4115

Addresses of some major printer manufacturers

Advanced Matrix Technology
765 Flynn Rd.
Camarillo, CA 93012
(800) 637-7878, (805) 494-4221

AEG Olympia, Inc.
P.O. Box 3800
Somerville, NJ 08876
(800) 999-6872, (201) 231-8300

AT & T Computer Systems
55 Corporate Dr.
Bridgewater, NJ 08807
(800) 247-1212

Axonix Corp.
1214 Wilmington Ave.
Salt Lake City, UT 84106
(800) 866-9797, (801) 466-9797

Brother International Corp.
200 Cottontail Ln.
Somerset, NJ 08873
(800) 284-HELP, (908) 356-8880

Canon USA, Inc.
Printer Division
1 Canon Plaza
Lake Success, NY 11042
(516) 488-6700, (800) 848-4123

CIE America, Inc.
2515 McCabe Way
Irvine, CA 92714
(800) 877-1421, (714) 833-8445

Citizen America Corp.
2450 Broadway, Suite 600
P.O. Box 4003
Santa Monica, CA 90404-3060
(213) 453-0614

Dataproducts Corp.
6200 Canoga Ave.
Woodland Hills, CA 91637
(818) 887-8000

DCS/Fortis Inc.
1820 West 20th Street, #220
Torrance, CA 90501
(800) 736-4847, (213) 782-6090

Epson America
Torrance, CA
(800) 922-8911

Fujitsu America, Inc.
3055 Orchard Dr.
San Jose, CA 95134
(800) 626-4686, (408) 432-1300

Genicom Corp.
1 Genicom Dr.
Waynesboro, VA 22980
(800) 443-1347, (703) 949-1000

IBM Corp.
(800) IBM 2468

Laser Computer, Inc.
800 North Church St.
Lake Zurich, IL 60047
(708) 540-8086

Mannesmann Tally Corp.
8301 South 180th St.
Kent, WA 98032
(800) 843-1347, (206) 251-5524

Memorex Telex Corp.
6422 East 41st St.
Tulsa, OK 74135
(800) 331-2623, (918) 627-1111

Okidata, an Oki America Co.
532 Fellowship Rd.
Mount Laurel, NJ 08054
(800) OKI-DATA, (609) 235-2600

Olivetti Office USA
765 U.S. Highway 202
Somerville, NJ 08876
(800) 527-2960, (201) 526-8200

Packard Bell Electronics
9425 Canoga Ave.
Chatsworth, CA 91311
(800) 733-4422, (818) 773-4400

Panasonic Communications & Systems Co.
2 Panasonic Way
Secaucus, NJ 07094
(800) 742-8086, (201) 348-7000

Printek, Inc.
1517 Townline Rd.
Benton Harbor, MI 49022
(800)368-4636, (616)925-3200

Sanyo Business Systems Corp.
51 Joseph St.
Moonachie, NJ 07074
(800)524-0047, (201)440-9300

Seikosha-Epson America
10 Industrial Ave.
Mahwah, NJ 07430
(800)338-2609, (201)327-7227

Star Micronics America, Inc.
420 Lexington Ave., Suite 2702
New York, NY 10170
(800)447-4700, (212)986-6770

Texas Instruments, Inc.
P.O. Box 202230
Austin, TX 78720-2230
(800)527-3500

Toshiba America Information Systems, Inc.
9740 Irvine Blvd.
Irvine, CA 92718
(800)587-6300, (714)583-3000

Unisys Corp.
P.O. Box 500
Blue Bell, PA 19424
(215)986-4011

Telephone numbers of manufacturers by printer type

Dot matrix printers

Advanced Communications, Inc. ....(408)749-9845
ALPS America ....(800)828-2577
Amstrad, Inc..(214)518-0668
Anritsu America, Inc. ....(800)255-7234
Apple Computer, Inc..(408)996-1010
Bull HN Information Systems, Inc..(508)294-6000
C-Tech Electronics, Inc..(800)347-4017
Computer Products Plus, Inc. ....(800)274-4277
Craden Peripherals Corp. ....(609)488-0700
Data General Corp...(800)328-2436
Data Systems Hardware ....(800)937-DSHI
Datasouth Computer Corp. ....(800)476-2120
Decision Data...(800)523-6529
DeRex, Inc...(800)245-7282
Dianachart, Inc. ....(201)625-2299
Digital Equipment Corp...(508)493-5111
Digitec...(614)387-3444
Epson America, Inc. ....(800)289-3776
Facit Inc. ....(800)733-2248
Florida Digital, Inc...(407)242-2842
GCC Technologies, Inc. ....(800)422-7777
General Business Technology, Inc. ....(800)521-1891
Gulton Graphic Instruments ....(800)343-7929
Harris Adacom Corp. ....(214)386-2000
Hyundai Electronics America...(800)544-7808
Idea Courier/Servcom, Inc. ....(800)528-1400
Infoscribe/CTSI International, Inc. ....(800)233-4442
Interface Systems, Inc..(800)544-4072
Lee Data...(800)533-3282
Magnetic Corp. ....(203)243-8941
NCR Corp. ....(800)544-3333
NEC Technologies, Inc. ....(800)826-2255
Novatek Corp. ....(305)341-7700

Output Technology Corp. .... (800)468-8788
Packard Bell .... (818)773-4400
QANTEL Business Systems, Inc. .... (800)227-1894
Shinwa of America, Inc. .... (708)470-1600
Singer Data Products .... (708)860-6500
Stafford Computer Corp. .... (317)566-3724
Syntest Corp. .... (508)481-7827
Tandy Corp. .... (817)390-3011
Texas Instruments, Inc. .... (800)527-3500
TopLink Computer, Inc. .... (415)226-8600
TrendCOM .... (415)490-1291
Wang Laboratories, Inc. .... (800)835-9264
Xtron Computer Equipment Corp. .... (800)854-4450

Thermal printers

Digitec .... (614)387-3444
Gulton Graphic Instruments .... (800)343-7929
IBM .... (800)426-2468
Syntest Corp. .... (508)481-7827
TrendCOM .... (415)490-1291

Ink jet printers

Apple Computer, Inc. .... (408)996-1010
Canon U.S.A., Inc. .... (516)488-6700
Chinon America, Inc. .... (213)533-0274
Data General Corp. .... (800)328-2436
Digital Equipment Corp. .... (508)493-5111
Eastman Kodak Co. .... (800)242-2424
Epson America, Inc. .... (800)289-3776
GCC Technologies, Inc. .... (800)422-7777
Hewlett-Packard Co. .... (800)752-0900
Howtek, Inc. .... (800)44HOWTEK
IBM .... (800)426-2468
Sharp Electronics Corp. .... (201)529-8731
Tektronix, Inc. .... (800)835-9433
Xerox Corp. .... (800)832-6979

Laser printers

Abaton .... (800)444-5321
AccuPrint, Inc. .... (619)931-9316
Acer America Corp. .... (800)538-1542
Advanced Matrix Technology, Inc. .... (800)992-2264

Advanced Technologies International..(408)942-1780
AEG Olympia, Inc...(800)999-6872
Agfa-Compugraphic..(800)822-5524
American Computer Hardware Corp. ....(800)447-1237
Apollo Computer, Inc. ....(508)256-6600
Apple Computer, Inc...(408)996-1010
AT&T Computer Systems ....(800)247-1212
Autographix, Inc...(800)548-8558
Autologic, Inc...(805)498-9611
BDT Products, Inc..(800)346-3238
BGL Technology Corp. ....(805)987-7305
Brother International Corp..(908)356-8880
Bull Worldwide Information Systems Inc. ....(508)294-6000
Canon U.S.A., Inc..(516)488-6700
Colorocs Corp. ....(800)966-2579
Computer Language Research, Inc...(800)FORM-FREE
CPT Corp...(800)447-1189
CSS Laboratories, Inc...(714)852-8161
Data General Corp...(800)328-2436
Data Systems Hardware ....(800)937-DSHI
Dataproducts Corp. ....(800)624-8999
DCS/Fortis ....(800)736-4847
Decision Data...(800)523-6529
Desktop Systems, Inc...(800)444-5321
Digital Design, Inc..(800)733-0908
Digital Equipment Corp. ....(508)493-5111
Eastman Kodak Co..(800)242-2424
Epson America, Inc. ....(800)289-3776
Facit, Inc. ....(800)733-2248
Fujitsu America, Inc. ....(800)233-1798
GCC Technologies, Inc..(800)422-7777
General Business Technology, Inc. ....(800)521-1891
General Parametrics Corp..(800)223-0999
Harris Adacom Corp. ....(214)386-2000
Hewlett-Packard Co...(800)752-0900
IBM ....(800)426-2468
Image Systems, Inc. ....(800)347-4027
Kentek Information Systems, Inc. ....(303)440-5500
Konica Business Machines USA, Inc. ....(800)456-6422
Kyocera Unison, Inc..(800)367-7437
Lanier Worldwide, Inc. ....(404)329-8000
LaserMaster ....(612)944-9696
LaserSmith, Inc...(408)727-7700

Linotype-Hell..(800)633-1900
Mannesmann Tally Corp. ....(800)843-1347
Microtek Lab, Inc. ....(800)654-4160
Minolta Corp. ....(201)825-4000
Mirror Technologies, Inc. ....(800)654-5294
NCR Corp. ....(800)544-3333
NEC Technologies, Inc. ....(800)826-2255
NewGen Systems Corp. ....(714)641-8600
NeXT, Inc..(800)848-NEXT
Nissei Sangyo America, Ltd. (NSA) ....(617)893-5700
Nissho Electronics (U.S.A.) Corp. ....(800)233-1837
Oce Graphics USA, Inc. ....(800)545-5445
Office Automation Systems, Inc...(619)452-9400
Okidata Corp. ....(800)654-3282
Olivetti Office USA ....(800)447-4700
Output Technology Corp. ....(800)468-8788
Packard Bell ....(818)773-4400
Panasonic Communications & Systems Co..(201)348-7000
Pentax Technologies Corp. ....(800)543-6144
Personal Computer Products, Inc. (PCPI)..(619)485-8411
Philips Information Systems Co...(800)527-0204
Printer Systems Corp. (PSC)..(800)638-4041
Printronix, Inc. ....(800)826-3874
Q/Cor ....(800)548-3420
QMS, Inc..(800)631-2692
Qume Corp. ....(408)942-4000
Ricoh Corp..(800)327-8349
Rosetta Technologies Corp..(800)937-4224
Seiko Instruments U.S.A., Inc. ....(800)873-4561
Sharp Electronics Corp. ....(201)529-8731
Spear Technology, Inc...(708)480-7300
Star Micronics America, Inc...(800)447-4700
Sun Microsystems, Inc..(415)960-1300
Synergystex International, Inc. ....(216)225-3112
Talaris Systems, Inc. ....(619)587-0787
Tandy Corp..(817)390-3011
TEC America Electronics, Inc..(415)651-5333
Tektronix, Inc..(800)835-9433
Texas Instruments, Inc. ....(800)527-3500
Toshiba America Information Systems, Inc...(800)334-3445
Troy..(800)332-MICR
UNISYS Corp. ....(215)542-2239
Varityper ....(800)631-8134

Vistron, Inc. ....(408)996-1824
Wang Laboratories, Inc. ....(800)835-9264
Xerox Corp. ....(800)832-6979
Xpoint Corp. ....(404)446-2764

Appendix B

Font samples

NOTE: These font samples have been photographically reduced.

```
-------- PORTRAIT FONTS --------
```

```
FONT                            POINT SYMBOL
 ID        NAME          PITCH  SIZE  SET      PRINT SAMPLE
----   ------------------ ----- ----- ------   ------------------------
```

"PERMANENT" SOFT FONTS

LEFT FONT CARTRIDGE

RIGHT FONT CARTRIDGE

FONT ID	NAME		PITCH	POINT SIZE	SYMBOL SET	PRINT SAMPLE
R01	Helv	ITALIC	PS	14	OU	*ABCDEfghij#$@[\]^`{|}~123*
R02	Helv	ITALIC	PS	18	OU	*ABCDEfghij#$@[\]^`{|}~1*
R03	Helv	BOLD	PS	18	OU	**ABCDEfghij#$@[\]^`{|}~**
R04	Helv	BOLD	PS	24	OU	**ABCDEfghij#$@[\]^**
R05	Helv	BOLD	PS	30	OU	**ABCDEfghij#$**
R06	Helv	BOLD	PS	36	OU	**ABCDEfghij#**
R07	Helv	BOLD	PS	48	OU	**ABCDEfg**
R08	Helv	BOLD ITALIC	PS	24	OU	***ABCDEfghij#$@[\]^***
R09	Helv	BOLD ITALIC	PS	30	OU	***ABCDEfghij#$***
R10	Park Ave	ITALIC	PS	12	OU	*ABCDEfghij#$@[\]^`{|}~123*
R11	Park Ave	ITALIC	PS	14	OU	*ABCDEfghij#$@[\]^`{|}~123*
R12	Park Ave	ITALIC	PS	18	OU	*ABCDEfghij#$@[\]^`{|}~123*
R13	Park Ave	ITALIC	PS	24	OU	*ABCDEfghij#$@[\]^`*
R14	Park Ave	ITALIC	PS	30	OU	*ABCDEfghij#$@*
R15	Park Ave	ITALIC	PS	48	OU	*ABCDEfg*

B-1 UDP TurboGold type sample.

Description	Points	Pitch	Sample
Prestige Elite Bld Legal/Rmn 8 8U*	10	12	**ABCDrstz1234'~!@#$%^&*(]\;',./<>?:"{}|áíóúñÑªº¿½¼¡«»¯ °ÇçÑ**
Prest Elite Norm ASCII 0U*/Rmn 8 8U*	10	12	ABCDrstz1234'~!@#$%^&*(]\;',./<>?:"{}|áíóúñÑªº¿½¼¡«»¯°ç¿§ê
Prestige Elite Normal Legal 1U	10	12	ABCDEFGpqrstuvwxyz1234567890°™!@#$%©&_*()[]®;',./_¢?:"§†¶
Prestige Elite Italic Roman 8 8U*	10	12	*ABCDrstz1234'~!@#$%^&*()_+[]\;',./<>?:"{}|áíóúñÑªº¿½¼¡«»¯*
Prestige Elite Ita ASCII 0U/Legal 1U	10	12	*ABCDEFGHIJKlmnopqrstuvwxyz1234°™!@#$%©&*()_+[]®;',./_¢?:"§*
Prestige Elite Roman 8 8U	7	16.66	ABCDEFGHIJKlmnopqrstuvwxyz1234'~!@#$%^&*()_+[]\;',./<>?:"{}|áíóúñÑªº¿ ½¼¡«»¯ °Çç
Prestige Elite ASCII 0U*/Legal 1U*	7	16.66	ABCDEFGHIJKLMNOhijklmnopqrstuvwxyz1234567890°=™!@#$%©&*()_+[]®;',./_¢?:"§†¶
Math Elite Math 7 0A	10	12	αβψφε∂ληιθκωμνρπγθστξΔδχυζαβψφε∂ληιθκωμνρπγθστξΔδχυζ¹²³⁴¶←
Math Elite Math 8 8M/8A 0Q	10	12	ΑΒΓΔΕΖΗΘΙΚΛΜΝΞΟΠΡΣΤΤΦΧΨΩ∇∂αβγδεζηθικλμνξοπρστυφχψωθφ1234·:≠
Math Elite Math 8B 1Q	10	12	↑→↓←⇑⇒⇓⇐↕↔⇕⇔ ⊤⊥∪∩⊇⊄⊂⊃⊆⊕⊗⊘⊘∧∨⊻¬··•∘†‡Å+ ∫∮∠∅ℵ⊃⊐ℭ𝔖ℜ𝔍
Math Elite Pi 15U/A 2Q	10	12	Δ_Fℏ ℒ℘℘ℝ∑ ¬ ┤┴ ‖∏‖ ˘ˇ˙ ↗Δ▷§' :: "" '™⟨⟩ ℠▪[]‖◁®® ◈¶▽ ‖♦■
Math Elite Math 8 8M/8A 0Q	7	16.66	ΑΒΓΔΕΖΗΘΙΚΛΜΝΞΟΠΡΣΤΤΦΧΨΩ∇∂αβγδεζηθικλμνξοπρστυφχψωθφ1234567890-=·≠/:·∞÷≥∝×()_+ç≠
Math Elite Math 8B 1Q	7	16.66	→↓←⇒⇓⇐↕↔⇕⇔ ⊤⊥∪∩⊇⊄⊂⊃⊆⊕⊗⊘∧∨⊻¬··•∘†‡Å+ ⊆⊕⊗⊘∧∨⊻¬··•∘†‡Å+ ∫∮∠∅ℵ⊃⊐ℭ𝔖ℜ𝔍⌈⌊⌈
Courier Bold ASCII 0U/Roman 8 8U	12	10	**ABCDrstz12340~@#$%^&(]\;>{|áíóúñÑªº¿ ½¼¡«¯ °ÇÑ¡¤**
Courier Bold French 0F	12	10	**ABCDrstwxyz12340'¨!à£$%^&*()_+°§ç;',./<>?:"éèù**
Courier Bold German 0G	12	10	**ABCDrstwxyz12340'ß!§£$%^&*()_+ÄÜÖ;',./<>?:"äüö**
Courier Bold Italian 0I	12	10	**ABCDrstwxyz12340ùì!§£$%^&*()_+°éç;',./<>?:"àèò**
Courier Bold Spanish 1S	12	10	**ABCDrstwxyz12340'~!@#$%°&*()_+¡¿Ñ;',./<>?:"{}ñ**
Courier Bold Swedish/Finnish 0S	12	10	**ABCDrstwxyz12340éü!É#¤%Ü&*()_+ÄÅÖ;',./<>?:"äåö**
Courier Bold Danish/Norweg 0D	12	10	**ABCDrstwxyz12340'~!@#$%^&*() +ÆÅØ;',./<>?:"æåø**
Courier Bold United Kingdom 1E	12	10	**ABCDrstwxyz12340'~!@£$%^&*()_+[]\;',./<>?:"{}|**
Courier Italic ASCII 0U/Roman 8 8U	12	10	*ABCDrstz12340'~|áíóúñÑªº¿ ½¼¡«¯ °Çç¿¤£¥§ƒ¢âêôûá*
Courier Italic French 0F	12	10	*ABCDrstwxyz12340'¨!à£$%^&*()_+°§ç;',./<>?:"éèù*
Courier Italic German 0G	12	10	*ABCDrstwxyz12340'ß!§£$%^&*()_+ÄÜÖ;',./<>?:"äüö*
Courier Italic Italian 0I	12	10	*ABCDrstwxyz12340ùì!§£$%^&*()_+°éç;',./<>?:"àèò*
Courier Italic Spanish 1S	12	10	*ABCDrstwxyz12340'~!@#$%°&*()_+¡¿Ñ;',./<>?:"{}ñ*
Courier Italic Swedish/Fin 0S	12	10	*ABCDrstwxyz12340éü!É#¤%Ü&*()_+ÄÅÖ',./<>?:"äåö*
Courier Italic Danish/Norweg 0D	12	10	*ABCDrstwxyz12340'~!@#$%^&*()_+ÆÅØ',./<>?:"æåø*
Courier Italic United Kingdom 1E	12	10	*ABCDrstwxyz12340'~!@£$%^&*()_+[]\',./<>?:"{}|*
Courier ASCII 0U/Roman 8 8U	12	10	ABCDrstwxyz12340`¯!@#$%^&*()_+[]\',./<>?:"{}|
Courier French 0F	12	10	ABCDrstwxyz12340'¨!à£$%^&*()_+°§ç;',./<>?:"éèù
Courier German 0G	12	10	ABCDrstwxyz12340'ß!§£$%^&*()_+ÄÜÖ;',./<>?:"äüö
Courier Italian 0I	12	10	ABCDrstwxyz12340ùì!§£$%^&*()_+°éç;',./<>?:"àèò
Courier Spanish 1S	12	10	ABCDrstwxyz12340'~!@#$%°&*()_+¡¿Ñ;',./<>?:"{}ñ
Courier Swedish/Finnish 0S	12	10	ABCDrstwxyz12340éü!É#¤%Ü&*()_+ÄÅÖ;',./<>?:"äåö
Courier Danish/Norweg 0D	12	10	ABCDrstwxyz12340'~!@#$%^&*()_+ÆÅØ;',./<>?:"æåø
Courier United Kingdom 1E	12	10	ABCDEFGHrstwxyz1234567890'~!@£$%^&*()]\>?:"{}|
PC Line Draw Bold PC Line 4Q*	14	10	┴┬├┼╞╟╚╔╩╦╠═╬╧╨╤╥╙╘╒╓╫╪┘┌ ▪•░▒▓│┤╡╢╖╕╣║╗╝╜╛ ▪ ▪ └
Tax Line Draw Bold Tax 0B	12	10	╢█▌ └ ┐ └ ┼┘ ┌┘ ┌┬▐▄┘ ┼▌▀▲┴┬↑←├└
Line Printer PC Set 10U*/Roman 8 8U*	8.5	16.66	ABCDEFGHIJKLMhijklmnopqrstuvwxyz1234590-=`¯!@#$%^&*()_+[]\;',./<>?:"{}|
Prsntatn Bold ASCII 0U*	18	6.5	**ABCDRSTZ1234'~!@#$%^&*()_+[]\;'**
Prsntatn Bold Legal 1U*	18	6.5	**ABCDRSTZ1234°™!@#$%©&*()_+[]®;'**
Prsntatn Bold ASCII 0U*	16	8.1	**ABCDRSTZ1234'~!@#$%^&*()_+[]\;',./<>?:"**
Prsntatn Bold Legal 1U*	16	8.1	**ABCDRSTZ1234°™!@#$%©&*()_+[]®;',./_¢?:"**
Prsntatn Bold ASCII 0U*	14	10	**ABCDRSTWXYZ12340'~!@#$%^&*()_+[]\;',./<>?:"{}|**
Prsntatn Bold Legal 1U*	14	10	**ABCDRSTWXYZ12340°™!@#$%©&*()_+[]®;',./_¢?:"§†¶**
AFS ASCII*	3.6	27.27	ABCDEFGHIJKLMNOPQRSTUVWXYZabcdefghijklmnopqrstuvwxyz1234567890-=`~!@#$%^&*()_+[]\;',./<>?:"{}|

B-2 Pacific Data Products 25 in One! type sample.

FONT ID	NAME			PITCH	POINT SIZE	SYMBOL SET	PRINT SAMPLE
----	------------------------			-----	-----	------	------------------------

"PERMANENT" SOFT FONTS

FONT ID	NAME			PITCH	POINT SIZE	SYMBOL SET	PRINT SAMPLE
S01	CG CentSchl			PS	10	OU	ABCDEfghij#$@[\]^'{|}~123
S02	CG CentSchl			PS	12	OU	ABCDEfghij#$@[\]^'{|}~123
S03	CG CentSchl			PS	18	OU	ABCDEfghij#$@[\]^'{|}~1
S04	CG CentSchl	Bd	BOLD	PS	10	OU	ABCDEfghij#$@[\]^'{|}~123
S05	CG CentSchl	Bd	BOLD	PS	12	OU	ABCDEfghij#$@[\]^'{|}~123
S06	CG CentSchl	It	ITALIC	PS	10	OU	ABCDEfghij#$@[\]^'{|}~123
S07	CG CentSchl	It	ITALIC	PS	12	OU	ABCDEfghij#$@[\]^'{|}~123
S08	CG CentSchl	It	ITALIC	PS	18	OU	ABCDEfghij#$@[\]^'{|}~1
S09	CG CentSchl	BdIt	BOLD ITA	PS	10	OU	ABCDEfghij#$@[\]^'{|}~123
S10	CG CentSchl	BdIt	BOLD ITA	PS	12	OU	ABCDEfghij#$@[\]^'{|}~123
S11	Futura II	Bd	BOLD	PS	12	OU	ABCDEfghij#$@[\]^'{|}~123
S12	Cooper	Blk	BOLD	PS	14	OU	ABCDEfghij#$@[\]^'{|}~123
S13	Cooper	Blk	BOLD	PS	24	OU	ABCDEfghij#$
S14	Futura II	Bd	BOLD	PS	18	OU	ABCDEfghij#$@[\]^'{|
S15	Futura II	Bk		PS	12	OU	ABCDEfghij#$@[\]^'{|}~123

FONT ID	NAME			PITCH	POINT SIZE	SYMBOL SET	PRINT SAMPLE
----	------------------------			-----	-----	------	------------------------

"PERMANENT" SOFT FONTS

FONT ID	NAME			PITCH	POINT SIZE	SYMBOL SET	PRINT SAMPLE
S16	Futura II	Bk		PS	18	OU	ABCDEfghij#$@[\]^'{|}~1
S17	Futura II	BdIt	BOLD ITA	PS	12	OU	ABCDEfghij#$@[\]^'{|}~123
S18	Futura II	BdIt	BOLD ITA	PS	18	OU	ABCDEfghij#$@[\]^'{|}
S19	Futura II	BkIt	ITALIC	PS	12	OU	ABCDEfghij#$@[\]^'{|}~123
S20	Futura II	BkIt	ITALIC	PS	18	OU	ABCDEfghij#$@[\]^'{|}~1
S21	ITCZapfChncyMdIt	ITALIC		PS	14	OU	ABCDEfghij#$@[\]^'{|}~123
S22	ITCZapfChncyMdIt	ITALIC		PS	24	OU	ABCDEfghij#$@[\]^'{|
S23	Revue	Lt	LIGHT	PS	12	OU	ABCDEfghij#$@[\]^'{|}~123
S24	Revue	Lt	LIGHT	PS	14	OU	ABCDEfghij#$@[\]^'{|}~123
S25	Revue	Shdw	160	PS	12	OU	ABCDEfghij#$@[\]^'{|}~123
S26	Revue	Shdw	160	PS	14	OU	ABCDEfghij#$@[\]^'{|}~123
S27	Uncial			PS	10	OU	ABCDEfghij#$@[\]^'{|}~123
S28	Uncial			PS	12	OU	ABCDEfghij#$@[\]^'{|}~123
S29	University	Rmn		PS	10	OU	ABCDEfghij#$@[\]^'{|}~123
S30	University	Rmn		PS	12	OU	ABCDEfghij#$@[\]^'{|}~123

B-3 HP Type Director soft fonts type sample.

Fonts in printer's memory

AvantGarde-Book	The quick brown fox jumps over the lazy dog.
AvantGarde-BookOblique	*The quick brown fox jumps over the lazy dog.*
AvantGarde-Demi	**The quick brown fox jumps over the lazy dog.**
AvantGarde-DemiOblique	***The quick brown fox jumps over the lazy dog.***
Bookman-Demi	**The quick brown fox jumps over the lazy dog.**
Bookman-DemiItalic	***The quick brown fox jumps over the lazy dog.***
Bookman-Light	The quick brown fox jumps over the lazy dog.
Bookman-LightItalic	*The quick brown fox jumps over the lazy dog.*
Courier	The quick brown fox jumps over the lazy dog.
Courier-Bold	**The quick brown fox jumps over the lazy dog.**
Courier-BoldOblique	***The quick brown fox jumps over the lazy dog.***
Courier-Oblique	*The quick brown fox jumps over the lazy dog.*
Helvetica	The quick brown fox jumps over the lazy dog.
Helvetica-Bold	**The quick brown fox jumps over the lazy dog.**
Helvetica-BoldOblique	***The quick brown fox jumps over the lazy dog.***
Helvetica-Narrow	The quick brown fox jumps over the lazy dog.
Helvetica-Narrow-Bold	**The quick brown fox jumps over the lazy dog.**
Helvetica-Narrow-BoldOblique	***The quick brown fox jumps over the lazy dog.***
Helvetica-Narrow-Oblique	*The quick brown fox jumps over the lazy dog.*
Helvetica-Oblique	*The quick brown fox jumps over the lazy dog.*
NewCenturySchlbk-Bold	**The quick brown fox jumps over the lazy dog.**
NewCenturySchlbk-BoldItalic	***The quick brown fox jumps over the lazy dog.***
NewCenturySchlbk-Italic	*The quick brown fox jumps over the lazy dog.*
NewCenturySchlbk-Roman	The quick brown fox jumps over the lazy dog.
Palatino-Bold	**The quick brown fox jumps over the lazy dog.**
Palatino-BoldItalic	***The quick brown fox jumps over the lazy dog.***
Palatino-Italic	*The quick brown fox jumps over the lazy dog.*
Palatino-Roman	The quick brown fox jumps over the lazy dog.
Symbol	Τηε θυιχκ βροων φοξ φυμπσ οϖερ τηε λαζψ δογ.
Times-Bold	**The quick brown fox jumps over the lazy dog.**
Times-BoldItalic	***The quick brown fox jumps over the lazy dog.***
Times-Italic	*The quick brown fox jumps over the lazy dog.*
Times-Roman	The quick brown fox jumps over the lazy dog.
ZapfChancery-MediumItalic	*The quick brown fox jumps over the lazy dog.*
ZapfDingbats	✳✳✳ ❏◆✳✳✳ ◗❏◗❒■ ✳❏❙ ✳◆○❏▲ ❏✦✳❏ ▼✳✳ ●◗❙❙ ✳❏

B-4 LaserWriter Plus PostScript type sample.

Times-Roman 36 points

ÁÂÄÀÅÃÇÉÊËÈÍÎÏÌÑ
ÓÔÖÒÕŠÚÛÜÙŸŽáâäà
 !"#$%&'()*+,-./
0123456789:;<=>?
@ABCDEFGHIJKLMNO
PQRSTUVWXYZ[\]^_
'abcdefghijklmno
pqrstuvwxyz{|}~
åãçéêëèíîïìñóôöò
õšúûüùÿž
 ¡¢£/¥ƒ§¤'"«‹›fifl
–†‡·¶•‚„"»…‰ ¿
ˋˆ˜ˉˇ˙ ˝ ˚ ˝ ˇ
          ˌ ˛

——

Æ ª ŁØŒº
æ 1 łøœß

B-5 Freedom of Press PostScript-compatible type sample.

JetPage

Times-Roman equivalent

Times-Bold equivalent

Times-Italic equivalent

Times-BoldItalic equivalent

Helvetica equivalent

Helvetica-Bold equivalent

Helvetica-Oblique equivalent

Helvetica-BoldOblique equivalent

Courier equivalent

Courier-Bold equivalent

Courier-Oblique equivalent

Courier-BoldOblique equivalent

Palatino-Roman equivalent

Palatino-Italic equivalent

Palatino-Bold equivalent

Palatino-BoldItalic equivalent

AvantGarde-Book equivalent

AvantGarde-Demi equivalent

AvantGarde-BookOblique equivalent

AvantGarde-DemiOblique equivalent

Helvetica-Narrow equivalent

Helvetica-Narrow-Bold equivalent

Helvetica-Narrow-Oblique equivalent

Helvetica-Narrow-BoldOblique equivalent

Bookman-Light equivalent

Bookman-Demi equivalent

Bookman-LightItalic equivalent

Bookman-DemiItalic equivalent

NewCenturySchlbk-Roman equivalent

NewCenturySchlbk-Bold equivalent

NewCenturySchlbk-Italic equivalent

NewCenturySchlbk-BoldItalic equivalent

ZapfChancery-MediumItalic equivalent

✿✛✢❀✪❅☞✦✔ < ZapfDingbats equivalent >

ABXαβχ123 < Symbol equivalent >

Helvetica-Light equivalent

Helvetica-LightOblique equivalent

Helvetica-Black equivalent

Helvetica-BlackOblique equivalent

Garamond-Light equivalent

Garamond-LightItalic equivalent

Garamond-Bold equivalent

Garamond-BoldItalic equivalent

Korinna-Regular equivalent

Korinna-KursivRegular equivalent

Korinna-Bold equivalent

Korinna-KursivBold equivalent

JetWare *By Computer Peripherals, Inc.*

B-6 CPI's JetPage PostScript-compatible type sample.

Index

A

Adobe PostScript (*see* PostScript)
Adobe PostScript emulator cartridges, 143
Adobe Type Manager soft fonts, 221-222
Apple dot matrix printers printers, ROM expansion, 45-48
Apple page printers
  RAM expansion, 127-130
  ROM expansion, 131-134
AppleTalk as printer-sharing connections, 194

B

Bubble Jet ink-jet printers, 84
  RAM and ROM memory expansion, 109-111
buffers
  dot matrix printers, 8-9
  printer-sharing connections, 175
  RAM expansion, dot matrix printers, 8-9
  sources, 250-253
  spooling buffers, software, 205-211

C

cabling for printer connections, 194-196, 250-253
Canon CX engine, PostScript for page printers, 148-150
Canon LPB-4 printers, PostScript emulators, 145
Canon SX engine, PostScript for page printers, 150-153
cartridges (*see* font options for page printers)
cassettes, paper-handling mechanisms, 200-202
Centronics parallel interfaces, dot matrix printers, 49-51
chip handling precautions, xiii
Citizen dot matrix printers
  color options, upgrades, 65-68
color options for dot matrix printers, 63-73, 245-246
  Citizen printers, 65-68
  color-capabilities by manufacturer, 72-73
  Panasonic printers, 68-72
  ribbon selection, 64

D

controller boards, high-resolution, 154-155, 249
converters, printer-sharing connections, 175-177

daisy wheel printers, 165-169
data converters, sources, 250-253
data managers, printer-sharing connections, 177-182
DeskJet ink-jet printers, 83-84
  DeskWriter from DeskJet upgrade, 102-109
  font-cartridge compatibility table, 90
  fonts, internal fonts table, 89
  logic-board upgrades, 91, 247
  paper skew settings, 99-102
  RAM expansion, 87-89
  ROM expansion, 89-91
  ROM upgrades to Plus or 500 level, 91-102
DeskWriter ink-jet printers
  DeskJet to DeskWriter upgrade, 102-109
Diconix ink-jet printers, 84

directory of printer manufacturers, 257-264
dot matrix printers, 1-79
  Apple printers, ROM expansion, 45-48
  Centronics parallel interfaces, 49-51
  Citizen printers, color options and upgrades, 65-68
  color options, 63-73, 245-246
  color-capabilities by manufacturer, 72-73
  electronic circuitry, 5
  Epson FX-80 RAM upgrade, 29-34
  Epson printers, ROM expansion, 39-45, 45-48
  Epson serial interfaces, 52-56
  font options and upgrades, 75-79
  font-card acceptable printers, 78-79
  interface, parallel vs. serial, 6, 49-61, 244-246
  motors, pulse or stepper, 5
  Okidata Microline 192 RAM upgrade, 14-16
  Okidata printers, ROM expansion, 37-39
  Okidata serial interfaces, 59-61
  Panasonic KX RAM upgrades, 16-24
  Panasonic printers, color options and upgrades, 68-72
  Panasonic serial interfaces, 56-59
  platen and paper-transport, 4-5
  power supplies, 3-4
  RAM chips, 5-6
  RAM chips, expanding internal RAM (see RAM memory, dot matrix)
  ROM chips, 5-6
  ROM memory expansion, 37-48, 244
  Seikosha printers, ROM expansion, 45-48
  Seikosha SP-2000 RAM upgrade, 10-14
  Smith-Corona RAM upgrades, 26-29
  soft-font software, 213-215
Dots-Perfect (Dresselhaus), 244
  Epson DIP switch functions, 45
  function selection table, 41
download-area RAM expansion, dot matrix printers, 8

E
electric shock hazards, xiii
electronic circuitry, dot matrix printers, 5
emulators, PostScript, 142-148
  Adobe cartridges, 143
  Canon LPB-4 printers, 145
  compatibility issues, 148
  JetPage by CPI, 143
  Pacific Page by Pacific Data, 142
  PostScript vs. emulator performance, 145-148
  speed of emulator vs. PostScript, 146-148
  TurboScript cartridge by UDP, 143-145
Epson dot matrix printers
  DIP switch functions using Dots-Perfect, 45
  interfaces, 244
  language set selection by DIP switch, 45
  RAM expansion, 29-34
  ROM expansion, 39-45, 45-48
  serial interfaces, 52-56
Ethernet as printer-sharing connections, 194

F
feed (see paper-handling mechanisms)
fixed-form font cartridges, page printers, 134-137
font cards, 75-76
font options for dot matrix printers, 75-79
  font cards, 75-76
  font-card acceptable printers, 78-79
  font samples, 265-271
  ROM chips as font cards, 76-78
  soft-font software, 213-215
font options for ink-jet printers
  DeskJet cartridge compatibility table, 90
  DeskJet internal fonts table, 89
  extending print cartridge life, 102
  font samples, 265-271
  soft-font software, 215-225
font options for page printers, 134-148
  custom font cartridges, 137-139

fixed-form font cartridges, 134-137
font samples, 265-271
Hewlett-Packard PCL, 141
page-control languages (PCL), 140-141
PostScript (see PostScript), 141-161
scalable font cartridges, 139-140
soft-font software, 215-225
Freedom of Press PDL for PostScript, 232-239
  font sample, 270

G
GoScript PDL for PostScript, 239

H
hardware sources, miscellaneous items, 250-253
Hewlett-Packard page printers PCL, 141
  RAM expansion, 121-127
high-resolution controller boards, 154-155, 249

I
ink-jet printers, 81-111
  Bubble Jet development, 84
  BubbleJet memory expansion, 109-111
  cartridges, extending print cartridge life, 102
  DeskJet development, 83-84
  DeskJet font cartridge compatibility table, 90
  DeskJet internal fonts table, 89
  DeskJet logic board upgrades, 91
  DeskJet RAM expansion, 87-89
  DeskJet ROM expansion, 89-91
  DeskWriter from DeskJet upgrade, 102-109
  developmental history of ink-jet printers, 83-84
  Diconix development, 84
  logic board upgrades, DeskJet, 91, 247
  operation and mechanics of ink-jet printers, 84-86
  paper motor suppliers, 247
  RAM memory expansion, 87-111
  ROM memory expansion, 87-111

ROM upgrade, DeskJet to Plus to 500 level, 91-102
soft-font software, 215-225
Thinkjet development, 83
upgrade sources, 246-247
interfaces, parallel and serial
Centronix dot matrix printers, 49-51
dot matrix printers, 6, 49-61, 244-246
Epson serial interface, 52-56
Okidata dot matrix printers, 59-61
Panasonic serial interface, 56-59

J

JetPage PostScript emulator, 143, 271
JetWay printer-sharing device, 182-187

L

laser printers (*see* page printers)
laser-beam danger, xiii
LaserWriter Plus PostScript font sample, 269
LCS printers (*see* page printers)
LED printers (*see* page printers)
local area networks (LANs), printer-sharing connections, 194
logic boards, 247

M

MacPrint, printer-sharing connections, 190-194
manufacturers' addresses and telephone numbers, 257-264
memory, chip manufacturers, 242-243
motors, pulse or stepper, dot matrix printers, 5

O

Okidata dot matrix printers
interfaces, 244-245
RAM expansion, 14-16
ROM memory upgrades, 37-39, 244
serial interfaces, 59-61

P

Pacific Data Products 25 in One!

type sample, 267
Pacific Page PostScript emulator, 142
page description languages (PDLs), 225-239
Freedom of Press for PostScript, 232-239
GoScript for PostScript, 239
PCL, 225-227
PostScript, 225-239
PreScript for PostScript, 239
T-Script for PostScript, 239
UltraScript for PostScript, 227-231
page printers (laser printers), 113-161
Apple printers, RAM expansion, 127-130
Apple printers, ROM expansion, 131-134
Canon CX engine and PostScript use, 148-150
Canon SX engine and PostScript use, 150-153
cartridges and font upgrades, 134-148
custom font cartridges, 137-139
fixed-form font cartridges, 134-137
Hewlett-Packard PCL, 141
Hewlett-Packard printers, RAM expansion, 121-127
high-resolution controller boards, 154-155, 249
laser printer operation, 115-118
LCS printers, 118-120
LED printers, 118-120
page-control languages (PCL), 140-141
paper-handling mechanisms, cassettes, 200-202
PostScript (*see* PostScript)
RAM memory expansion, 121-130
ROM memory expansion, 131-161
scalable font cartridges, 139-140
soft-font software, 215-225
step-by-step high-resolution, 300+ dpi upgrade, 155-161
upgrade sources, 248
Panasonic dot matrix printers printers
color options, upgrades, 68-72

interfaces, 56-59, 245
RAM expansions, 16-24
paper-handling mechanisms, 197-202
automatic sheet feeder, 198-200
bottom-feeding types, 197
cassettes, 200-202
platen, dot matrix printers, 4-5
parallel interface
Centronix dot matrix printers, 49-51
dot matrix printers, 6, 49-61
PCL page-description language, 225-227
platen and paper-transport, dot matrix printers, 4-5
PostScript, 141-161
beyond the 300 dpi horizon, 153-161
Canon CX engine, 148-150
Canon SX engine, 150-153
compatibility of emulators, 148
emulator performance vs. PostScript, 145-148
emulators (*see* emulators, PostScript)
Freedom of Press PDL, 232-239, 270
GoScript PDL, 239
high-resolution controllers, 154-155
JetPage font sample, 271
LaserWriter Plus font sample, 269
page description languages (PCLs), 225-239
PreScript PDL, 239
speed of emulators vs. PostScript, 146-148
T-Script PDL, 239
UltraScript PDL, 227-231
power supplies, dot matrix printers, 3-4
precautions, xiii
PreScript PDL for PostScript, 239
printer-sharing connections, 171-196
buffers, 175
cabling for printer connections, 194-196
converters, 175-177
data managers, 177-182
JetWay printer-sharing device, 182-187

printer-sharing connections (*cont.*)
local area networks (LANs), 194
MacPrint for Macintosh users, 190-194
ServerJet IO card, 187-190
sources of supply, 250-253
switch boxes, manual and automatic, 171-175

Q

Quick Font! soft fonts, 222-225

R

RAM memory
RAM chip manufacturers, 242-243
SIMM chip manufacturers, 242-243
SIPP chip manufacturers, 242-243
RAM memory, dot matrix printers
buffer-area RAM expansion, 8-9
chip removal procedure, 12
chip replacement procedure, 12
chip selection for upgrades, 9
download-area RAM expansion, 8
Epson FX-80 printer example, 29-34
expanding internal RAM, 7-35
Okidata Microline 192 example, 14-16
Panasonic KX printers example, 16-24
performance improvements possible with upgrade, 34
Seikosha SP-2000 example, 10-14
Smith-Corona printer example, 26-29
standard, 5-6
upgrade considerations: cost vs. benefit, 24
RAM memory, ink-jet printers, 87-111
BubbleJet expansion, 109-111
DeskJet printers, 87-89
DeskWriter from DeskJet upgrade, 102-109
RAM memory, page printers, 121-130

Apple printers, 127-130
Hewlett-Packard printers, 121-127
ribbons, color ribbon selection, dot matrix printers, 64
ROM memory, dot matrix printers, 37-48, 244
Apple ROM expansion, 45-48
Dots-Perfect, function selection table, 41
Dots-Perfect, Epson DIP switch functions, 45
Epson ROM expansion, 39-45, 45-48
font selections and upgrades, 76-78
Okidata printer examples, 37-39
Seikosha ROM expansion, 45-48
standard, 5-6
ROM memory, ink-jet printers, 87-111
BubbleJet expansion, 109-111
DeskJet logic-board upgrades, 91
DeskJet printers, 89-91
DeskJet upgrade to Plus or 500 level, 91-102
DeskWriter from DeskJet upgrade, 102-109
logic-board upgrades, DeskJet, 91
ROM memory, page printers (*see also* font options
for page printers), 131-161
Apple printers, 131-134

S

safety, xiii
Seikosha dot matrix printers
parts substitution table, 48
RAM expansion, 10-14
ROM expansion, 45-48, 244
serial interface
dot matrix printers, 6, 51-61
Epson dot matrix printers, 52-56
Okidata dot matrix printers, 59-61
Panasonic dot matrix printers, 56-59
ServerJet IO card, printer-sharing connections, 187-190
sharing printers (*see* printer-shar-

ing connections)
sheet-paper feeders, automatic, 198-200
SIMM chip manufacturers, 242-243
SIPP chip manufacturers, 242-243
Smith-Corona dot matrix printers, RAM expansions, 26-29
soft fonts software, 211-225
Adobe Type Manager, 221-222
custom-created soft fonts, 222-225
dot matrix printers, 213-215
ink jet printers, 215-225
page (laser) printers, 215-225
page description languages (PDLs), 225-239
Quick Font!, 222-225
sources of supply, 253-254
TrueType, 222
Type Director, 216-221
software, 203-239
soft fonts, 211-225
sources of supply, 253-256
spooling buffers, 205-211
sources, information and supplies, 241-264
spooling buffers, software, 205-211
static electricity, xiii
switch boxes
manual and automatic, 171-175
sources, 250-253

T

25 in One! font sample, 267
T-Script PDL for PostScript, 239
thermal printers, 170
TrueType soft fonts, 222
TurboGold font sample, UDP, 266
TurboScript PostScript emulator, 143-145
Thinkjet ink-jet printers, 83
Type Director soft fonts, 216-221, 268
Type Manager (Adobe) soft fonts, 221-222

U

UltraScript PDL for PostScript, 227-231